WHEN?

by

F. Kenton Beshore

with

R. William Keller

World Bible Society
Costa Mesa, California

iUniverse books may be ordered through booksellers or by contacting:

iUniverse
1663 Liberty Drive
Bloomington, IN 47403
www.iuniverse.com
1-800-Authors (1-800-288-4677)

ISBN: 978-1-4502-8870-5 (sc)
ISBN: 978-1-4502-8871-2 (hc)
ISBN: 978-1-4502-8872-9 (ebook)

Library of Congress Control Number: 2011900422

Printed in the United States of America

iUniverse rev. date: 01/05/2011

Dedication

We dedicate this book to our Lord and Savior Jesus Christ for His infallible holy Word, and to all students of Bible prophecy (past and present), who have labored diligently to learn **When** Christ will return to take us home to be with Him. Without their searching of the Scriptures, this book would not be possible.

CONTENTS

FOREWORD

Growing up the son of a pastor created many wonderful opportunities. Along with hearing many messages, I was able to see the church as a wonderful expression of Jesus Christ. I heard my father teach and was infected by my father's love for God's Word. You cannot hear my father teach without seeing his passion to put the whole story of God's Word together. I was able to see the beginning of the creation story all the way to redemption and then to its final fulfillment in the glorious appearing of Jesus Christ.

As a young child, I was not sure I wanted Jesus to return before I experienced all of life. But in time I realized the return of Christ really means there would be no more hatred or war, no more souls tortured by addiction or battered children, injustice is eliminated, the cruelty of people destroyed, no more cancer, disease or death, ambulances or hospitals, no more poverty, greed or corruption. Everyone is loved and experiences the thrill of being loved by their heavenly Father. It is when the lion and the lamb lie down together. Death is destroyed. All creation is again filled with singing. I want that to happen today. I want heaven to come to earth. The beauty of God's creation restored. The prayer Jesus taught us to pray, *"Our Father who art in heaven, hollowed be Thy name. Thy kingdom come, Thy will be done in earth as it is in heaven, will be fulfilled."*

In this book, you will see my father's passion for people to know God's Word and to know it well. You will see the hand of God from the beginning of time and where it is headed. When you know where you are going, you know how to live today. My dad is a lifelong learner. He has an inquisitive mind, always asking questions. He has passion to know God and His Word. He never stops studying. He has a fascinating, brilliant mind which you will experience in this book. As a result, this is my father's greatest legacy. I love God's Word. It is truth to live by.

Kenton Beshore

8

PREFACE

Why write this book? Why is another book on prophecy important? Why should you read this book? Here are some reasons why this book needed to be written, and why it is important for all Christians to read it:

We are rapidly moving toward a **New World Order**. The current economic crisis will pave the way for the creation of a **world economic system** that the **Antichrist** will take control of, and eventually force everyone to take his **"mark"** to be able to buy or sell:

> And it was given unto him to give breath to it, even to the image to the beast, that the image of the beast should both speak, and cause that as many as should **not worship** the **image of the beast** should **be killed**. And **he causeth all**, the small and the great, and the rich and the poor, and the free and the bond, that there **be given them a mark** on their **right hand**, or upon their **forehead**; and that no man should be able to **buy or to sell**, save he that hath the **mark**, even the name of the beast or the number of his name. Here is wisdom. He that hath understanding, let him count the **number of the beast**; for it is the number of a man: and his number is **Six hundred and sixty and six.** (Revelation 13.15-18, emphasis added, mine)

We can use the movement to create a **"New World Order"** and the **mark of the beast technology** to alert the unsaved to the reliability of the Bible, and warn them to **not take the mark**.

When the dramatic prophecies of the **destruction of Russia**; the rebuilding of the **Jewish Temple;** the rebuilding of the ancient **city of Babylon**; and the formation of a **world government, world economic system** and **world church** are fulfilled, we will have a great opportunity to share the gospel. We should be prepared to share the gospel at all times in a clear and concise manner, today and tomorrow:

> But sanctify in your hearts Christ as Lord: being ready always to give answer to every man that asketh you a reason concerning the hope that is in you, yet with meekness and fear. (1 Peter 3.15)

As we **see prophecies fulfilled**, our confidence that the **Lord will return in our lifetime** will grow stronger:

> Even so ye also, when ye see all these things, know ye that he is nigh, even at the doors. (Matthew 24.33)

There is a **special reward** for those who **"look"** for the **Christ's return:**

*Henceforth there is laid up for me the **crown of righteousness,** which the Lord, the righteous judge, shall give to me at that day; and not to me only, but also to all them that have **loved his appearing**.* (2 Tim 4.8)

Watching for the **return** of **our Lord purifies us:**

*Beloved, now are we children of God, and it is not yet made manifest what we shall be. We know that, if he shall be manifested, we shall be like him; for we shall see him even as he is. And every one that hath this hope set on him **purifieth himself**, even as he is pure.* (1 John 3.2-3)

We are **commanded to resist evil and expose their evil deeds**, including the coming **New World Order:**

*Be sober, be watchful: your adversary the devil, as a roaring lion, walketh about, seeking whom he may devour, whom **withstand stedfast** in your faith, knowing that the same sufferings are accomplished in your brethren who are in the world.* (1 Peter 5.8-9)

*And have no fellowship with the unfruitful works of darkness, but rather even **reprove them**; for the things which are done by them in secret it is a shame even to speak of. But all things when they are **reproved** are made manifest by the light: for everything that is made manifest is light.* (Ephesians 5.11-13)

*Put on the whole armor of God, that ye may be able to **stand against the wiles of the devil**.* (Ephesians 6.11)

He that saith unto the wicked, Thou art righteous;
Peoples shall curse him, nations shall abhor him:
*But to them that **rebuke** him shall be delight,*
And a good blessing shall come upon them. (Proverbs 24.24-25)

They that forsake the law praise the wicked;
*But such as **keep the law contend** with them.* (Proverbs 28.4)

*For consider him that hath endured such gainsaying of sinners against himself, that ye wax not weary, fainting in your souls. Ye have not yet resisted unto blood, **striving against sin**.* (Hebrews 12.3-4)

As a troubled fountain, and a corrupted spring,
*So is a righteous man that **giveth way before the wicked**.* (Proverbs 25.26) (Emphasis mine)

Remember the Golden Rule of Interpretation as you study the Bible and this book, "When the plain sense of Scripture makes common sense, seek no other sense; therefore, take every word at its primary, ordinary, usual, literal meaning unless the facts of the immediate content, studied in the light of related passages and axiomatic and fundamental truths, indicates clearly otherwise."

INTRODUCTION

All students of Bible prophecy understand that there will be many *warning signs* prior to the Rapture and the start of the Tribulation. Jesus commanded us to *"watch"* for His return (Matthew 24.42-44; 25.13; Mark 13.33-37; Luke 12.40). The only way to do this is to *"watch"* the prophecies (*warning signs*) that will be fulfilled before the Rapture/Tribulation. As we see more prophecies fulfilled before the Tribulation starts (Appendix A) we will know the Rapture is drawing that much nearer.

When Jesus made His startling prophecy that the Temple would be destroyed Peter, James, John and Andrew approached to question Him privately (Mark 13.3-4). They asked the all-important question that every student of Bible prophecy desires to know the answer to, *"And as he sat on the Mount of Olives over against the temple, Peter and James and John and Andrew asked him privately, Tell us, when shall these things be? and what shall be the sign when these things are all about to be accomplished?"*

They asked three specific questions:

1. When will the Temple be destroyed?
2. What will the *sign* be of its destruction?
3. What will the *sign* be of the return of Jesus and the end of the age?

The disciples asked the **When** and the **What**. The **What** are the *warning signs* of the Tribulation, and the **When** is the start of the Tribulation. Since the Rapture takes place before the Tribulation all prophecies that have been fulfilled alert us to the nearness of the Rapture. Two primary examples are the establishment of the nation of Israel in 1948 and the retaking of Jerusalem in 1967.

Ever since the Disciples asked the Lord that all important question, *"When shall these things be? and what shall be the sign of thy coming, and of the end of the world?"* (Matthew 24.3), Bible students have tried to determine **when** the Lord will return to Rapture His bride. Unfortunately, many have stumbled over the doctrine of *imminence*. In their search for **When** they have spent much time in futility as did Ponce de Leon in his search for the fountain of youth which he discovered did not exist. They, like him, have been led astray by a word that does appear in the Bible or a doctrine that is not taught anywhere in sacred Scripture. As long as they keep looking for that elusive fountain of youth of *imminence* they will never be able to know **When,** because they do not know the answer to **What**. And so, until the answer to **What** is discovered we will never know **When.**

This book answers the **When**, but before one can know the **When**, one must first know the **What** (the *warning signs* of the approaching Tribulation).

Dr. Timothy LaHaye, co-author of the *Left Behind* series, believes that all Christians must be prepared for the greatest opportunity for worldwide evangelism of the last 2000 years. In his book, *The Beginning of the End*, he said the greatest *sign* that will produce a ripe crop of souls for harvesting is the destruction of Russia and its allies when they attack Israel:

> If the magnifying and sanctifying of the Lord, as indicated in Ezekiel 38:16, 23 and 39:7, 13, 22 does indeed mean a short period of time when men call upon the Lord as a result of his miraculous preservation of Israel, then we should work diligently to prepare for it. Since we can expect the period to be brief, we should begin now to train ourselves and find positions of service where we can reach a maximum number of people with the gospel (p. 84).

The invasion of Israel by Russia is a *super-sign*. After the Russian-led forces are defeated, the world will see their defeat was a divine judgment. People all over the world will be receptive to the gospel, and we must be prepared to share the gospel in a clear, concise and loving manner. (Christians should always be prepared to share the gospel – 1 Peter 3.15.)

In their 1999 book, *Are We Living in the End Times?*, Tim LaHaye and Jerry Jenkins emphasized the importance of *signs*:

> We are surrounded by so **many obvious signs** that one would have to be blind not to see them – yet some fail to recognize them even when they are called to their attention. So **many signs exist today** that you could write a book about them. In fact, I [LaHaye] did, *The Beginning of the End*, first published in 1972 and then again in 1991. Many changes in the twenty-seven years since that book's first publication have only brought further confirmation that we are indeed living in "the **times of the signs**." Never in history have so **many legitimate signs** of Christ's return existed (pp. 26-27, emphasis mine).

There are so many *warning signs* of the approaching Tribulation that we must be living in "the times of the signs." Numerous *warning signs* have already been given to us, with many more to follow. God gave Noah and the people of his day 120 years of warning (Genesis 6.3); Lot and his family were given a warning; the Egyptians were given 10 *warning signs* (Exodus 5.1-12.36); a 40-day warning was given to Nineveh (Jonah 3.4); and Jesus gave the nation of Israel a warning 37 years before her destruction (Matthew 24.1-2).

God warns His people before judgment falls, and saves those who are obedient. He will do this before the start of the Tribulation with specific *signs*, and then save them by snatching them off the planet (the Rapture).

> *Surely the Lord Jehovah will do nothing, except he reveal his secret unto his servants the prophets.* (Amos 3.7)

Jesus also gave a promise to all of His disciples in the ι
in the letter to the church of Philadelphia:

And bring us not into temptation, but deliver us from the e
6.13)

Because thou didst keep the word of my patience, I also will ke
the hour of trial, that hour which is to come upon the whole w
them that dwell upon the earth. (Revelation 3.10)

Jesus taught all Christians to pray (Matthew 6.13) that they not be brought
into temptation (*peirasmos*). In His revelation He promises to keep His
disciples from the hour of trial (*peirasmos*). The "*temptation*" of the prayer is
the "*trial*" of the Tribulation (Revelation 3.10). Jesus answered that prayer, "*I
will keep thee from the hour of trial.*"

This book is written from a Pre-Tribulation Rapture perspective. We quote
men of various denominations who are considered to be knowledgeable in
eschatology. While we do not necessarily agree with their eschatology or other
doctrines, or necessarily endorse them or their ministries, we quote them to
show what some of the most notable prophecy preachers teach.

This book is written for all Christians, but especially for students of
prophecy who want to know exactly what the Bible teaches about the Rapture
and the Tribulation. Do not accept what we write or what anyone else writes as
fact. Instead, examine the Scriptures daily to see whether or not that which is
written by prophecy teachers is true:

*Now these were more noble than those in Thessalonica, in that they
received the word with all readiness of the mind, examining the Scriptures
daily, whether these things were so.* (Acts 17:11)

We all need to study Bible prophecy carefully, using the Bible as our map.
See for yourself if the claims in this book are based on Scripture. We urge you,
as Paul urged Timothy:

*Give diligence to present thyself approved unto God, a workman that
needeth not to be ashamed, handling aright the word of truth.* (2 Timothy
2.15)

As you study the Bible and this book remember the "Golden Rule of
Interpretation":

When the plain sense of Scripture makes common sense, seek no other
sense; therefore, take every word at its primary, ordinary, usual, literal
meaning unless the facts of the immediate content, studied in the light of
related passages and axiomatic and fundamental truths, indicate clearly
otherwise.

PART I

THE RAPTURE

For this we say unto you by the word of the Lord, that we that are alive, that are left unto the coming of the Lord, shall in no wise precede them that are fallen asleep. For the Lord himself shall descend from heaven, with a shout, with the voice of the archangel, and with the trump of God: and the dead in Christ shall rise first; then we that are alive, that are left, shall together with them be caught up in the clouds, to meet the Lord in the air: and so shall we ever be with the Lord. Wherefore comfort one another with these words. (1 Thessalonians 4.15-18)

Behold, I tell you a mystery: We all shall not sleep, but we shall all be changed, in a moment, in the twinkling of an eye, at the last trump: for the trumpet shall sound, and the dead shall be raised incorruptible, and we shall be changed. For this corruptible must put on incorruption, and this mortal must put on immortality. (1 Corinthians 15.51-53)

16

ONE

THE VALLEY

The Old Testament prophets saw two distinct comings of the Messiah. They saw the first coming in which the Messiah would die for mankind. They also saw the second coming in which the Messiah would establish His physical kingdom on Earth. Between the two comings (mountain peaks) is a valley (the duration between the two comings). They did not know how large that valley is, but they gave some definite hints of its size.

Isaiah 61

The key to Pre-Millennial and Pre-Tribulation eschatology is found in the 61st chapter of the book of Isaiah:

The Spirit of the Lord Jehovah is upon me; because Jehovah hath anointed me to preach good tidings unto the meek; he hath sent me to bind up the broken-hearted, to proclaim liberty to the captives, and the opening of the prison to them that are bound; to proclaim the year of Jehovah's favor, and the day of vengeance of our God; to comfort all that mourn; to appoint unto them that mourn in Zion, to give unto them a garland for ashes, the oil of joy for mourning, the garment of praise for the spirit of heaviness; that they may be called trees of righteousness, the planting of Jehovah, that he may be glorified. And they shall build the old wastes, they shall raise up the former desolations, and they shall repair the waste cities, the desolations of many generations. And strangers shall stand and feed your flocks, and foreigners shall be your plowmen and your vine-dressers. But ye shall be named the priests of Jehovah; men shall call you the ministers of our God: ye shall eat the wealth of the nations, and in their glory shall ye boast yourselves. Instead of your shame ye shall have double; and instead of dishonor they shall rejoice in their portion: therefore in their land they shall possess double; everlasting joy shall be unto them. For I, Jehovah, love justice, I hate robbery with iniquity; and I will give them their recompense in truth, and I will make an everlasting covenant with them. And their seed shall be known among the nations, and their offspring among the peoples; all that see them shall acknowledge them, that they are the seed which Jehovah hath blessed. I will greatly rejoice in Jehovah, my soul shall be joyful in my God; for he hath clothed me with the garments of salvation, he hath covered me with the robe of righteousness, as a bridegroom decketh himself with a garland, and as a bride adorneth herself with her jewels. For as the earth bringeth forth its bud, and as the garden causeth the things that are sown in it to spring forth; so the Lord

Jehovah will cause righteousness and praise to spring forth before all the nations. (Isaiah 61.1-11)

This prophecy shows the Messiah will usher in three different periods of time:

1. A long time likened to a year (at His First Coming).
2. A short period of time likened to a day (at the Rapture).
3. A time of comfort to all that mourn in Zion (at His Glorious Appearing).

These three periods of time are:

1. The Christian dispensation.
2. The seven-year Tribulation.
3. The Millennial Kingdom.

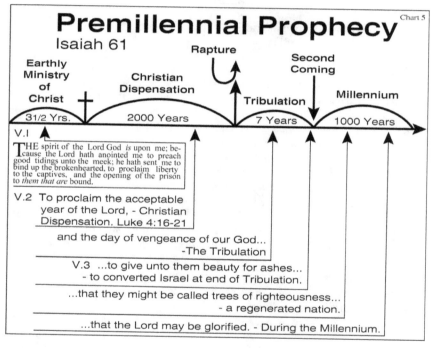

Jesus began his ministry by bringing in the first period of time – the Christian dispensation (Luke 4.18-19). On the day that He raptures the Church, He will usher in the second period – the Tribulation. Then at the end of the Tribulation with His glorious appearing, He will bring in the third period of time – the Millennial Kingdom.

The length of the Tribulation in relation to the Christian dispensation is like one day is to a year. The Tribulation will be seven years in length, so the

Christian dispensation would be about 360 times as long, or approximately 2520 years. Remember, it is not an exact relationship, but an approximate one. That means if we took it absolutely literally it would be, but we believe He is showing an approximate period of time.

It has been a tradition for more than 2000 years for Jews in every congregation to read the same passage on the Sabbath. On the Sabbath that Jesus went to the synagogue and read the passage in Isaiah 61, that same passage was read in every synagogue in the world. Jesus stopped reading after the phrase, *"to proclaim the year of Jehovah's favor."* He rolled up the scroll, gave it back to the attendant and then said, *"Today hath this scripture been fulfilled in your ears"* (Luke 4.21). He did not read on and say, *"and the day of vengeance of our God"* (the Tribulation) and *"to comfort all that mourn; to appoint unto them that mourn in Zion"* (Millennial Kingdom), because those prophecies would not be fulfilled for nearly 2000 years. This is the foundational passage for the doctrine of Pre-Millennialism, which teaches that the Second Coming of Jesus will take place before the Millennial Kingdom.

Isaiah 61 teaches three periods of time – a long one like a year (Christian dispensation), followed by a short period of time like a day (Tribulation) and then the Millennial Kingdom.

The Olivet Discourse follows the same pattern. The First Coming of Christ and the Church Age are described in Matthew 24.4-8, and the Tribulation and Second Coming are covered in verses 9-31. The beginning of the Millennial Kingdom is then described in Matthew 25.31-34.

Chapters 1-3 of Revelation describe the First Coming of Christ and the Church dispensation. Chapters 4-5 give the scene in Heaven after the Rapture (*"Come up hither,"* 4.1), and chapters 6-19 describe the Tribulation and the Second Coming. Chapters 20-22 describe the Millennial and Eternal Kingdoms.

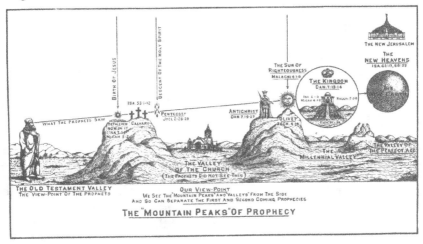

The early dispensationalists did not believe the prophets saw the Church Age. They would draw a chart like the one above picturing the prophets seeing the mountain of his First Coming and the mountain peak of his Second Coming, but not the valley of the church age in between. However the following passages show that their position is incorrect, and that prophets clearly saw the valley of the church age and its length.

Peter affirmed the long gap of time between the two comings of the Messiah

Peter explained that Jesus had to return to Heaven until the *"times of restoration of all things"* and he said this was foretold by the prophets:

> *Repent ye therefore, and turn again, that your sins may be blotted out, that so there may come seasons of refreshing from the presence of the Lord; and that he may send the Christ who hath been appointed for you, even Jesus: whom the **heaven must receive until the times of restoration of all things**, whereof God spake by the mouth of His holy prophets that have been from of old.* (Acts 3.19-21, emphasis mine)

There are four types of Messianic prophecies and the fourth shows there is a gap between the first and second comings of the Messiah:

First – The prophecies that only refer to Christ's first coming (Deuteronomy 18.18; Psalm 16.8-11; 34.20; 40.6-10; 41.9; 69.13-28; Isaiah 7.14; 52.13-53.12; Zechariah 13.7)

Second – The prophecies that only refer to Christ's second coming (Psalm 2.48; 72.1-19; Isaiah 2-4; 24; 32; 33; 35; 60; Jeremiah 3.11-18; 23.1-8; Ezekiel 34; Amos 9.11-15; Habakkuk 3; Zephaniah 3.8-20; Zechariah 14)

Third – the prophecies that blend the two comings together (Genesis 49.10; Psalm 22; Isaiah 9.5-7; 11.1-12; 6; Zechariah 6.9-15; 9.9-10)

Fourth – The prophecies giving Christ's first coming, His second coming, and the interval of time between (Psalm 110; Hosea 5.14-6.3; Isaiah 42.1-4; 61.1-4).

The prophets prophesied two different comings of the Messiah. The first in which the Messiah would die for mankind (Isaiah 52.13-53.12), and the second in which He would defeat the forces of wickedness and establish His Millennial Kingdom (Isaiah 11.1-16; 65.17-25). It is obvious that there would be a period of time separating the two comings. There were several hints given by the Old Testament prophets that the valley would be very large as noted previously. Yet the Lord Himself made it perfectly clear that this valley would be very large. His parables of the nobleman (Luke 19.12) and talents (Matthew

25.19) as noted above emphasized this truth. The phrases, *"went to a distant country"* and *"after a long time,"* show there would be a long period of time between the two comings of the Messiah, and that the valley would be very large.

The prophets said the Messiah would come to Earth, go back to Heaven and then return a long time later? David, Isaiah and Hosea:

Jehovah saith unto my Lord, Sit thou at my right hand, **until** (the entire Church Age) *I make thine enemies thy footstool. Jehovah will send forth the rod of thy strength out of Zion: Rule thou in the midst of thine enemies.* (Psalm 110.1-2)

Behold, my servant, whom I uphold; my chosen, in whom my soul delighteth: I have put my Spirit upon him; he will bring forth justice to the Gentiles. He will not cry, nor lift up his voice, nor cause it to be heard in the street. A bruised reed will he not break, and a dimly burning wick will he not quench: he will bring forth justice in truth. He will not fail nor be discouraged, **till** (the entire Christian dispensation) *he have set justice in the earth; and the isles shall wait for his law.* (Isaiah 42.1-4)

To proclaim the **year** *of Jehovah's favor* (Church Age), *and the* **day** *of vengeance of our God* (Tribulation); *to comfort all that mourn...* (Isaiah 61.2)

For I will be unto Ephraim as a lion, and as a young lion to the house of Judah: I, even I, will tear and go away; I will carry off, and there shall be none to deliver. I will **go and return to my place**, **till** *they* **acknowledge their offence**, *and* **seek my face**: *in their affliction they will seek me earnestly. Come, and let us return unto Jehovah; for he hath torn, and he will heal us; he hath smitten, and he will bind us up.* **After two days** *will he* **revive us: on the third day** *he will* **raise us up**, *and we shall live before him. And let us know, let us follow on to know Jehovah: his going forth is sure as the morning; and he will come unto us as the rain, as the latter rain that watereth the earth.* (Hosea 5.14-6.3, emphasis mine)

22

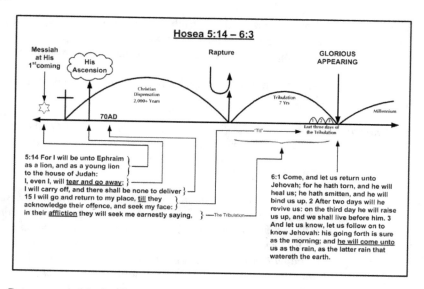

Peter noted this in his sermon under inspiration of the Holy Spirit. The phrase *"even Jesus: whom the heaven must receive until times of restoration of all things"* is the key. The times of restoration would not be a few decades, but will be nearly 2000 years.

According to Hosea 6.2, *"After two days will he revive us: on the third day he will raise us up, and we shall live before him"* we understand there is two days between the resurrection of Jesus and His return. Remember a "day" in some instances can be 1000 years (2 Peter 3.8).

It should also be noted that some theologians argue the Lord offered the kingdom to the Jews at His first coming. This hypothesis is not valid because, as shown, Scripture specified there would be a *gap* between the two comings. Jesus also said this *gap* would be a very long period of time.

If Jesus intended to offer the "kingdom" to the Jews that offer would have been recorded in the Bible. Instead, He made an offer to Jews and Gentiles alike to believe in Him. When Nicodemus, a high-ranking Pharisee, came to Jesus secretly early in His ministry, He made the offer of salvation to him and to everyone (John 3.1-16). This meeting took place at the beginning of His ministry. He prophesied that He would die for the world:

> *"And as Moses lifted up the serpent in the wilderness, even so must the Son of man be lifted up; that whosoever believeth may in him have eternal life."* (John 3.14-15)

We know from other statements by Jesus that He came to die for all the people of the world (Matthew 20.28; 26.28). We also know from the Old Testament that the Messiah would die for the world (Isaiah 52.13-53.12). It is pure speculation to declare that Jesus intended to make the offer of the "kingdom" to Israel, and if accepted then offer Himself as the Passover lamb, followed by His resurrection from the dead and the establishment of His "kingdom."

The idea that the Lord offered the "Kingdom of Heaven" to the nation of Israel is not biblical. Those who spend time arguing that there is a difference between the terms, the "Kingdom of Heaven" and the "Kingdom of God" are wasting their time. The Lord Himself said:

> *And Jesus said unto his disciples, "Verily I say unto you, It is hard for a rich man to enter into the kingdom of heaven. And again I say unto you, It is easier for a camel to go through a needle's eye, than for a rich man to enter into the kingdom of God."* (Matthew 19.23-24)

Since the Lord used the two interchangeably, it is a serious mistake to claim they are different. There is no difference between the "Kingdom of God" and the "Kingdom of Heaven." There is only one gospel as Paul boldly declared, and any other gospel is a false gospel (Galatians 1.6, 9). At the end of his ministry Paul was preaching the gospel of the kingdom (Acts 28.30).

Conclusion

The apostles and early Church fathers may not have guessed how long the Church Age would be, but we know that it will be almost 2000 years. Thusly, the understanding that the valley between the two mountain peaks of the first and second comings of Christ is a long period of time of approximately 2000 years is the only acceptable understanding.

STUDY QUESTIONS

Chapter 1

1. Which period did Jesus usher in?

2. Which period will He bring in next?

3. What is the third period that He will inaugurate, and when will He do it?

TWO

THE RAPTURE

The "Rapture" is a word that refers to the catching away of all believers from Earth to meet Jesus Christ in the air when He returns. The Greek word, *harpazo*, that is translated "*caught up*" (1 Thessalonians 4.17), means to "snatch or catch away" with "forceful seizure" (Vine's Expository Dictionary, p. 174). The Rapture of believers from Earth is not a point of disagreement among Christians; it is the timing of the Rapture that is not agreed upon.

The Blessed Event

Paul described this event in his first letter to the church at Thessalonica, Greece:

For this we say unto you by the word of the Lord, that we that are alive, that are left unto the coming of the Lord, shall in no wise precede them that are fallen asleep. For the Lord himself shall descend from heaven, with a shout, with the voice of the archangel, and with the trump of God: and the dead in Christ shall rise first; then we that are alive, that are left, shall together with them be caught up in the clouds, to meet the Lord in the air: and so shall we ever be with the Lord. (1 Thessalonians 4.15-17)

The announcement of the catching up from Earth of all believers, dead and alive, takes place in a matter of several moments. The archangel shouts the command, "*Come up here!*" (Revelation 4.1), and then the trumpet of God is blown. We do not know how long the trumpet blast is, but it could be from several seconds to a minute or more because more than one trumpet is blown. Paul said believers will be changed "*at the last trumpet*" (1 Corinthians 15.52).

The dead in Christ are raised first, and then the bodies of all living believers are transformed from mortal bodies to immortal ones. Once they are transformed they are "*caught up*" to meet the Lord in the air.

Paul gave more information in his first letter to the church in Corinth:

Behold, I tell you a mystery: We all shall not sleep, but we shall all be changed, in a moment, in the twinkling of an eye, at the last trump: for the trumpet shall sound, and the dead shall be raised incorruptible, and we shall be changed. For this corruptible must put on incorruption, and this mortal must put on immortality. (1 Corinthians 15.51-52)

The entire Rapture event will take several moments to as long as a few minutes. It will not take place in the *"twinkling of an eye,"* as most teach.

According to many eschatologians, the entire Rapture event will take about one-thousandth of a second. It is hard to imagine how the shout from the archangel, the blowing of the trumpet blasts, and the resurrection and rapture of believers can take place in just one-thousandth of a second.

Hal Lindsey believes the entire Rapture event takes place in the "twinkling of an eye":

> Someone said that the twinkling of an eye is about one-thousandth of a second. The Greek word *is atomos* from which we get the word atom. It means something that cannot be divided. In other words, the Rapture will occur so quickly and suddenly that the time frame in which it occurs cannot be humanly divided.
>
> Just think of it...in the flash of a second every living believer on earth will be gone! Suddenly, without warning, only unbelievers will be populating Planet Earth. (*Vanished Into Thin Air*, pp. 56-57)

Timothy LaHaye also believes that the entire Rapture event takes only a fraction of a second:

> Through the years some have tried to discredit the pre-Trib Rapture theory by calling it the *secret rapture*. Of course, nowhere in Scripture is the term *secret* applied to this event. However, anyone who does not participate in the Rapture will not actually see it, for it will occur in the *twinkling of an eye*. The word twinkling has been defined as a *gleam in your eye*, which is faster than the eye can see. The occurrence would much better be labeled the *sudden rapture*. (*No Fear of the Storm*, pp. 33-34, emphasis T.L.)

Some say that only Christians hear the shout and the trumpet blasts. That is a guess, but it does not explain how an event, that must take a minute or more, can take place in one-thousandth of a second. When the archangel shouts, *"Come up here!"* (Revelation 4.1), he does not say it in less than one-thousandth of a second. The duration of the trumpet blasts are also not less than one-thousandth of a second.

Most prophecy teachers do not explain the various parts of the Rapture. Instead, they teach that the entire event takes place in a fraction of a second. They do not break down the four primary parts, and they never go into detail on how long it will take. Here are the four major parts of the Rapture event:

1. The descent of Christ with a shout of the archangel and the command, *"Come up here!"* (1 Thessalonians 4.16; Revelation 4.1)
2. The blowing of the trumpets (1 Corinthians 15.52; 1 Thessalonians 4.16)
3. The resurrection and catching up of dead believers (1 Thess. 4.17)
4. The changing of the bodies of living believers from mortal to immortal, and their being *caught up* to be with Christ in the air (1 Cor. 15.51-54).

The Rapture must take longer than a fraction of a second because Jesus commanded those on the housetops and in the field to not return to their home to get anything (Luke 17.31). It is common sense that if the Rapture takes a split second no one could even think of going back to their house.

Partial Rapture doctrine

Some pastors teach the Partial-Rapture doctrine, and when they were asked if backslidden Christians who miss the Rapture might take the mark of the Beast, they said they were not certain and hoped none would.

We do not believe the Partial-Rapture doctrine is biblical. All Christians will be *"caught up"* when Christ returns, as Paul said (1 Corinthians 15.51). Even if a Christian is in the middle of committing a sin he will be *"caught up."*

The Resurrections

There are two general resurrections. The second resurrection, of the unsaved, takes place at the end of the Millennial Kingdom (Revelation 20.5). The unsaved are resurrected, judged, found guilty and cast into the Lake of Fire where they will spend all eternity (Revelation 20.11-15).

The first resurrection is divided into four parts. The resurrection of Jesus and a select number of Old Testament saints (Matthew 27.52-53) was the first part. They were the first fruits (1 Corinthians 15.23). The second part is the resurrection of all believers of the Church Age (1 Thessalonians 4.15-17). They will be the harvest. The third part is the resurrection of the two witnesses (Revelation 11.11-12). The final part of the first resurrection is that of believers who are martyred during the Tribulation, and the Old Testament saints (Revelation 20.4). The two witnesses, the Tribulation martyrs and the Old Testament saints will be the gleaning.

Conclusion

1 Thessalonians 4.16-17 and 1 Corinthians 15.51-53 teach that the entire Rapture event will take from several seconds to a minute or more. The announcement of the catching up of believers takes place in a few seconds as the archangel shouts the command, *"Come up here!"* (Revelation 4.1).

Next the trumpet of God is blown more than once. The duration of the blowing of the trumpet could take several seconds to several minutes, depending on how many trumpet blasts there are. (If the Rapture takes place on Rosh Hashanah, and forty trumpets are blown, it will take more than several minutes to blow them all. They will be blown by angels, not men.) We do not know the duration of the trumpet blasts, because more than one trumpet blast is blown. Paul said believers will *"be changed in a moment, at the last trumpet,"* (1 Corinthians 15.52). The trumpet blasts could be similar to the blasts that were blown to prepare the people to move out. When the first trumpet was blown the tribes on the east side set out, and the tribes on the south side set out on the second blast (Numbers 10.5-6). There may be just two blasts. The dead in Christ will rise on the first blast, and the living Christians will be caught up when the second blast is blown.

Dead believers will be resurrected and *"caught up"* after the trumpet is blown. The living believers will then be changed from mortals to immortals in the *"twinkling of an eye,"* and be *"caught up."* The transformation of living Christians from mortals to immortals takes place in the *"twinkling of an eye,"* not the entire Rapture event.

STUDY QUESTIONS

Chapter 2

1. Will the entire Rapture event take place in the *"twinkling of an eye,"* or will it take a few minutes or more?

2. What are the four things that happen during the Rapture event?

    A.

    B.

    C.

    D.

3. What are the four parts of the first general resurrection?

    A.

    B.

    C.

    D.

PART II

WARNING SIGNS OF THE TRIBULATION

Seven major *signs* of the Tribulation have already been fulfilled, 5 major *signs* are currently being fulfilled and 15 more major *signs* have yet to be fulfilled.

Those who are "watching" for specific *warning signs* to take place before the Tribulation are obedient servants. The Lord Jesus Christ commanded us to "*watch*" for His return:

Watch therefore: for ye know not on what day your Lord cometh. (Matthew 24.42)

Watch therefore, for ye know not the day nor the hour. (Matthew 25.12)

Looking for the blessed hope and appearing of the glory of the great God and our Saviour Jesus Christ. (Titus 2.13)

THREE

WARNING SIGNS THAT HAVE BEEN FULFILLED

Scripture teaches us that numerous *warning signs* will be fulfilled prior to the Tribulation. These are the major *signs* that have already been fulfilled:

1-Balfour Declaration (Zephaniah 2.1a)
2-Return of the Jews to the Holy Land, (Ezekiel 37.1-14; Zeph. 2.1-2)
3-The two World Wars – birth pains (Matthew 24.6-8)
4-Founding of the United Nations (Luke 21.29-32)
5-Israel becomes a nation (Matthew 24.32)
6-Capture of Jerusalem – end of the *Times of the Gentiles* (Luke 21.24)
7-Gaza abandoned by Israel (Zephaniah 2.4).

The Balfour Declaration
(Zephaniah 2.1a)

The Balfour Declaration was the preparation for the re-gathering of the Jews to the Holy Land:

Gather yourselves together, yea, gather together…

After World War I, the British took control of the Ottoman Empire and officially declared that it favored the return of the Jews to the Holy Land to establish a Jewish nation:

Foreign Office,
November 2nd, 1917.

Dear Lord Rothschild,

I have much pleasure in conveying to you, on behalf of His Majesty's Government, the following declaration of sympathy with Jewish Zionist aspirations which has been submitted to, and approved by, the Cabinet:

His Majesty's Government view with favour the establishment in Palestine of a national home for the Jewish people, and will use their best endeavours to facilitate the achievement of this object, it being clearly understood that nothing shall be done which may prejudice the civil and religious rights of existing non-Jewish communities in Palestine, or the rights and political status enjoyed by Jews in any other country.

I should be grateful if you would bring this declaration to the knowledge of the Zionist Federation.

Yours Sincerely,
Alfred James Balfour

The Return of the Jews to the Holy Land
(Ezekiel 37.12-14; Zephaniah 2.1-2)

The re-gathering of the Jews to the Holy Land was prophesied in detail by Ezekiel:

Therefore prophesy, and say unto them, Thus saith the Lord Jehovah: Behold, I will open your graves, and cause you to come up out of your graves, O my people; and I will bring you into the land of Israel. And ye shall know that I am Jehovah, when I have opened your graves, and caused you to come up out of your graves, O my people. And I will put my Spirit in you, and ye shall live, and I will place you in your own land: and ye shall know that I, Jehovah, have spoken it and performed it, saith Jehovah. (Ezekiel 37.12-14)

The re-gathering of the Jews to their ancient homeland before the Tribulation was also prophesied by Zephaniah:

Gather yourselves together, yea, gather together, O nation that hath no shame; before the decree bring forth, before the day pass as the chaff, before the fierce anger of Jehovah come upon you, before the day of Jehovah's anger come upon you. (Zephaniah 2.1-2)

The re-gathering of the nation of Israel began in the latter part of the 19th century, culminating on May 14, 1948, with the re-establishment of the nation of Israel. Jews from all over the world flooded into Israel and turned an agrarian land into a thriving industrial nation.

The truth that the Jewish people must return to their ancient homeland had been known among some theologians throughout the Church Age. The most famous theologian who wrote about the physical return of the Jews to the Holy Land was Sir Isaac Newton (1642-1727). He stated around 250 years before the nation of Israel was re-established that the Jews would return to the Holy Land and form a nation again:

So then the mystery of this restitution of all things is to be found in all the Prophets: which makes me wonder with great admiration that so few Christians of our age can find it there. For they understand not that the final return of the Jews captivity... (Moore, Philip N., *The End of History Messiah Conspiracy*, pp. 493-494; citing Franz Kobler, *Newton on the Restoration of the Jews*, 1943, *Yahudah Manuscript* 6)

The two world wars
(The First Birth Pains - Matthew 24.6-8)

The two world wars were the first birth pains that Jesus spoke of in His briefing to His disciples on eschatology. Called the Olivet Discourse, it is found in Matthew chapters 24 and 25, Mark 13 and Luke 21:

And ye shall hear of wars and rumors of wars; see that ye be not troubled: for these things must needs come to pass; but the end is not yet. For nation shall rise against nation, and kingdom against kingdom; and there shall be famines and earthquakes in divers places. But all these things are the beginning of travail.

World Wars I and II, the first birth pains, were followed by other wars, as well as by many famines and major earthquakes. A woman's labor pains come closer together as the time of birth draws near. The wars, famines, and earthquakes will take place in shorter intervals the closer we get to the Rapture/Tribulation. World War I prepared the land of Israel for the Jews, and World War II prepared the Jews for the land.

Founding of the United Nations
(Luke 21.29-32)

The founding of the United Nations in 1945 was prophesied by Jesus in the Olivet Discourse:

And he spake to them a parable: Behold the fig tree, and all the trees: when they now shoot forth, ye see it and know of your own selves that the summer is now nigh. Even so ye also, when ye see these things coming to pass, know ye that the kingdom of God is nigh. Verily I say unto you, this generation shall not pass away, till all things be accomplished.

The putting-forth of the leaves of all the trees was the establishment of the United Nations in 1945. That political organization is the foundation for the creation of the "end-times" world government that is still many years away. In 1948, the fig tree (Israel) put forth its leaves – it became a nation. Israel could not have been recognized as a nation without the United Nations to do it.

Israel becomes a nation
(Matthew 24.32-33)

The re-establishment of the nation of Israel in her ancient homeland on May 14, 1948, is considered to be the most important *sign* of the "end times" by most eschatologians. The parable of the fig tree is about Israel's rebirth:

Now from the fig tree learn her parable: when her branch is now become tender, and putteth forth its leaves, ye know that the summer is nigh; even so ye also, when ye see all these things, know ye that he is nigh, even at the doors.

Capture of Jerusalem
(Luke 21.24)

The next *sign* was the end of the "times of the Gentiles" that Jesus prophesied of:

And they shall fall by the edge of the sword, and shall be led captive into all the nations: and Jerusalem shall be trodden down of the Gentiles, until the times of the Gentiles be fulfilled.

The fulfillment of the beginning of the end of the *times of the Gentiles* was the taking of the city of Jerusalem by the Jews on June 17, 1967.

Abandonment of Gaza
(Zephaniah 2.4)

The abandonment of the Gaza Strip was prophesied more than 2500 years ago:

For Gaza shall be forsaken, and Ashkelon a desolation; they shall drive out Ashdod at noonday, and Ekron shall be rooted up.

Israel abandoned Gaza in August of 2005.

Conclusion

Seven major Bible prophecies have been fulfilled alerting the world that the "last days" are upon us. Everyone should "watch" for the *warning signs* that have yet to be fulfilled before the start of the Tribulation.

STUDY QUESTIONS

Chapter 3

1. Have a few major prophecies been fulfilled that had to be fulfilled before the Tribulation could start?

2. Could the Tribulation have started before the Jews returned to Israel and became a nation?

3. Were the Rapture and the start of the Tribulation *imminent* events before 1948?

FOUR

WARNING SIGNS THAT ARE BEING FULFILLED

We have seen 7 warning signs of the Tribulation already having been fulfilled, and we are currently "watching" 5 more as they are being fulfilled:

1-The *"falling away"* (2 Thessalonians 2.3; 2 Timothy 2.1-5; 4.3-4)
2-Increase in travel and knowledge (Daniel 12.4)
3-Rise of anti-Semitism (Psalm 83)
4-Mark of the Beast technology (Revelation 13.15-18).
5-Israel dwelling securely (*betach*) (Ezekiel 38.8, 11, 14).

The first *sign* began in the 19th century, the second and third began before the start of the Second World War, and the fourth began after that war. They will not be fully completed until the Second Coming of Jesus Christ.

The falling away
(2 Thessalonians 2.1-3; 2 Timothy 4.3-4)

The *"falling away"* or "apostasy" of the Church from the faith began in the 19th century. It was prophesied by Paul almost 2000 years ago:

Now we beseech you, brethren, touching the coming of our Lord Jesus Christ, and our gathering together unto him; to the end that ye be not quickly shaken from your mind, nor yet be troubled, either by spirit, or by word, or by epistle as from us, as that the day of the Lord is just at hand; let no man beguile you in any wise: for it will not be, except the falling away come first, and the man of sin be revealed, the son of perdition. (2 Thessalonians 2.1-3).

The *"falling away"* of the Church from the faith in the "last days" began with the acceptance of higher criticism, which was spearheaded by the Graf-Wellhausen hypothesis in the late 19th century. Karl Graf and Julius Wellhausen argued that the Old Testament was not inspired by God. According to them, it is a compilation of books that were written by priests and scribes, rather than the men that tradition says wrote the books. They taught that the Pentateuch (Genesis through Deuteronomy) was not written by Moses, but by four groups of scribes. One group in Judah preferred to use the proper name of God (Yahweh). They wrote their account around 950 BC. A second group in the northern kingdom used Elohim for God. They wrote their account around 850 BC. The third group focused on the law and wrote their account around 650 BC. The fourth group focused on the priestly duties and wrote their account around 550 BC. One scribe, maybe Ezra, used these four accounts to create the Pentateuch. According to the high-priests of higher criticism, four teams of scribes wrote the book of Isaiah, and Daniel was written around 170 BC.

Soon after the Graf-Wellhausen hypothesis was adopted by several Protestant denominations, they began to question fundamental doctrines of the Christian faith. Some eventually rejected the historicity of the first eleven chapters of the book of Genesis. They did not believe that Adam and Eve were the progenitors of the Human race. They also rejected the universal flood of Noah's time, along with many other miracles recorded in the Old Testament. They rejected the divine judgment of Sodom and Gomorrah, the ten plagues of Egypt, the parting of the Red Sea by Moses, the collapse of the walls of Jericho by trumpet blasts, the sun standing still for about 24 hours and Jonah being swallowed by a large fish. They even rejected the virgin birth of Jesus and most of His miracles, along with the miracles of the apostles. Some denominations have gone so far as to claim that Jesus Christ is not God the Son, but was just a good and wise teacher.

The men of the Jesus Seminar (a group of 150 people, founded in 1985, who vote to decide what Jesus did or did not do and say) do not believe Jesus is the Christ, the Son of God. Instead, they have determined, by their votes, that Jesus did not say all the things that the Bible says He said, nor did He ever claim to be God, or the Son of God.

The rejection of the Bible's divine inspiration by some denominations has led to the preaching of sermons that have little substance and do not edify believers to live holy lives. Teaching in some churches is shallow, and most members know little about the Bible. Few churches have solid discipleship programs, and only a few dedicated believers study the Bible on their own.

The theory of evolution, which was published in the middle of the 19th century, also struck a blow against Christianity. In the 20th century, some denominations and churches declared that God used the mechanism of evolution to bring about the Human race. The Roman Catholic Church is one of those churches.

There have been many other aspects of the "apostasy." Far too many congregations no longer desire to be taught the Scriptures; instead, they seek out pastors who preach feel-good sermons and give them all kinds of social programs to make them happy. This sad situation is ubiquitous in the Western world. It was also prophesied by Paul:

For the time will come when they will not endure the sound doctrine; but, having itching ears, will heap to themselves teachers after their own lusts; and will turn away their ears from the truth, and turn aside unto fables. (2 Timothy 4.3-4)

The pastors hired by the apostate congregations do not feed their souls. Many Christians in the Western world are fed lukewarm, sour milk and remain spiritual babies until death, as Paul warned about:

Of whom we have many things to say, and hard of interpretation, seeing ye are become dull of hearing. For when by reason of the time ye ought to be teachers, ye have need again that someone teach you the rudiments of the first principles of the oracles of God; and are become such as have need of milk, and not of solid food. For every one that partaketh of milk is without experience of the word of righteousness; for he is a babe. But solid food is for fullgrown men, even those who by reason of use have their senses exercised to discern good and evil. (Hebrews 5.11-14)

The abandonment of the fundamental doctrines of the Christian faith has led many Christians to accept some of the unscriptural practices of the world such as pre-marital sex, intoxication, use of illegal drugs, watching illicit television shows and movies, and listening to inappropriate music. The lifestyle of these so-called Christians is similar to that of non-Christians. Paul prophesied that in the last days people would basically be evil:

But know this, that in the last days grievous times shall come. For men shall be lovers of self, lovers of money, boastful, haughty, railers, disobedient to parents, unthankful, unholy, without natural affection, implacable, slanderers, without self-control, fierce, no lovers of good, traitors, headstrong, puffed up, lovers of pleasure rather than lovers of God; holding a form of godliness, but having denied the power therefore. From these also turn away. (2 Timothy 3.1-5)

While it is understandable that the unsaved live unholy lives, it is tragic that these negative attributes are found among far too many Christians. Today most Christians do not know that we are living in the "apostasy" of the "last days." Some think they are living in a time of revival.

All Christians should take to heart a quote by General George Smith Patton, Jr: "It is better to fight for something than to live for nothing." Christians should fight the *"good fight"* for Jesus Christ as Paul did (2 Timothy 4.7) rather than live for their desires of the flesh (1 John 2.15-17).

Increase in travel and knowledge
(Daniel 12.4)

The increase in travel and knowledge that was prophesied by Daniel began to be fulfilled just before World War II, when the militaries of the great powers started an arms race:

But thou, O Daniel, shut up the words, and seal the book, even to the time of the end: many shall run to and fro, and knowledge shall be increased.

The need by both sides to win the second great war sped the development of several key technologies that have increased man's knowledge and his ability to travel anywhere in the world at fantastic speeds.

Rocket technology skyrocketed during the war, and eventually enabled mankind to send men to the moon. It also enabled mankind to send unmanned probes throughout the solar system and beyond. The American space shuttles routinely circle the earth in less than 90 minutes.

Just before World War II, the jet engine was invented separately by Dr. Hans von Ohain (Germany) and Sir Frank Whittle (Britain). Shortly after the war, jets were put into military service by America, Britain, France and the Soviet Union. Commercial air travel by jet quickly became commonplace, enabling a person to fly anywhere in the world in hours, rather than days.

The number of people flying today has increased dramatically. In 1930, only 300,000 people flew by plane. Today, more than 600,000,000 passengers take to the air each year in America alone. The speed of air travel has gone from a couple of hundred miles-per-hour in 1930, to 1450 mph in supersonic jets. The speed of military aircraft has increased ten-fold from the end of World War II. The fastest pre-jet fighter was the World War II P-38 Lightning Bolt, with a top speed of 450 mph. Then the X-15 reached a record speed of 4,519 mph (Flight 188, October 3, 1967, Pete Knight). Current experimental aircraft are capable of flying at even greater speeds. The super-secret Aurora spacecraft is said to fly at more than twice the speed of the X-15.

The speed of ground travel by train, bus and cars has increased greatly, with massive railway networks and highway systems abounding. Improvement in engine technology has enabled automobiles to travel from an original speed of about 20 mph to more than 200 mph. The bullet trains in Japan travel at more than 200 mph, and experimental magnetic-levitation trains have reached speeds of 362 mph.

During World War II, a tool was developed which has enabled mankind to double its knowledge about every eighteen months. Man's knowledge doubled from the flood of Noah's day to 1800, and again from 1800 to 1900. It doubled again from 1900 to 1950. Since then, it has been doubling about every 18 months. The tool that has enabled man's knowledge to explode is the computer. The first British computer (Colossus) was put into use in 1941 for code breaking. An American computer was built from 1943-1946 to calculate artillery firing tables. It was named ENIAC (Electronic Numerical Integrator and Computer), but was not put into use until after the war in 1946. Since then the power and capabilities of the computer have gone into orbit. The ability to keep track of virtually everything people do, say and buy with the world computer networks will give the future world ruler total control over everyone on the planet. No one will be able to buy or sell or function in society without the permission of the False Prophet and the Antichrist (Revelation 13.15-18).

The Rise of anti-Semitism
(Psalm 83.1-5 - A prayer for Ezekiel 38 to occur)

The rise of anti-Semitism in the last days was prophesied nearly 3000 years ago:

O God, keep not thou silence:
Hold not thy peace, and be not still, O God.
For, lo, thine enemies make a tumult;
And they that hate thee have lifted up the head.
They take crafty counsel against thy people,
And consult together against thy hidden ones.
They have said, Come, and let us cut them off from being a nation;
That the name of Israel may be no more in remembrance.
For they have consulted together with one consent;
Against thee do they make a covenant.

Anti-Semitism has been around since the enslavement of the Jews in Egypt (Exodus 5.10-19). It was during the 20th century that anti-Semitism became so unbearable that without the creation of the state of Israel, the survival of the Jewish people would have been in doubt. Hitler systematically exterminated one-third of them during World War II. It was this crime that forced the Jewish people to establish their own nation in Israel as soon as possible after the war. Since the creation of the modern state of Israel, anti-Semitism has continued throughout the world. It will continue, as prophesied by Asaph (Psalm 83), and not stop until Jesus Christ returns. It should be noted that in this psalm the Islamic nations seek to destroy Israel as a nation! God will remove the Islamic presence with the events of Ezekiel 38.1-39.16.

Mark of the Beast technology
(Revelation 13.15-18)

It is at the mid-point of the seven-year Tribulation that the Antichrist forces everyone on Earth to worship him and his image, and take his mark to be able to buy or sell:

And it was given unto him to give breath to it, even to the image to the beast, that the image of the beast should both speak, and cause that as many as should not worship the image of the beast should be killed. And he causeth all, the small and the great, and the rich and the poor, and the free and the bond, that there be given them a mark on their right hand, or upon their forehead; and that no man should be able to buy or to sell, save he that hath the mark, even the name of the beast or the number of his name. Here is wisdom. He that hath understanding, let him count the number of the beast; for it is the number of a man: and his number is Six hundred and sixty and six.

The technology to make this possible must be developed before the start of the Tribulation. It is logistically impossible to develop and implement a technology to track what everyone on Earth buys and sells in 3½ years.

Before the Tribulation starts, a large number of people will have some kind of device implanted in their bodies that will allow them to make purchases. When the Antichrist requires everyone to take his "mark" during the Tribulation, whatever it may be, most people will accept it without a second thought. The penalty for taking his "mark" and worshipping him is eternal punishment in the Lake of Fire:

> *And another angel, a third, followed them, saying with a great voice, If any man worshippeth the beast and his image, and receiveth a mark on his forehead, or upon his hand, he also shall drink of the wine of the wrath of God, which is prepared unmixed in the cup of his anger; and he shall be tormented with fire and brimstone in the presence of the holy angels, and in the presence of the Lamb: and the smoke of their torment goeth up for ever and ever; and they have no rest day and night, they that worship the beast and his image, and whoso receiveth the mark of his name.* (Revelation 14.9-11)

Israel living securely
(Ezekiel 38.8, 11, 14)

Israel is currently dwelling securely (*betach*). This sets the stage for the *imminent* attack by Russia and its Muslim allies:

> *After many days thou shalt be visited: in the latter years thou shalt come into the land that is brought back from the sword, that is gathered out of many peoples, upon the mountains of Israel, which have been a continual waste; but it is brought forth out of the peoples, and they shall dwell securely, all of them. ...and thou shalt say, I will go up to the land of unwalled villages; I will go to them that are at rest, that dwell securely, all of them dwelling without walls, and having neither bars nor gates. ...Therefore, son of man, prophesy, and say unto Gog, Thus saith the Lord Jehovah: In that day when my people Israel dwelleth securely, shalt thou not know it?*

The Hebrew word *betach* means "a place of refuge" and "safety," "both the fact (safety) and the feeling (trust)" (Strong's 983). Israel is living securely at this time. The attack by Russia is an event that will take place in the very near future.

Conclusion

Five major Bible prophecies are being fulfilled before our eyes. These *warning signs* along with the seven *signs* that have been fulfilled should make every Christian take notice that the Tribulation is racing toward us. We can determine how close it is by "watching" the remaining 15 *warning signs* as they are fulfilled.

STUDY QUESTIONS

Chapter 4

1. Are we living in a time of apostasy, and has there been a massive increase in knowledge and travel in the last few decades?

2. Has technology been developed that could be used by the Antichrist to control what everyone on Earth buys and sells?

3. Is Israel living "securely," and is the attack by Russia an imminent event?

FIVE

WARNING SIGNS YET TO BE FULFILLED

Christians should "watch" for the final *warning signs* of the Tribulation to be fulfilled. They may not necessarily be fulfilled in the order given, but they must all be fulfilled before the start of the Tribulation. Christians may see some or all of them fulfilled before the Rapture:

1-Destruction of Russia, Islam and Egypt (Ezekiel 38.1-39.16; 30.1-5)
2-First stage of the conversion of Israel and also Gentiles (Ezekiel 39.7)
3-Rebuilding the ancient city of Babylon (Zechariah 5.5-11)
4-World church & the rise of the False Prophet (Rev. 17.1-5, 18; 13.11-17)
5-World economy (Revelation 13.15-18)
6-World government (Daniel 7.23)
7-World government breaks into 10 divisions (Daniel 7.24)
8-Rebuilding of the Temple (Revelation 11.1-2; 2 Thessalonians 2.4)
9-Rise of Antichrist (Is. 28.15; Dan. 9.27; 7.20, 24; Rev. 6.1-2; 13.1-10)
10-The *"overflowing scourge"* (Joel 2.1-11; Isaiah 28.18-19)
11-A time of *"peace and safety"* (1 Thessalonians 5.3)
12-Appearing of Elijah (Malachi 4.5)
13-Indications of the impending covenant between Israel and the Antichrist (Isaiah 28.15).
14-Signs in space and on Earth (Joel 2.30-31)
15-Distress and fear among the nations (Luke 21.25-27).

Destruction of Russia, Islam and Egypt
(Ezekiel 38.1-9, 21-23; 39.6-8; 30.1-5)

Russia will be destroyed when it attacks Israel, along with its Arab and Muslim nation allies. These Muslim nations (Russia has a large Muslim population) must be removed before a world government and a world religion can be established. The Russian-Islamic invasion of Israel will put an end to the Islamic religion and Muslim influence in the world. Once the military and economic power of the Muslim nations is eliminated, the "New World Order" of the Antichrist will be established with little resistance:

And the word of Jehovah came unto me, saying, Son of man, set thy face toward Gog, of the land of Magog, the prince of Rosh, Meshech, and Tubal, and prophesy against him, and say, Thus saith the Lord Jehovah: Behold, I am against thee, O Gog, prince of Rosh, Meshech, and Tubal: and I will turn thee about, and put hooks into thy jaws, and I will bring thee forth, and all thine army, horses and horsemen, all of them clothed in full armor, a great company with buckler and shield, all of them handling swords; Persia, Cush, and Put with them, all of them with shield and helmet; Gomer, and all his hordes; the house of Togarmah in the uttermost parts of the north, and all his hordes; even many peoples with thee. Be thou prepared, yea, prepare thyself, thou, and all thy companies that are assembled unto thee, and be thou a guard unto them. After many days thou shalt be visited: in the latter years thou shalt come into the land that is brought back from the sword, that is gathered out of many peoples, upon the mountains of Israel, which have been a continual waste; but it is brought forth out of the peoples, and they shall dwell securely, all of them. And thou shalt ascend, thou shalt come like a storm, thou shalt be like a cloud to cover the land, thou, and all thy hordes, and many peoples with thee. (Ezekiel 38.1-9)

And I will call for a sword against him unto all my mountains, saith the Lord Jehovah: every man's sword shall be against his brother. And with pestilence and with blood will I enter into judgment with him; and I will rain upon him, and upon his hordes, and upon the many peoples that are with him, an overflowing shower, and great hailstones, fire, and brimstone. And I will magnify myself, and sanctify myself, and I will make myself known in the eyes of many nations; and they shall know that I am Jehovah. (Ezekiel 38.21-23)

And I will send a fire on Magog, and on them that dwell securely in the isles; and they shall know that I am Jehovah. And my holy name will I make known in the midst of my people Israel; neither will I suffer my holy name to be profaned any more: and the nations shall know that I am Jehovah, the Holy One in Israel. Behold, it cometh, and it shall be done, saith the Lord Jehovah; this is the day whereof I have spoken. (Ezekiel 39.6-8)

The small number of Muslims that remain will understand that Jehovah is the true God, and submit to a world government. During this battle, Egypt will fight with Russia against Israel, and be judged by God:

The word of Jehovah came again unto me, saying, Son of man, prophesy, and say, Thus saith the Lord Jehovah: Wail ye, Alas for the day! For the day is near, even the day of Jehovah is near; it shall be a day of clouds, a time of the nations. And a sword shall come upon Egypt, and anguish shall be in Ethiopia, when the slain shall fall in Egypt; and they shall take away her multitude, and her foundations shall be broken down. Ethiopia, and Put, and Lud, and all the mingled people, and Cub, and the children of the land that is in league, shall fall with them by the sword. (Ezekiel 30.1-5)

The Russian/Islamic invasion of Israel must take place at least 3½ years before the Tribulation starts. Ezekiel 39.9 says, "*they that dwell in the cities of*

Israel shall go forth, and shall make fires of the weapons and burn them" for 7 years. At the mid-point of the Tribulation, when the Antichrist commits the abomination of desolation, the residents of Jerusalem are commanded to flee to the mountains (Matthew 24.15-18). If the residents of the cities burn the weapons for 7 years, Russia will attack Israel at least 3½ years before the Tribulation starts, because most people will not be living in the city of Jerusalem from the mid-point of the Tribulation on.

Will Israel put a stop to Iran's nuclear weapons program? If they do, it may prompt Russia and its allies to attack Israel.

First stage of the conversion of Israel and also Gentiles
(Ezekiel 39.7)

After Russia and its allies are destroyed, the people of Israel will realize that it was due to divine judgment:

And my holy name will I make known in the midst of my people Israel; neither will I suffer my holy name to be profaned any more: and the nations shall know that I am Jehovah, the Holy One in Israel.

Many Jews will come to Jesus Christ in faith for salvation by calling on the name of Jesus (Romans 10.13). This will be the first stage of the conversion of the nation of Israel. During the Tribulation more will be saved after seeing the divine judgments that fall upon the world (Revelation 6.12-17; 8.1-13; 9.1-21; 11.3-6, 13; 16.1-21; 18.8-11, 15-19). Since the War of Ezekiel 38-39 takes place 3½ years prior to the start of the Tribulation the first stage of the conversion of the nation of Israel will also take place before the Tribulation.

Rebuilding the ancient city of Babylon
(Zechariah 5.5-11)

The ancient city of Babylon will be rebuilt before the start of the Tribulation. The first world religion was created in Babylon by Nimrod and his wife Semiramis. The final world religion (church) will be headquartered there. (For details concerning this see my book *The Millennium, the Apocalypse and Armageddon*.)

Saddam Hussein of Iraq began to rebuild the ancient city, but his efforts were cut short. A future ruler of Iraq will resume the rebuilding project, and it will be nearly completed (if not completely finished) prior to the start of the Tribulation:

Then the angel that talked with me went forth, and said unto me, Lift up now thine eyes, and see what is this that goeth forth. And I said, What is it? And he said, This is the ephah that goeth forth. He said moreover, This is their appearance in all the land (and, behold, there was lifted up a talent of lead); and this is a woman sitting in the midst of the ephah. And he said,

This is Wickedness: and he cast her down into the midst of the ephah; and he cast the weight of lead upon the mouth thereof. Then lifted I up mine eyes, and saw, and, behold, there came forth two women, and the wind was in their wings; now they had wings like the wings of a stork; and they lifted up the ephah between earth and heaven. Then said I to the angel that talked with me, Whither do these bear the ephah? And he said unto me, To build her a house in the land of Shinar: and when it is prepared, she shall be set there in her own place.

The destruction of most of the Muslim and Arab nations in the Middle East will open the door for the Western nations to rebuild the ancient city of Babylon. The Bible says this city will be rebuilt and become the center of the world economy. The rebuilding project will begin before the Tribulation because it is virtually impossible to build a thriving city that is the economic capital of the world (Revelation 18.9-19) in just 3½ years. We should "watch" for this *warning sign* to be fulfilled.

The call to rebuild the ancient city of Babylon has already begun:

Iraq's Ancient Babylon To Be Restored
February 12, 2009

BAGHDAD – The Iraqi government will invite UNESCO to visit ancient Babylon this month to evaluate damage at the site, parliamentarian Mufid al-Jazaeri told RFE/RL's Radio Free Iraq.

Al-Jazaeri, former Iraqi culture minister and chairman of parliament's committee on culture and antiquities, said that repairs and reconstruction at the ruins will begin once a report on the extent of the damage is complete.

The Hanging Gardens of Babylon, which is about 100 kilometers south of Baghdad, were built in 600 B.C. and were considered one of the seven wonders of the world.

Al-Jazaeri told RFI that Babylon's ruins sustained heavy damage under Saddam Hussein's regime and during the U.S.-led invasion in 2003 when a portion of the site was used as a military base by coalition forces.

Al-Jazaeri urged that Babylon remain closed to the public until restoration is complete. (Radio Free Europe Radio Liberty, 2.12.2009)[1]

While Babylon is being rebuilt the archeological find of the last two millennia will be made. Excavators will find the "bones" of the apostle Peter. This sensational discovery will compel the Roman Catholic Church to move its headquarters to that city as described in Zechariah 5.5-11.

The land of Shinar is the location of the ancient city of Babylon. The woman is the World Church, which will be led by the Roman Catholic Church. After Peter's "bones" are found the World Church will move from Rome to Babylon (Zechariah 5.5-11). (More details concerning the bones of Peter can be found in Appendix E.)

World church and rise of the False Prophet
(Revelation 17.1-5, 18; 13.11-17)

A world church must be in place before the Tribulation as John prophesied:

And there came one of the seven angels that had the seven bowls, and spake with me, saying, Come hither, I will show thee the judgment of the great harlot that sitteth upon many waters; with whom the kings of the earth committed fornication, and they that dwell in the earth were made drunken with the wine of her fornication. And he carried me away in the Spirit into a wilderness: and I saw a woman sitting upon a scarlet-colored beast, full of names of blasphemy, having seven heads and ten horns. And the woman was arrayed in purple and scarlet, and decked with gold and precious stone and pearls, having in her hand a golden cup full of abominations, even the unclean things of her fornication, and upon her forehead a name written, MYSTERY, BABYLON THE GREAT, THE MOTHER OF THE HARLOTS AND OF THE ABOMINATIONS OF THE EARTH. (Revelation 17.1-5)

And the woman whom thou sawest is the great city, which reigneth over the kings of the earth. (Revelation 17.18)

This false church will be formed before the start of the Tribulation. We have seen efforts to unite all of the religions of the world into one super religion. This effort will intensify and eventually be obvious to everyone. In the next chapter we describe the work to create a "World Church." Even though a world religion may be a good idea to the natural man, it will be used by the Antichrist to deceive mankind into worshipping him instead of Jehovah.

This coming world church will have a leader – the False Prophet:

And I saw another beast coming up out of the earth; and he had two horns like unto lamb, and he spake as a dragon. And he exerciseth all the authority of the first beast in his sight. And he maketh the earth and them that dwell therein to worship the first beast, whose death-stroke was healed. And he doeth great signs, that he should even make fire to come down out of heaven upon the earth in the sight of men. And he deceiveth them that dwell on the earth by reason of the signs which it was given him to do in the sight of the beast; saying to them that dwell on the earth, that they should make an image to the beast who hath the stroke of the sword and lived. And it was given unto him to give breath to it, even to the image to the beast, that the image of the beast should both speak, and cause that as many as should not worship the image of the beast should be killed. And he causeth all, the small and the great, and the rich and the poor, and the free and the bond, that there be given them a mark on their right hand, or upon their forehead; and that no man should be able to buy or to sell, save he that hath the mark, even the name of the beast or the number of his name. (Revelation 13.11-17)

The False Prophet will be the head of this world church. When it is formed he will be a leader in its creation. He may be the Pope of the Roman Catholic Church which will be the driving force behind it. He will be the top henchman of the Antichrist who will enforce his dictates, especially the one requiring everyone on Earth to worship the Antichrist or his image, and to take his "mark" to be able to buy or sell. Those who refuse the "mark" will be beheaded. Since 1996 there has been a provision for execution by guillotine in America.[2] That has been the preferred method of execution in France since the French Revolution.

A world church must be established prior to the Tribulation. It is unthinkable that the False Prophet could unite all of the religions of the world in 3½ years. There have been great efforts to do this for the last 100 years without success (Chapter 15).

World economy
(Revelation 13.15-18)

There must also be a world economic system in place before the Rapture and the start of the Tribulation, because midway through the seven-year Tribulation the Antichrist and the False Prophet will take total control of a world economic system. As we have noted previously, at that point, the False Prophet will force everyone on Earth to worship the Antichrist and take his "mark" to be able to buy and sell. Everyone will be forced to worship the Antichrist or his image to get the "mark of the Beast":

And it was given unto him to give breath to it, even to the image to the beast, that the image of the beast should both speak, and cause that as many as should not worship the image of the beast should be killed. And he causeth all, the small and the great, and the rich and the poor, and the free and the bond, that there be given them a mark on their right hand, or upon their forehead; and that no man should be able to buy or to sell, save he that hath the mark, even the name of the beast or the number of his name. (Revelation 13.15-18)

Before the Tribulation starts, there will be a technology of some kind that will allow a world dictator to control what everyone on Earth buys and sells. In Chapter 18 we describe what that technology may be. It is virtually impossible to develop and implement that technology in 3½ years if it is not in place before the Tribulation starts. Remember, during the Tribulation the Antichrist will force everyone on Earth to take his mark to be able to buy or sell. If that technology, whatever it is, is not in use prior to the Tribulation the Antichrist will have just 3½ years to develop and implement it. That is a virtual impossibility.

People will not be able to receive government benefits, be able to work or hire employees, drive a vehicle, get any kind of license or do just about anything without the "mark of the Beast."

World government
(Daniel 7.23)

Once Russia and its allies are destroyed (Psalm 83; Ezekiel 38.1-39.16), the nations of the world will establish a world government:

Thus he said, The fourth beast shall be a fourth kingdom upon earth, which shall be diverse from all the kingdoms, and shall devour the whole earth, and shall tread it down, and break it in pieces.

Daniel prophesied that there would be a "world government" in the "end times." Note the phrase, *"the whole earth."* This final kingdom will be like the first world kingdom under Nebuchadnezzar. God gave him rule over the entire world (Daniel 2.36-38). Though he did not rule over everyone on Earth, he was given the entire Earth to rule over. The final world government will not only be given power over all the nations, it will rule over them.

The world government must be established before the Tribulation because it will break into 10 divisions (Daniel 7.24) before then. It is after it breaks into 10 divisions that the Antichrist rises to power (Daniel 7.24). If the Antichrist comes to power before the Tribulation, as Paul explained (2 Thessalonians 2.3), then the world government must also be established before the Tribulation. The Antichrist rises to power "*after*" the world government breaks into 10 divisions.

World government breaks into 10 divisions
(Daniel 7.24)

Sometime after the world government is established, it will break into 10 divisions:

And as for the ten horns, out of this kingdom shall ten kings arise: and another shall arise after them; and he shall be diverse from the former, and he shall put down three kings.

No one knows how long it will be before the "world government" is broken into 10 divisions. It will be divided before the start of the Tribulation because the Antichrist rises to power after the break up of the world government into 10 divisions. Notice that the Antichrist "*shall arise after them*" (after the 10 kings rise to power out of the world government). Since the Antichrist rises to power before the Tribulation, the world government will be formed and break into 10 divisions before then.

Antichrist will seek to be a member of the group of rulers that governs the world. This is why it is unwise to try to identify the Antichrist before this event. Once he joins the group of 10 it will be obvious to every student of Bible prophecy that he is the Antichrist.

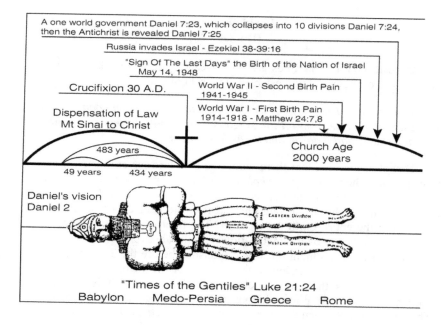

A one world government Daniel 7:23, which collapses into 10 divisions Daniel 7:24, then the Antichrist is revealed Daniel 7:25

Russia invades Israel - Ezekiel 38-39:16

"Sign Of The Last Days" the Birth of the Nation of Israel May 14, 1948

Crucifixion 30 A.D.

World War II - Second Birth Pain 1941-1945

Dispensation of Law Mt Sinai to Christ

World War I - First Birth Pain 1914-1918 - Matthew 24:7,8

483 years

Church Age 2000 years

49 years   434 years

Daniel's vision Daniel 2

EASTERN DIVISION

WESTERN DIVISION

"Times of the Gentiles" Luke 21:24

Babylon   Medo-Persia   Greece   Rome

Rebuilding of the Temple
(Revelation 11.1-2; 2 Thessalonians 2.4)

We know the Temple will be rebuilt and used to offer sacrifices by the mid-point of the Tribulation:

And there was given me a reed like unto a rod: and one said, Rise, and measure the temple of God, and the altar, and them that worship therein. And the court which is without the temple leave without, and measure it not; for it hath been given unto the nations: and the holy city shall they tread under foot forty and two months. (Revelation 11.1-2)

At the mid-point, the Antichrist will enter the Temple and declare himself to be God:

He that opposeth and exalteth himself against all that is called God or that is worshipped; so that he sitteth in the temple of God, setting himself forth as God. (2 Thessalonians 2.4)

The Temple must be rebuilt and in use before the Antichrist can enter it, claiming to be God. Once Russia and its Muslim/Arab allies are destroyed, Israel will begin to rebuild her Temple. That project will be completed before the Tribulation begins. If Israel waits until after the start of the Tribulation to begin the rebuilding project, it is unlikely that it could be completed in just 3½

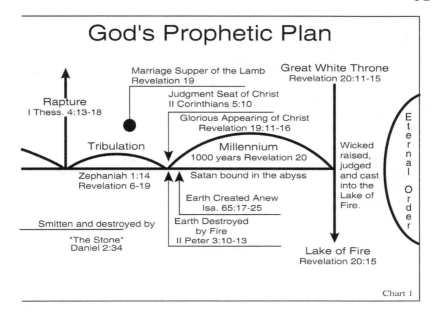

Chart 1

years. It must be completed by that time because it is at the mid-point of the seven-year Tribulation that the Antichrist enters it and claims to be God. It is a very important *warning sign* for which Christians must "watch."

Rise of Antichrist
(Isaiah 28.15; Daniel 9.27; 7.20, 24; Revelation 6.1-2; 13.1-10)

Once the world government breaks into 10 divisions, the Antichrist will rise to power out of obscurity. After the Antichrist has risen to a position of power on the world stage, he will sign the seven-year covenant of death with Israel that marks the beginning of the Tribulation:

Because ye have said, We have made a covenant with death, and with Sheol are we at agreement; when the overflowing scourge shall pass through, it shall not come unto us; for we have made lies our refuge, and under falsehood have we hid ourselves. (Isaiah 28.15)

This peace treaty with Israel is the official start of the seven-year Tribulation:

And he shall make a firm covenant with many for one week: and in the midst of the week he shall cause the sacrifice and the oblation to cease; and upon the wing of abominations shall come one that maketh desolate; and even unto the full end, and that determined, shall wrath be poured out upon the desolate. (Daniel 9.27)

The Antichrist will then seek to join the club of ten rulers who control the world government. Three of those rulers will not want him to join their club. They will hinder his schemes and prevent him from becoming dictator of the world. At the mid-point of the Tribulation, those three rulers unite and go to war against him. They are the hindering force of 2 Thessalonians 2.6. He defeats them, yet they give him a mortal wound. Satan then resuscitates him. The wounds he receives will be evident – a damaged right arm and right eye (Zechariah 11.17). After his victory, he becomes the world dictator:

And concerning the ten horns that were on its head, and the other horn which came up, and before which three fell, even that horn that had eyes, and a mouth that spake great things, whose look was more stout than its fellows. (Daniel 7.20)

And as for the ten horns, out of this kingdom shall ten kings arise: and another shall arise after them; and he shall be diverse from the former, and he shall put down three kings. (Daniel 7.24)

And I saw when the Lamb opened one of the seven seals, and I heard one of the four living creatures saying as with a voice of thunder, Come. And I saw, and behold, a white horse, and he that sat thereon had a bow; and there was given unto him a crown: and he came forth conquering, and to conquer. (Revelation 6.1-2)

And he stood upon the sand of the sea. And I saw a beast coming up out of the sea, having ten horns, and seven heads, and on his horns ten diadems, and upon his heads names of blasphemy. And the beast which I saw was like unto a leopard, and his feet were as the feet of a bear, and his mouth as the mouth of a lion: and the dragon gave him his power, and his throne, and great authority. And I saw one of his heads as though it had been smitten unto death; and his death-stroke was healed: and the whole earth wondered after the beast; and they worshipped the dragon, because he gave his authority unto the beast; and they worshipped the beast, saying, Who is like unto the beast? And who is able to war with him? and there was given to him a mouth speaking great things and blasphemies; and there was given to him authority to continue forty and two months. And he opened his mouth for blasphemies against God, to blaspheme his name, and his tabernacle, even them that dwell in the heaven. And it was given unto him to make war with the saints, and to overcome them: and there was given to him authority over every tribe and people and tongue and nation. And all that dwell on the earth shall worship him, every one whose name hath not been written from the foundation of the world in the book of life of the Lamb that hath been slain. If any man hath an ear, let him hear. If any man is for captivity, into captivity he goeth: if any man shall kill with the sword, with the sword must he be killed. Here is the patience and the faith of the saints. (Revelation 13.1-10)

It is at the mid-point of the Tribulation that the Antichrist enters the Holy of Holies of the rebuilt Temple in Jerusalem and sets up a statue of himself (Matthew 24.15). He declares that he is God Almighty (2 Thessalonians 2.4) and stops the daily sacrifices of the nation of Israel (Daniel 9.27). At this point, the Antichrist begins a pogrom against the Jewish people, and tries to destroy them (Revelation 12.13). The people of Israel flee and are given supernatural help to escape the Antichrist (Revelation 12.14-16).

There has been a desire for a world dictator for some time. Paul Manzur, a proponent of world government, said we must eventually have a dictator:

So, in order to control the diverse bureaucracies required, a politburo will develop, and over this group organization there is likely to arise the final and single arbitrator – the master of the order, the **total dictator**. (Malachi Martin, *The Keys of this Blood*, p. 343, emphasis mine)

The Antichrist meets his final doom when Jesus Christ returns to Earth at the end of the Tribulation. He has the Antichrist and the False Prophet cast into the Lake of Fire:

And the beast was taken, and with him the false prophet that wrought the signs in his sight, wherewith he deceived them that had received the mark of the beast and them that worshipped his image: they two were cast alive into the lake of fire that burneth with brimstone. (Revelation 19.20)

The *"overflowing scourge"*
(Joel 2.1-11; Isaiah 28.15, 18-19)

Just prior to the start of the Tribulation, an army of demonic creatures is set loose by God to terrorize the Middle East, including the nation of Israel. Joel sees the following events take place before the Tribulation starts. Notice that he says the "*day of Jehovah is nigh at hand*":

Blow ye the trumpet in Zion, and sound an alarm in my holy mountain; let all the inhabitants of the land tremble: for the day of Jehovah cometh, for it is nigh at hand; a day of darkness and gloominess, a day of clouds and thick darkness, as the dawn spread upon the mountains; a great people and a strong; there hath not been ever the like, neither shall be any more after them, even to the years of many generations. A fire devoureth before them; and behind them a flame burneth: the land is as the garden of Eden before them, and behind them a desolate wilderness; yea, and none hath escaped them. The appearance of them is as the appearance of horses; and as horsemen, so do they run. Like the noise of chariots on the tops of the mountains do they leap, like the noise of a flame of fire that devoureth the stubble, as a strong people set in battle array. At their presence the peoples are in anguish; all faces are waxed pale. They run like mighty men; they climb the wall like men of war; and they march every one on his

54

ways, and they break not their ranks. Neither doth one thrust another; they march every one in his path; and they burst through the weapons, and break not off their course. They leap upon the city; they run upon the wall; they climb up into the houses; they enter in at the windows like a thief. The earth quaketh before them; the heavens tremble; the sun and the moon are darkened, and the stars withdraw their shining. And Jehovah uttereth his voice before his army; for his camp is very great; for he is strong that executeth his word; for the day of Jehovah is great and very terrible; and who can abide it? (Joel 2.1-11)

The army of demonic creatures described in Joel continues into the Tribulation for an undisclosed period of time. (This demonic army is different from the demonic armies in Revelation Chapter 9.)

When the Antichrist rises to power he exerts control over the *"overflowing scourge."* He promises mankind to stop the demonic army. This promise is what prompts the unsaved to celebrate, saying they finally have, *"Peace and safety"* (1 Thessalonians 5.3). The Antichrist will keep the *"overflowing scourge"* idle for a brief period. During this time he convinces Israel to sign a covenant with him:

Because ye have said, We have made a covenant with death, and with Sheol are we at agreement; when the overflowing scourge shall pass through, it shall not come unto us; for we have made lies our refuge, and under falsehood have we hid ourselves. (Isaiah 28.15)

Israel reluctantly signs a covenant, trusting the Antichrist to control the demonic army. Included in this covenant is a provision that allows the nation of Israel to resume her daily sacrifices. It is the signing of this covenant that begins the Tribulation. The covenant is kept by the Antichrist for a time. The demonic army then resumes its campaign of terrorizing Israel and other nations:

And your covenant with death shall be annulled, and your agreement with Sheol shall not stand; when the overflowing scourge shall pass through, then ye shall be trodden down by it. As often as it passeth through, it shall take you; for morning by morning shall it pass through, by day and by night: and it shall be nought but terror to understand the message. (Isaiah 28.18-19)

Time of *"peace and safety"*
(1 Thessalonians 5.1-3)

Paul clearly taught the church in Thessalonica that before the Tribulation starts there will be a time of *"peace and safety"*:

But concerning the times and the seasons, brethren, ye have no need that aught be written unto you. For yourselves know perfectly that the day of the Lord so cometh as a thief in the night. When they are saying, Peace and safety, then sudden destruction cometh upon them, as travail upon a woman with child; and they shall in no wise escape.

The "*day of the Lord*" is the Tribulation. Right before the start of the "*day of the Lord*" (Tribulation), the unsaved believe they have achieved worldwide peace. At that time, they say that they have entered a period of "*peace and safety.*" (We know it is a period of false "*peace and safety*" because the Antichrist will not keep his promise to keep the "*overflowing scourge*" under control, but the unsaved do not know that.)

Paul goes on to say that believers should not be caught by surprise the period of false peace ends:

But ye, brethren, are not in darkness, that that day should overtake you as a thief: for ye are all sons of light, and sons of the day: we are not of the night, nor of darkness; so then let us not sleep, as do the rest, but let us watch and be sober. (1 Thessalonians 5.4-6)

They will know that shortly after the "*overflowing scourge*" stops its campaign of terror, and the false peace has been achieved that the Rapture has finally become an *imminent* event. Israel will quickly sign the "*covenant with death*" with the Antichrist. On the day that Israel signs that covenant the Rapture will take place.

The Appearing of Elijah
(Malachi 4.5-6)

Another *sign* to watch for is the appearing of Elijah. Malachi prophesied that before the Tribulation starts Elijah will return:

Behold, I will send you Elijah the prophet before the great and terrible day of Jehovah comes. And he shall turn the heart of the fathers to the children, and the heart of the children to their fathers; lest I come and smite the earth with a curse.

Elijah may appear during the time of "*peace and safety.*" He will do his work, but the nation of Israel will not respond to his ministry. Instead, they will sign the covenant with the Antichrist and suffer the consequences.

Indications of the impending covenant between Israel and the Antichrist
(Isaiah 28.15)

The Antichrist will sign a covenant with the nation of Israel. Christians will not see Israel sign this covenant (Daniel 9.27) because they will have been raptured earlier, but they should see preparation for the signing of the covenant. When they see the *"overflowing scourge"* terrorizing mankind they will know the signing of the covenant is imminent:

> *Because ye have said, We have made a covenant with death, and with Sheol are we at agreement; when the overflowing scourge shall pass through, it shall not come unto us; for we have made lies our refuge, and under falsehood have we hid ourselves.* (Isaiah 28.15)

Signs on the day of the Rapture

Signs in space and on Earth
(Joel 2.30-32)

On the day the Tribulation starts, there will be a few other significant *warning signs*:

> *And I will show wonders in the heavens and in the earth: blood, and fire, and pillars of smoke. The sun shall be turned into darkness, and the moon into blood, before the great and terrible day of Jehovah cometh. And it shall come to pass, that whosoever shall call on the name of Jehovah shall be delivered* (by the rapture); *for in mount Zion and in Jerusalem there shall be those that escape* (believers will escape the Tribulation judgments by the Pre-Tribulation Rapture), *as Jehovah hath said, and among the remnant those whom Jehovah doth call.*

These *warning signs* will be clear to every student of Bible prophecy. They will then know that the Rapture is *imminent* and is about to take place. The Tribulation will start shortly after the Rapture with the signing of the covenant by the Antichrist and Israel (Daniel 9.27).

Distress and fear among the nations
(Luke 21.25-27)

Those who are not saved and unlearned Christians will have no idea that the Tribulation will soon start. They will be greatly afraid because of these *signs*, just as the Bible says:

> *And there shall be signs in sun and moon and stars; and upon the earth distress of nations, in perplexity for the roaring of the sea and the billows; men fainting for fear, and for expectation of the things which are coming on the world: for the powers of the heavens shall be shaken. And then shall they see the Son of man coming in a cloud with power and great glory.*

These signs begin before the rapture and will increase in severity and intensity throughout the Tribulation (Revelation 4.5; 8.5; 11.19; 16.18) up to the glorious appearing. But then in verse 28 Jesus said, *"But when these things begin to come to pass, look up, and lift up your heads; because your redemption* (the rapture with the redemption of your body) *draweth nigh.*

Conclusion

There are numerous *warning signs* of the approaching Tribulation for which all disciples of Jesus Christ should be diligently "watching."

Seven major *end-times* prophecies have already been fulfilled:

1-Balfour Declaration (Zephaniah 2.1a)
2-The Return of the Jews to the Holy Land (Ezekiel 37.1-14; Zeph. 2.1-2)
3-The two World Wars – birth pains (Matthew 24.6-8)
4-Founding of the United Nations (Luke 21.29-32)
5-Israel becomes a nation (Matthew 24.34)
6-The Capture of Jerusalem – end of *"times of Gentiles"* (Luke 21.24)
7-Gaza abandoned by Israel (Zephaniah 2.4).

Five other major *end-times* prophecies are currently being fulfilled:

1-The *"falling away"* (2 Thessalonians 2.3)
2-Increase in travel and knowledge (Daniel 12.4)
3-Rise of anti-Semitism (Psalm 83)
4-Mark of the Beast technology (Revelation 13.15-18).
5-Israel dwelling securely (*betach*) (Ezekiel 38.8, 11, 14).

The eight *warning signs* that take place, from a few years to several months, before the Tribulation are:

1-Destruction of Russia, Islam and Egypt (Ezekiel 38.1-39.16; 30.1-5)
2-First stage of the conversion of Israel and also Gentiles (Ezekiel 39.7)
3-Rebuilding the ancient city of Babylon (Zechariah 5.5-11)
4-World church & the rise of the False Prophet (Rev. 17.1-5, 18; 13.11-17)
5-World economy (Revelation 13.15-17)
6-World government (Daniel 7.23)
7-World government breaks into 10 divisions (Daniel 7.24)
8-Rebuilding of the Temple (Revelation 11.1-2; 2 Thessalonians 2.4).

The five *warning signs* that take place a short time before the Tribulation are:

1-Rise of Antichrist (Daniel 7.20, 24; Revelation 6.1-2; 13.1-10)
2-The *"overflowing scourge"* (Joel 2.1-11)
3-A time of *"peace and safety"* (1 Thessalonians 5.3)
4-Appearing of Elijah (Malachi 4.5)
5-Indications of a covenant between Israel and the Antichrist (Is. 28.15).

The final *warning signs* that take place on the day the Tribulation starts are:

1-Signs in space and on Earth (Joel 2.30-31)
2-Distress and fear among the nations (Luke 21.25-27).

We must remember Jesus rebuked the religious leaders of His time for not knowing the time they were living in:

Ye hypocrites, ye know how to interpret the face of the earth and the heaven; but how is it that ye know not how to interpret this time? (Luke 12.56)

Jesus rebuked the Pharisees for not knowing the time of His First Coming. They failed to analyze the time they were living in. They missed the **What** (*signs* of the First Coming of the Messiah). If we do not "watch" for the **What** (*signs* of the Tribulation), we will also not be ready **When** Christ returns.

All of these *warning signs* must be fulfilled before the start of the Tribulation. Christians should keep close "*watch*" of their fulfillment. As they are fulfilled we will understand that the Rapture is that much closer.

STUDY QUESTIONS

Chapter 5

1. How many major prophecies have yet to be fulfilled prior to the Tribulation?

2. Will it be several years at least before those *warning signs* are fulfilled?

3. Will a world government and economic system be firmly in place before the Tribulation starts?

4. Will a world church be formed before the Tribulation starts?

5. Will the demonic army of Joel 2.1-11 (the *"overflowing scourge"*) terrorize mankind before the Tribulation starts?

6. Will there be a time of *"peace and safety"* before the Tribulation starts?

7. Will the Antichrist be identified before the start of the Tribulation?

8. Is it possible that Christians may see some of these prophecies fulfilled before the Rapture?

9. Are the *warning signs* of the Tribulation also *warning signs* of the Rapture?

PART III

ARGUMENTS CONCERNING SIGNS

...that two advents of Christ have been announced: the one, in which He is set forth as suffering, inglorious, dishonored, and crucified; but the other, in which He will come from heaven with glory, when the **man of apostasy**, who speaks strange things against the Most High, shall venture to do **unlawful deeds on the earth against us the Christians**... (Justin Martyr)

And that the city of fornication may receive from the ten kings its deserved doom, and that the beast **Antichrist with his false prophet may wage war on the Church of God**... (Tertullian)

We ought to understand thoroughly therefore, my brothers, what is imminent or overhanging. Already there have been hunger and plagues, violent movements of nations and **signs**, which have been **predicted** by the Lord, they have already been fulfilled (consummated), and **there is not another which remains, except the advent of the wicked one in the completion of the Roman kingdom**. Why therefore are we occupied with worldly business, and why is our mind held fixed on the lusts of the world or the anxieties of the ages? (Ephrem)

I believe that **all the signs** which are to precede the last days **have already appeared**. Let us **not think that the Coming of Christ is far off**; let us look up with heads lifted up; let us expect our Redeemer's coming with longing and cheerful minds. (Martin Luther)

The Scripture declares plainly that the **Lord Jesus will not come until the Apostasy shall have taken place, the Man of Sin, the son of perdition shall have been revealed as seen in 2 Thessalonians 2:1-5**. Many other portions also of the Word of God distinctly teach that **certain events are to be fulfilled before the return of our Lord Jesus Christ**. (George Muller)

Even most of those who **looked for Antichrist's appearance** prior to the second advent, saw that event as occurring suddenly and just as suddenly **being followed by the rescue and rapture of the saints** by Christ. (Conservative Theological Journal)

We are **surrounded by so many obvious signs** that one would have to be blind not to see them – yet some fail to recognize them even when they are called to their attention. (Timothy LaHaye)

Obviously, in context, the generation that would see the **signs** – chief among them the **rebirth of Israel**. A generation in the Bible is something like forty years. If this is a correct deduction, then **within forty years** or so **of 1948, all these things could take place. Many scholars** who have studied Bible prophecy all their lives **believe that this is so.** (Hal Lindsey)

The Lord has not left us in spiritual darkness concerning the **approximate time** of Christ's Second Coming. Although we are specifically warned that we cannot know *"the day nor the hour wherein the Son of Man cometh"* (Matthew 25:13), the **fulfillment of dozens of specific prophecies in our generation strongly suggests** that Jesus Christ's Second Coming will occur in our lifetime. (Grant Jeffrey)

SIX

THE EARLY CHURCH FATHERS

The early Church fathers were not experts on prophecy and the major doctrines of Scripture. Most of them did not have access to all the books in the Bible. It took them a few hundred years to come to a consensus on the major doctrines. The doctrine of the Trinity was not confirmed until the First Council of Nicaea (325 AD). Athanasius (293-373 AD) properly formulated it, and in 381, at the First Council of Constantinople, the doctrine was finalized. It is folly to base any doctrine, or to derive support for a doctrine on the teachings of the early Church fathers. All doctrines must be based solely on Scripture. Yet we can learn by studying what they wrote for us.

The early Church fathers did not believe in the doctrine of *imminence*, which teaches that Jesus Christ can return at *any moment* to rapture the Church. Some of them expected Him to return in their lifetime because they thought the signs of His return were being fulfilled. The last sign they awaited for was the rise of the Antichrist. The consensus among the early Church fathers was that the Antichrist would rise to power before the Rapture.

Larry V. Crutchfield, writing in the *Conservative Theological Journal,* admitted that the early Church fathers looked for the coming of the Antichrist before the Rapture:

Even most of those who **looked for Antichrist's appearance** prior to the second advent, saw that event as occurring suddenly and just as suddenly **being followed by the rescue and rapture of the saints** by Christ. (*Conservative Theological Journal*, August 1999, p. 195, emphasis mine)

And Irenaeus still spoke of Antichrist's "sudden coming," **and** the church "suddenly" being caught up. (Ag. Her. V, XXX, 2 and V, XXIX, *Conservative Theological Journal*, August 1999, p. 195, emphasis mine)

Crutchfield understood that the early Church fathers looked for the appearing of the Antichrist, and taught that the Church would be raptured after he rose to power, just as the Bible says (2 Thessalonians 2.3).

Dr. John Walvoord admitted that the view of the early Church fathers concerning eschatology does not "correspond to what is advanced by pretribulationists today except for the one important point that both subscribe to the imminency of the rapture" ("The Blessed Hope and the Tribulation," p. 25, *Conservative Theological Journal*, August 1999, p. 196).

Walvoord also stated in his book, *The Rapture Question*, that the early Church fathers believed in the *imminence* of the return of Jesus:

The early church believed in the imminency of the Lord's return, which is an essential doctrine of pretribulationalism. (p. 192, 11th printing, 1973)

Roland Rasmussen refuted that claim by Dr. Walvoord, which is clearly not true. This is what he wrote in his 1996 book, *The Post-Trib, Pre-Wrath Rapture*:

In our chapter, "Posttribulationalism Is the Historical Position," we will show that Walvoord, Stanton, and Pentecost all try to convince their readers that the early church fathers taught imminency. They did not teach imminency; they taught expectancy. It is one thing to eagerly expect Christ's coming, but it is an entirely different thing to believe that Christ may come at any moment. (pp. 275-276)

The view of the early Church fathers does not agree with today's doctrine of the Pre-Tribulation Rapture, because they did not believe the Rapture was an *imminent* event. They taught that the Antichrist had to rise to power before the Rapture.

If the early Church fathers were correct, and the Antichrist comes before the Rapture, then his appearing is a *sign*. Christians should not overlook the rise of the Antichrist, along with the formation of a ten-nation confederacy which is formed before the Antichrist comes to power. It is possible we may see that confederacy come into being. (It is not edifying to try to identify the Antichrist before the confederacy is formed.)

According to the book of Daniel, a world government will be established. Then the leaders of the ten most prominent nations will form a confederacy and take control of it:

Thus he said, "The fourth beast will be a fourth kingdom upon earth, which will be diverse from all the kingdoms, and will devour the whole earth, and will tread it down, and break it in pieces. And as for the ten horns, out of this kingdom will ten kings arise: and another will arise after them; and he will be diverse from the former, and he will put down three kings." (Daniel 7.23-24)

Shortly after the ten rulers form this coalition, another national leader will rise up. This eleventh prominent ruler is the Antichrist, who will then become a member of this ruling coalition. The early Church fathers understood and they taught that the Antichrist would come first, then the Rapture.

The Didache
(110 AD)

The *Didache* was a Church manual written around 110 AD. It clearly taught that the Antichrist would rise to power before the Rapture:

Be you watchful for your life; let your lamps not be quenched and your loins not ungirded, but be ready; for you know not the hour when our Lord comes. And will gather yourselves together frequently, seeking what is fitting for your souls; for the whole time of your faith will not profit you, if you be not perfected at the last season. For in the last days the false prophets and corrupters will be multiplied, and the sheep will be turned into wolves, and love will be turned into hate. For as lawlessness increases, they will hate one another and will persecute and betray. And then the **world-deceiver will appear as a son of God**; and will work signs and wonders, and the earth will be delivered into his hands; and he will do unholy things, which have never been since the world began. Then all created mankind will come to the fire of testing, and many will be offended and perish; but **they that endure in their faith will be saved** by the Curse Himself. And then will the signs of the truth appear; first a sign of a rift in the heaven, then a sign of a voice of a trumpet, and thirdly, a resurrection of the dead; yet not of all, but as it was said: The Lord shall come and all his saints with Him. Then will the world see the Lord coming on the clouds of heaven. (Lightfoot, J.B., *The Apostolic Fathers,* p. 129, emphasis mine)

These early Church fathers understood the Antichrist would come to power before the Rapture takes place. Notice the statements they make about *"false prophets"* being multiplied (Matthew 24.5, 11, 24) and that *"lawlessness increases"* (Matthew 24.12). They also say that believers will *"hate and persecute and betray one another"* (Matthew 24.10), and then the "world-deceiver will appear" (Matthew 24.15). The context shows that the early Church fathers who wrote the Didache believed Christians of the Church Age would go through the entire Tribulation.

Some eschatologians argue that the phrase – *"for you do not know the hour when our Lord is coming"* – means that Jesus could return at *any moment* since Pentecost. The context shows that they used it to tell believers that they must be "alert" and living holy lives or they would not see the events taking place before the Tribulation. These things are: the rise of false prophets, the increase of lawlessness, believers betraying each other, and the rise of the Antichrist. Christians who are living backslidden lives, and not studying their Bibles will not see the clear *signs* that will precede the Tribulation. The most notable *sign* will be the rise of the Antichrist.

Clement of Rome
(??-99 AD)

Clement was the bishop of Rome from 88 until his death in 99 AD. Tradition says he is the Clement that Paul mentions in Philippians 4.3 as a fellow laborer in Christ. In a letter to the church at Corinth in 95 AD, Chapter 23, "Be humble and believe that Christ will come again," he briefly discusses the return of Christ:

Ye perceive how in a little time the fruit of a tree comes to maturity. Of a truth, soon and suddenly shall His will be accomplished, as the Scripture also bears witness, saying, "Speedily will He come, and He will not tarry;" and, "The Lord shall suddenly come to His temple, even the Holy One, for whom ye look." (Roberts, Alexander, *The Ante-Nicene Fathers,* vol. 1, p. 11)

The so-called *Second Epistle of St. Clement to the Corinthians* was written by an unknown author around 120-140 AD. It is titled, *An Ancient Homily*, of which a small section deals with the return of Christ:

If therefore we will do what is just in the sight of God, we will enter His kingdom, and will receive the promises, which neither eye has seen, nor ear heard, nor have entered into the heart of man. Let us therefore await the kingdom of God betimes in love and righteousness, since we know not the day of the God's appearing. (*The Apostolic Fathers*, p. 48)

The context of the paragraph from which the first quote above is taken, and those following, are about the resurrection. A careful study of the surrounding passages makes it clear that the author did not believe in the *imminent* return of Christ. Instead, he believed in the certainty of His return.

The second quotation does not support the doctrine of *imminence*. The context is about living a holy life. The statement "Let us therefore await the kingdom of God betimes in love and righteousness, since we know not the day of the God's appearing" is similar to a statement by James:

Be patient therefore, brethren, until the coming of the Lord. Behold, the husbandman waiteth for the precious fruit of the earth, being patient over it, until it receive the early and latter rain. Be ye also patient; establish your hearts: for the coming of the Lord is at hand. (James 5.7-8)

Both statements were given to inspire Christians to live holy lives. They are not doctrinal statements, nor are they clear enough to build a doctrine on.

Why are we commanded to "wait" for the return of the Lord? No believer in the Church Age can know the exact day of His return (Matthew 24.36), but we can know the approximate time by "waiting" and "watching." The way we "wait" and "watch" for His return is by "looking" for the *warning signs* of the Tribulation. The commands to "wait" and "watch" cannot be construed to mean that the Rapture has been an *imminent* event since Pentecost.

Justin Martyr
(100-165 AD)

Justin Martyr was born at the end of the 1st century. He knew people who lived through the destruction of Jerusalem in 70 AD. He was the first Christian apologist whose works survive. He believed that the Second Coming of Jesus

Christ was still to come. This is important because it refutes the belief that Christ returned in 70 AD, as Full-Preterism teaches. He also agreed with the other early Church fathers that the Antichrist would rise to power prior to the Rapture. This is what he wrote in *Dialogue with Trypho* (chapter 110):

> ...that two advents of Christ have been announced: the one, in which He is set forth as suffering, inglorious, dishonored, and crucified; but the other, in which He will come from heaven with glory, when the **man of apostasy**, who speaks strange things against the Most High, shall venture to do **unlawful deeds on the earth against us the Christians**, who, having learned the true worship of God from the law, and the word which went forth from Jerusalem by means of the apostles of Jesus, have fled for safety to the God of Jacob and God of Israel... (*The Ante-Nicene Fathers*, vol. 1, pp. 253-254, emphasis mine)

Justin Martyr believed the Antichrist would rise to power and persecute Christians before the return of Jesus Christ. The key is the phrase "us the Christians." The use of the word "us" means that he believed Christians of the Church Age would be persecuted by the Antichrist.

The General Epistle of Barnabas
(130 AD)

The General Epistle of Barnabas was written around 130 AD, allegedly by Barnabas, the disciple who traveled with the apostle Paul (Acts 13.1-5). It was quoted by Clemens of Alexandria, Origen, Eusebius, Jerome, and other Church fathers. Although Origen and Jerome considered it to be part of the canon of Scripture, most Church historians disagree and they do not believe it was written by Barnabas. The author did not believe the Rapture was an *imminent* event. Rather he believed it would not take place for another 2000 years. He writes in Chapter XV ("The False and the True Sabbath"):

> Further, also, it is written concerning the Sabbath in the Decalogue which [the Lord] spoke, face to face, to Moses on Mount Sinai, "And sanctify ye the Sabbath of the Lord with clean hands and a pure heart." And He says in another place, "If my sons keep the Sabbath, then will I cause my mercy to rest upon them." The Sabbath is mentioned at the beginning of the creation [thus]: "And God made in six days the works of His hands, and made an end on the seventh day, and rested on it, and sanctified it." Attend, my children, to the meaning of this expression, "He finished in six days." This implieth the Lord will finish all things in six thousand years, for a day is with Him a thousand years. And He Himself testifieth, saying, "Behold, to-day will be as a thousand years." Therefore, my children, in six days, that is, **in six thousand years, all things will be finished**. "And He rested the seventh day." This meaneth: When His Son, coming [again], shall destroy

the time of the wicked man, and judge the ungodly, and change the sun, and the moon, and the stars, then shall He truly rest on the seventh day. (Ibid., vol. 1, p. 146, emphasis mine)

The author believed the Rapture would take place about 1900 years after the time of his writing. There had been about 4000 years of human history from Adam to the birth of Jesus Christ, and there must be about 2000 more years until the return of Jesus. The final thousand years will be the Millennial Kingdom. The writer of this letter agreed with the early Church fathers that the Rapture was not an *imminent* event.

The author of this epistle also wrote in Chapter IV, "Antichrist is at Hand: Let Us Therefore Avoid Jewish Errors," the following warning to Christians:

It therefore behooves us, who inquire much concerning events at hand, to search diligently into those things which are able to save us. Let us then utterly flee from all the works of iniquity, lest these should take hold of us; and let us hate the error of the present time, that we may set our love on the world to come: let us not give loose reins to our soul, that it should have power to run with sinners and the wicked, lest we become like them. **The final stumbling-block** (or source of danger) **approaches**, concerning which it is written, as Enoch says, "For this end the Lord has cut short the times and the days, that His Beloved may hasten; and He will come to the inheritance." And the prophet also speaks thus: "**Ten kingdoms shall reign upon the earth, and a little king shall rise up after them, who shall subdue under one three of the kings.**" In like manner Daniel says concerning the same, "And I beheld the fourth beast, wicked and powerful, and more savage than all the beasts of the earth, and how **from it sprang up ten horns**, and **out of them a little budding horn**, and how **it subdued under one three of the great horns.**" Ye ought therefore to understand. And this also I further beg of you, as being one of you, and loving you both individually and collectively more than my own soul, to take heed now to yourselves, and not to be like some, adding largely to your sins, and saying, "The covenant is both theirs and ours." (Ibid., vol. 1, pp. 138-139, emphasis mine)

This warning was given to Christians of the 2nd century. They were warned to live holy lives so they would recognize the Antichrist (little horn). The writer believed Christians would recognize the Antichrist, and be persecuted by him. He understood that "ten kingdoms" would rise up, and that the Antichrist would subdue three of them. He was wrong in thinking the Antichrist would rise to power in his lifetime.

The Shepherd of Hermas
(150 AD)

The Shepherd of Hermas contains claims of visions, mandates and similitudes from the Lord to Hermas. It was written around 150 AD. From "Book One, Vision Fourth, Chapter II":

> You have escaped from great tribulation on account of your faith, and because you did not doubt in the presence of such a beast. Go, therefore, and tell the elect of the Lord His mighty deeds, and say to them that this beast is a type of the **great tribulation that is coming**. If then you prepare yourselves, and repent with all your heart, and turn to the Lord, it will be possible for you to escape it, if your heart be pure and spotless, and you spend the rest of the days of your life in serving the Lord blamelessly. Cast your cares upon the Lord, and He will direct them. Trust the Lord, ye who doubt, for He is all-powerful, and can turn His anger away from you, and send scourges on the doubters. Woe to those who hear these words, and despise them: better were it for them not to have been born. (Ibid., Vol. II, p. 18, emphasis mine)

This statement by the Shepherd of Hermas teaches that Christians who live holy lives will be preserved through the Tribulation, and backslidden Christians will not be preserved. Note that he writes to Christians who had already been preserved "through" (escaped) persecution. It can mean nothing else. The beast that they faced is a type of the beast to come. This writing also refutes Full-Preterism as all of the writings of the early Church fathers do.

Irenaeus
(140-202 AD)

Irenaeus was Bishop of Lugdunum in Gaul, which is now Lyon, France. He was an early Church father and apologist. His writings were formative in the development of Christian theology. He was said to be, but most likely not, a disciple of Polycarp, who was a disciple of the apostle John. He briefly touched on the subject of the Antichrist, the Tribulation and the Church in his treatise, *Against Heresies*:

> It is manifest, therefore, that of these [potentates], he who is to come shall slay three, and subject the remainder to his power, and that he shall be himself the eighth among them. And they shall lay Babylon waste, and burn her with fire, and shall give their kingdom to the beast, and **put the Church to flight**. After that they shall be destroyed by the coming of our Lord. (Ibid., vol. 1, vol. v, chap. 26, emphasis mine)

Irenaeus believed that the Church would be here when the Antichrist rises to power in the future, and that the Antichrist would persecute the Church.

Tertullian
(160-220 AD)

Tertullian was the first to write Christian literature in Latin. He was a notable early Christian apologist who helped develop the theology of the early Church. The most famous term he coined was "Trinitas" (Trinity), setting out the formula "three Persons, one Substance." He also coined the terms "Vetus Testamentum" (Old Testament) and "Novum Testamentum" (New Testament). He taught that the Church would go through the entire Tribulation period in Chapter 25 of his work, *Anti-Marcion, On the Resurrection of the Flesh*:

> In the Revelation of John, again, the order of these times is spread out to view, which "the souls of the martyrs" are taught to wait for beneath the altar, whilst they earnestly pray to be avenged and judged: (taught, I say, to wait), in order that the world may first drink to the dregs the plagues that await it out of the vials of the angels, and that the city of fornication may receive from the ten kings its deserved doom, and that the beast **Antichrist with his false prophet may wage war on the Church of God**; and that, after the casting of the devil into the bottomless pit for a while... (Ibid., vol. 3, emphasis mine)

Tertullian taught that the "Antichrist with his false prophet may wage war on the Church of God" after the angels pour out their vials of plagues on the world. The seven vials are poured out in Chapter 16 of Revelation at the end of the seven-year Tribulation.

Hippolytus
(170-236 AD)

Photius, an Eastern Orthodox Church patriarch of Constantinople from 858 to 867 AD, and from 877 to 886 AD, described Hippolytus in his Bibliotheca (cod. 121) as a disciple of Irenaeus, who was said to be a disciple of Polycarp. It is highly unlikely that Irenaeus was a disciple of Polycarp. Hippolytus became an enemy of the Church leaders and for some time led a separate group. Finally reconciled to the Church leaders, he eventually died as a martyr of the faith. Concerning the Antichrist, the Tribulation and the Church, he has this to say in his work, *Treatise on Christ and Antichrist*:

> It is proper that we take the Holy Scriptures themselves in hand, and find out from them what, and of **what manner, the coming of Antichrist is**; on **what occasion and at what time the impious pious one shall be revealed**; and whence and from **what tribe (he shall come)**; and **what his name is**, which indicated by the number in the Scripture; and how he shall

work terror among the people, gathering them from the ends of the earth; and (how) **he shall stir up tribulation and persecution against the saints**; and how he shall glorify himself as God; and what his end shall be; and how the sudden appearing of the Lord shall be revealed from heaven; and what the conflagration of the whole world shall be; and what the glorious and heavenly kingdom of the saints is to be, when they reign together with Christ; and what the punishment of the wicked by fire. (Ibid., vol. 5, p. 205, emphasis mine)

"And the dragon," he says, "saw and persecuted the woman which brought forth the man-*child*. And to the woman were given two wings of the great eagle, that she might fly into the wilderness, where she is nourished for a time, and times, and half a time, from the face of the serpent." That refers to the one thousand two hundred and threescore days (the half of the week) **during which the tyrant is to reign and persecute the Church**, which flees from city to city, and seeks concealment in the wilderness among the mountains, possessed of no other defense than the two wings of the great eagle, that is to say, the faith of Jesus Christ, who, in stretching forth His holy hands on the holy tree, unfolded two wings, the right and the left, and called to Him all who believed upon Him, and covered them as a hen her chickens. For by the mouth of Malachi also He speaks thus: "And unto you that fear my name shall the Sun of righteousness arise with healing in His wings." (Ibid., p. 217, emphasis mine)

Hippolytus believed the Church was to look for the appearing of the Antichrist. He said that Christians will be able to identify him: by his tribe, by his name, by his gathering the people together from around the world, by his persecution of the saints, and by claiming to be God. The above quote by him leads one to believe that he was certain that the Church would go through the entire Tribulation.

Cyprian
(200-258 AD)

Cyprian was bishop of Carthage and an important early Christian writer. He was born around the beginning of the third century in North Africa, received a classical education for that time, became a bishop after converting to Christianity around 249 AD, and died a martyr at Carthage. Cyprian wrote many volumes on Christian doctrine, and he stated emphatically that the Antichrist would persecute Christians and then they would be rescued by Christ. This is what he wrote in *Treatise XI. Exhortation to Martyrdom, Addressed to Fortunatus*:

You have desired, beloved Fortunatus that, since the burden of persecutions and afflictions is lying heavy upon us, and in the ending and completion of the world **the hateful time of Antichrist is already**

beginning to draw near, I would collect from the sacred Scriptures some exhortations for **preparing and strengthening the minds of the brethren**, whereby I might animate the soldiers of Christ for the heavenly and **spiritual contest**. I have been constrained to obey your so needful wish, so that as much as my limited powers, instructed by the aid of divine inspiration, are sufficient, some arms, as it were, and defenses might be brought forth from the Lord's precepts for **the brethren who are about to fight**. For it is little to arouse God's people by the trumpet call of our voice, unless we confirm the faith of believers, and their valor dedicated and devoted to God, by the divine readings. (Ibid., Vol. V, p. 496, emphasis mine)

Cyprian believed the Antichrist would rise to power in his time. He wanted to prepare Christians for the coming conflict. Agreeing with the teaching of the *Didache*, he believed the Antichrist would persecute Christians before they are delivered by Jesus Christ.

Victorinus
(???-304)

Victorinus of Poetovio was a Church writer who was martyred during the persecutions of Emperor Diocletian (284-305 AD). He wrote commentaries on several books of the Bible, with only portions of Revelation surviving. This is a short passage, written around 270 AD, concerning the last days, from his *Commentary on the Apocalypse*, 15.1:

"And I saw another great and wonderful sign, seven angels having the seven last plagues; for in them is completed the indignation of God." For the wrath of God always strikes the obstinate people with seven plagues, that is, perfectly, as it is said in Leviticus; and these shall be in the *last time, when the church shall have gone out of the midst.* (Ibid., vol. 7, p. 357)

The passage, from the commentary on the book of Revelation, does not prove that Victorinus or any of the early Church fathers knew or believed in the doctrine of *imminence*. Instead, the passage confirms that the early Church fathers believed the Antichrist would come to power before the Rapture.

According to the above statement, Victorinus believed Christians would escape the judgment on the unsaved that begins at the mid-point of the Tribulation. We know this because the passage that he was commenting on takes place at this time of the Tribulation. Chapters 6-9 cover the events of the first 3½ years of the Tribulation, and Chapter 10 describes what is taking place in Heaven at the mid-point. Chapter 15 announces the final judgment of God upon the unsaved that also starts at the mid-point of the Tribulation.

In another writing on the book of Revelation, *Commentary on the Apocalypse*, (20.1-3), he said that the Church would suffer persecution at the hands of the Antichrist during his last 3½ years of rule:

And he shut him up, says he, and put a seal upon him, that he should not deceive the nations until the thousand years should be finished. "He shut the door upon him," it is said, that is, he forbade and restrained his seducing those who belong to Christ. Moreover, he put a seal upon him, because it is hidden who belong to the side of the devil, and who to that of Christ. For we know not of those who seem to stand whether they shall not fall, and of those who are down it is uncertain whether they may rise. Moreover, that he says that he is bound and shut up, that he may not seduce the nations, **the nations signify the Church**, seeing that of them it itself is formed, and which being seduced, he previously held until, he says, the thousand years should be completed, that is, what is left of the sixth day, to wit, of the sixth age, which subsists for a thousand years; after this he must be loosed for a little season. The little season signifies three years and six months, in which with all his power the **devil will avenge himself under Antichrist against the Church**. Finally, he says, after that the devil shall be loosed, and will seduce the nations in the whole world, and will **entice war against the Church**, the number of whose foes shall be as the sand of the sea. (Ibid., vol. 7, p. 358, emphasis mine)

Victorinus believed the Antichrist will persecute the Church. His timing of this persecution is different than what the men who quote him say it is. He was certain the devil will be released from the abyss after the thousand years are completed, and then "avenge himself under Antichrist against the Church."

In his commentary on Revelation (12.7-9), he says the Antichrist will rise to power after the two witnesses of Chapter 11 have completed their 3½ years of ministry:

"There was a battle in heaven: Michael and his angels fought with the dragon; and the dragon warred, and his angels, and they prevailed not; nor was their place found any more in heaven. And that great dragon was cast forth, that old serpent: he was cast forth into the earth." This is the beginning of Antichrist; **yet previously Elias must prophesy**, and there must be **times of peace**. And afterwards, when the **three years and six months are completed** in the preaching of Elias, he also must be cast down from heaven, where up till that time he had had the power of ascending; and all the apostate angels, as well as Antichrist, must be roused up from hell. Paul the apostle says: *"Except there come a falling away first, and the man of sin shall appear, the son of perdition; and the adversary who exalted himself above all which is called God, or which is worshipped."* (Ibid., vol. 7, p. 356, emphasis mine)

When this passage is compared with the previous one, we see that Victorinus believed the Antichrist would reign for 3½ years prior to the

Second Coming of Christ. During that short period he will persecute the Church.

No Pre-Tribulationist should quote Victorinus, and claim he taught the doctrine of *imminence* and the Pre-Tribulation Rapture; he did not. His eschatology is unusual, to say the least.

Ephrem of Syria
(306-373 AD)

Ephrem was a hymnographer, theologian, and prolific writer (said to have written one million lines), of the 4th century. The following section includes key passages from a text written near the end of his life entitled, *On the Last Times, the Antichrist and the End of the World*:

We ought to understand thoroughly therefore, my brothers, what is imminent or overhanging. Already there have been hunger and plagues, violent movements of nations and **signs**, which have been **predicted** by the Lord, they have already been fulfilled (consummated), and **there is not another which remains, except the advent of the wicked one in the completion of the Roman kingdom**. Why therefore are we occupied with worldly business, and why is our mind held fixed on the lusts of the world or the anxieties of the ages? Why therefore do we not reject every care of earthly actions and prepare ourselves for the meeting of the Lord Christ, so that He may draw us from the confusion, which overwhelms the world? Believe you me, dearest brothers, because the coming (advent) of the Lord is nigh, believe you me, because it is the very last time. Or do you not believe unless you see with your eyes? See to it that this sentence be not fulfilled among you of the prophet who declares: *"Woe to those who desire to see the day of the Lord!"* **For all the saints and elect of God are gathered, prior to the tribulation that is to come, and are taken to the Lord lest they see the confusion that is to overwhelm the world because of our sins.** And so, brothers most dear to me, it is the eleventh hour, and the end of the world comes to the harvest, and angels, armed and prepared, hold sickles in their hands, awaiting the empire of the Lord. And we think that the earth exists with blind infidelity, arriving at its downfall early. Commotions are brought forth, wars of diverse peoples and battles and incursions of the barbarians threaten, and our regions will be desolated, and we neither become very much afraid of the report nor of the appearance, in order that we may at least do penance; because they hurl fear at us, and we do not wish to be changed, although we at least stand in need of penance for our actions! (*Vanished Into Thin Air*, pp. 115-116, emphasis mine)

Some eschatologians have used the writings of Ephrem to support their doctrine of *imminence*. They also claimed he believed in a Pre-Tribulation

Rapture. The statement below, taken from the quote above, shows that he expected the Antichrist would rise to power before the Raptures:

> Already there have been hunger and plagues, violent movements of nations and **signs**, which have been **predicted** by the Lord, they have already been fulfilled**, and there is not another which remains, except the advent of the wicked one in the completion of the Roman kingdom**.

Ephrem and the early Church fathers awaited the rise of the Antichrist before the Rapture. The key is the word "except." Ephrem had seen what he thought were the fulfillment of prophecies (*signs*) of the "last days." He was looking for the rise of the Antichrist. Clearly he did not believe in an *imminent* Rapture that has no *signs* preceding it. According to Ephrem, the Church will be here to watch the rise of the Antichrist, followed by the Rapture.

Cyril of Jerusalem
(313-386 AD)

Cyril of Jerusalem was a distinguished theologian of the early Church. He became the bishop of Jerusalem in 350 AD, and believed that Jesus Christ and God are of the "same substance" and are equally God (*homoousios* ὁμοούσιος). In 358 he was removed and forced to retire to the city of Tarsus because he taught that Jesus is fully God. His superior, Acacius, believed the Arian heresy that claimed Jesus was a created being who was inferior to God the Father. The church officially charged him with selling church property to help the poor. The Council of Seleucia in the following year, at which St. Cyril was present, deposed Acacius. In 360 Emperor Julian allowed him to return. The Arian Emperor Valens, who succeeded Julian, banished Cyril once more in 367. Yet he was able to return again, at the accession of Emperor Gratian, after which he remained undisturbed until his death in 386. Cyril's jurisdiction over Jerusalem was expressly confirmed by the First Council of Constantinople (381), at which he was present. At that council, he voted for acceptance of the term *homooussios*, convinced that there was no better alternative.

Cyril believed and taught that the Antichrist would rise to power and persecute Christians of the Church Age before the Rapture:

> 12. But this aforesaid **Antichrist** is to come when the times of the Roman empire shall have been fulfilled, and the end of the world is now drawing near. There shall rise up together ten kings of the Romans, reigning in different parts perhaps, but all about the same time; and after these an eleventh, the **Antichrist**, who by his magical craft shall seize upon the Roman power; and of the kings who reigned before him, *three he shall humble*, and the remaining seven he shall keep in subjection to himself. At first indeed he will put on a show of mildness (as though he were a learned and discreet person), and of soberness and benevolence having **beguiled**

the Jews, as though he were the expected Christ, he shall afterwards be characterized by all kinds of crimes of inhumanity and lawlessness, so as to outdo all unrighteous and ungodly men who have gone before him; displaying against all men, but especially against us Christians, a spirit murderous and most cruel, merciless and crafty. And after perpetrating such things for three years and six months only, he shall be destroyed by the glorious second advent from heaven of the only-begotten Son of God, our Lord and Saviour Jesus, the true Christ, who shall slay Antichrist *with the breath of His mouth*, and shall deliver him over to the fire of hell.

18. Guard thyself then, O man; thou hast the signs of Antichrist; and remember them not only thyself, but impart them also freely to all. If thou hast a child according to the flesh, admonish him of this now; if thou hast begotten one through catechizing put him also on his guard, lest he receive the false one as the True. For the *mystery of iniquity doth already work.* I fear these wars of the nations. I fear the schisms of the Churches; I fear the mutual hatred of the brethren. But enough on this subject; only God forbid that it should be fulfilled in our days; nevertheless, let us be on our guard. And thus much concerning Antichrist. (Philip Schaff, *The Nicene and Post Nicene Fathers*, vol. 7, Gregory Nazianzen, Lecture XV. On the Clause, And Shall Come in Glory to Judge the Quick and the Dead; Of Whose Kingdom There Shall Be No End. Daniel vii. 9–14)[1]

Commentary on the early Church fathers

Hal Lindsey's commentary on Ephrem's writing

Hal Lindsey, a noted televangelist, Christian author and graduate of Dallas Seminary, became a religious celebrity in 1970 with his first book, *The Late Great Planet Earth.* He believes that the writing of Ephrem supports a Pre-Tribulation Rapture:

No matter what else the writer of this sermon believed, the fact Pseudo-Ephraem taught a pre-tribulational Rapture is undeniable. (*Vanished Into Thin Air*, p. 123)

Lindsey believes that the Antichrist will not be identified as such until after the Rapture:
Antichrist's Unveiling Closely Connected to Beginning of the Day of the Lord

It begins shortly after the Antichrist is revealed, which is immediately after the removal of the Holy Spirit's restraining ministry (2 Thessalonians 2:1-12). (Ibid., p. 244)

On page 387 of his book, *Vanished Into Thin Air*, Lindsey has a chart that says the Antichrist is revealed immediately after the Rapture, and several weeks before the start of the Tribulation.

This is not what Ephrem taught. He clearly taught that the Antichrist would rise to power before the Rapture, ruling for just a few years. According to Ephrem, the reign of the Antichrist will start after the 70th week of Daniel is completed. He believed Christians would go through the seven-year Tribulation, and then be raptured before the Antichrist's reign of 2½ or 3½ years.

Grant Jeffrey's commentary on Ephrem's writing

Dr. Grant Jeffrey, a leading Pre-Tribulationist, chairman of Frontier Research Publications, host of the "Bible Prophecy Revealed" television program and author of numerous books on Bible prophecy, believes Ephrem taught the Rapture was an *imminent* event with no fulfilled prophecies beforehand:

To summarize the key points in Ephraem's text on the last days:

Ephraem's manuscript lays out the events of the last days in chronological sequence. Significantly he began with the Rapture using the word *imminent*, then, he described the Great Tribulation of three and a half years duration under the Antichrist's tyranny, followed by the second coming of Christ to earth with his saints to defeat the Antichrist. (*Final Warning*, p. 309)

The context of the use of the word *imminent* in the first passage of Ephrem's writing, a portion of which we quote below, is that the *signs* of the approaching Tribulation made him think it would start in his lifetime. The only thing that Ephrem thought had to take place next, before the start of the Tribulation, was the "advent of the wicked one" (the rise to power of the Antichrist). We quote Ephrem again from Lindsey's book:

We ought to understand thoroughly therefore, my brothers, what is **imminent** or overhanging. Already there have been hunger and plagues, violent movements of nations and signs, which have been predicted by the Lord, they have already been fulfilled (consummated), and **there is not other which remains, except the advent of the wicked one in the completion of the Roman kingdom.** (*Vanished Into Thin Air*, pp. 115, emphasis added, R.K.)

According to Ephrem's sermon, believers are commanded to look for the "advent of the wicked one" (Antichrist). The rise of the Antichrist is what he believed was *imminent*. We must also point out that Ephrem understood the importance of looking for *signs*. He said, "Already there have been hunger and plagues, violent movements of nations and signs, which have been predicted by the Lord, they have already been fulfilled (consummated)." He knew the **What** (*signs*) was very important. He simply did not understand that there were many more prophecies that had to be fulfilled before the **When** (Rapture) could take place.

Henry C. Theissen's commentary on the early Church fathers

Dr. Henry Theissen, a dispensational Pre-Tribulationist writer of the 20th century, is certain that the early Church fathers believed in the doctrine of *imminence*. His *Lectures in Systematic Theology* states:

It is clear that the Fathers regarded the Lord's coming as imminent. (*Lectures in Systematic Theology*, p. 372)

Theissen is mistaken in his understanding of what the early Church fathers believed. Some thought the Rapture was *imminent* because they believed that most, or all of the *signs* of the Rapture had been fulfilled except the rise of the Antichrist.

Thomas Ice's commentary on the early Church fathers

Dr. Thomas Ice, of the Pre-Trib Research Center and author of several books on Bible prophecy, has this to say about the beliefs of the early Church fathers:

Expressions of imminency abound in the Apostolic Fathers. Clement of Rome, Ignatius of Antioch, The Didache, The Epistle of Barnabas, and The Shepherd of Hermas all speak of imminency. (*Myths of the Origin of Pretribulationism*, Part 1)

He does not explain why he thinks the early Church fathers believed in the doctrine of *imminence*. There is no statement by any of them that supports that doctrine. Instead, they clearly taught that Christians were to "watch" for specific *signs*, with the rise of the Antichrist being the primary *sign*. He admitted that the early Church fathers had views of prophecy that were *contradictory*:

As was typical of every area of the early church's theology, their views of prophecy were undeveloped and sometimes contradictory, containing a seedbed out of which could develop various and diverse theological viewpoints. While it is hard to find clear pretribulationism spelled out in the fathers, there are also found clear pre-trib elements which if systematized with their other prophetic views contradict posttribulationism but support pretribulationism. (Ibid.)

Ice is correct that none of the early Church fathers taught a clear doctrine of the Pre-Tribulation Rapture. Most taught a Mid-Tribulation Rapture, and some taught the Post-Tribulation doctrine. If, as Ice admits, it is "hard to find clear pretribulationism spelled out in the fathers" how could they possibly believe in the doctrine of *imminence*? They could not and they did not! They were mistaken in thinking that all of the *warning signs* of the Rapture had been fulfilled except the rise of the Antichrist. Some thought the Rapture was *imminent* because of the fulfilled *warning signs*, not because Scripture says Christ can return at *any moment*. (You can read his full article at his website - www.pre-trib.org/article-view.php?id=50)

Gerald Stanton's commentary on the early Church fathers

Gerald Stanton, president of Ambassadors International, is a graduate of Dallas Seminary, a former professor of systematic theology at Talbot Theological Seminary and an author of several religious books. He believes the early Church fathers "held the coming of Christ to be an *imminent* event":

There is abundant literature to prove that they were almost without exception premillennial, down to the end of the third century. There is also sufficient evidence to prove that many of them held the coming of Christ to be an imminent event, as seen in the following quotations. (*Kept From the Hour*, p. 220)

Most early Church fathers were premillennial, but none believed in *imminence*. As noted previously, they thought most of the *signs* of the Rapture had been fulfilled, except the rise of the Antichrist. They were "looking" for him, not for the *any moment* return of Christ.

Timothy LaHaye's commentary on Victorinus

Dr. Timothy LaHaye, former pastor, founder of Christian Heritage College (now called San Diego Christian College), co-founder of the Council for National Policy and co-author of the best-selling *Left Behind* fiction series, cited the work of Victorinus and then commented on it to argue that the early Church fathers knew of the Pre-Tribulation Rapture:

And I saw another great and wonderful sign, seven angels having the seven last plagues; for in them is completed the indignation of God. For the wrath of God always strikes the obstinate people with seven plagues, that is, perfectly, as it is said in Leviticus; and these shall be in the *last time, when the church shall have gone out of the midst*.

So it is clear that the teaching of the church being taken out "in the last time," meaning the coming of Christ, was known as early as the third century. (*No Fear of the Storm*, p. 173, emphasis added, T.L.)

The passage, from the commentary on the book of Revelation, does not prove that Victorinus, or any early Church father believed in the Pre-Tribulation Rapture or the doctrine of *imminence*. Instead, the passage confirms that the early Church fathers believed the Antichrist would come to power before the Rapture.

He failed to mention that the passage from which Victorinus commented, was Revelation 15:1, which occurs at the mid-point of the Tribulation. It announces the final judgment of God upon the unsaved.

Victorinus believed that Christians would escape the judgment on the unsaved that begins at the mid-point of the Tribulation. At best he was a Mid-Tribulationist.

We can understand why LaHaye thinks the early Church fathers believed in the *imminent*, Pre-Tribulation Rapture:

> Frankly, one of my principal objections to the mid- and post-Trib theories is their **destruction of imminency**. For if Christ cannot come at any moment, these views cannot instruct us to look for His return. Instead they advise us to look for the inaugurating of the Tribulation period, when Antichrist signs a covenant with Israel for seven years for the rebuilding of the temple, the mark of the beast, the advent of Antichrist himself, and the thirty-one events listed in chapter four of this book. Only the pre-Tribulation view retains the **promise of imminency**! (Ibid., p. 66, emphasis added, mine)

Conclusion

The early Church fathers believed that all of the *warning signs* of the return of Christ had been fulfilled, except the rise of the Antichrist. The consensus among them was that the Antichrist would rise to power before the Rapture and persecute Christians. They did not teach the doctrine of *imminence*, and none of them taught a clear Pre-Tribulation Rapture doctrine. They admonished Christians to "watch" for the rise of the Antichrist before the return of Jesus Christ.

The claim by some eschatologians that the early Church fathers believed in a Pre-Tribulation Rapture, and in the modern doctrine of *imminence* is not based on the historical record. They were Mid-Tribulationists and Post-Tribulationists. Not even Ephrem taught a Pre-Tribulation Rapture doctrine. He clearly said the Antichrist would rise to power after the conclusion of the 70th week of Daniel, and the Rapture would take place before his 2½ or 3½ year reign. He taught the Post-Tribulation Rapture doctrine, and that the reign of the Antichrist will start at the conclusion of the seven-year Tribulation. It is a bit confusing, but Ephrem did not teach the modern doctrine of *imminence*, and he believed Christians of the Church Age would go through the entire 70th week of Daniel.

One must consider why all of the early Church fathers who wrote on eschatology stated clearly that the Antichrist would rise to power and persecute Christians of the Church Age before the Rapture. They came to that conclusion based on Scripture and on the teaching of the Holy Spirit (1 John 2.20, 27) or they came by it through a serious misunderstanding of Scripture. They either rejected the teaching of the Holy Spirit for their personal likes or they submitted to Scripture and the teaching of the Holy Spirit. It is possible that the men who teach the doctrine of *imminence* and who say the Rapture takes place before the Antichrist rises to power are the ones who are rejecting the clear teaching of Scripture and the Holy Spirit.

STUDY QUESTIONS

Chapter 6

1. Why did some of the early Church fathers mistakenly think they were living in the "last days," and that the Tribulation was just over the event horizon?

2. Who did most of the early Church fathers that wrote about prophecy say would ascend to a position of power before the Rapture?

3. What did they say this person would do to Christians of the Church Age?

4. Why did some of the early Church fathers believe Christ could not return at *any moment*?

5. Did some of the early Church fathers "*look*" for the return of Christ by "*watching*" for the rise of the Antichrist?

6. Did any of the early Church fathers quoted in this chapter believe in the modern-day doctrine of *imminence*.

SEVEN

REFORMERS

The Reformers wrote very little about eschatology. We gleaned a few of their statements from the monumental work, *Systematic Theology*, by Dr. Lewis Sperry Chafer, founder of Dallas Seminary.

Martin Luther
(1483-1546)

Martin Luther, considered to be the father of the Protestant Reformation, was a dedicated Catholic priest in Germany before he realized that some of the church's doctrines were wrong. He also knew that some of its practices were not biblical, such as the selling of indulgences. On October 31, 1517, he wrote to Albrecht, Archbishop of Mainz and Magdeburg, protesting the sale of indulgences. He enclosed a copy of his "Disputation of Martin Luther on the Power and Efficacy of Indulgences," which came to be known as *The 95 Theses*. On the same day, he also nailed a copy of *The 95 Theses* to the door of the Castle Church in Wittenberg, Germany. He eventually broke from the Catholic Church and became the leader of the Reformation. He thought the return of Christ was near in his day:

> I believe that **all the signs** which are to precede the last days **have already appeared**. Let us **not think that the Coming of Christ is far off**; let us look up with heads lifted up; let us expect our Redeemer's coming with longing and cheerful minds. (*Systematic Theology*, vol. 4, p. 279, emphasis mine)

He noted in his commentary on Second Peter that he was living in the "last days" and that the "day of judgment" was "now before the door" (*Commentary on Peter and Jude*, p. 280).

Luther exhorted believers to "not think that the Coming of Christ is far off," because he believed "all the signs which are to precede the last days" had "already appeared." He believed there are *warning signs* of the Lord's return, and he looked for them, but mistakenly thought they had "all" been fulfilled.

Hugh Latimer
(1485-1555)

Hugh Latimer was a devoted Catholic priest in England before converting to Protestantism. Thomas Bilney played a significant role in bringing him out of Catholicism. When King Edward VI's sister, Queen Mary I, came to the throne, Latimer was tried for his beliefs and imprisoned. In October of 1555 he was burned at the stake outside Balliol College, Oxford, beside Nicholas Ridley. He said to Ridley, "Be of good comfort, Master Ridley, and play the man; we shall this day light such a candle, by God's grace, in England, as I trust shall never be put out." This is what he wrote concerning the "last days":

> All those excellent and learned men whom, without doubt, God has sent into the world in these **latter days** to give the world **warning**, do gather out of the Scriptures that the **last days can not be far off**. Peradventure it may come in my day, old as I am, or in my children's days. (*Systematic Theology*, vol. 4, p. 279, emphasis mine)

Latimer was also mistaken in believing he was living just before the "last days." He thought that God had sent certain men, whom he did not name, "to give the world warning," and that these men had determined from "the Scriptures that the last days can not be far off." He went on to say that he was certain that Jesus would return "in my day, old as I am, or in my children's days." Latimer was wrong about the timing of the Rapture and Second Advent, as some of the other Reformers were, but he was correct in understanding that one can know the time of the "latter days" by studying Scripture.

John Calvin
(1509-1564)

John Calvin, a French theologian, broke from the Catholic Church by assisting Nicholas Cop escape after Cop gave a message on the need for reformation on November 1, 1533. They fled to Basel, Switzerland, where Calvin began his ministry as a Reformer. He published his most famous work, *Institutes of the Christian Religion* in 1536. He is best-known for his development of the doctrine of election, which is commonly called Calvinism. He went on to become equal to Martin Luther as a father of the Reformation and like Luther he "looked" for the return of Christ:

> Scripture uniformly enjoins us to **look** with expectation for the advent of Christ. (Ibid., emphasis mine)

The statement by Calvin, "Scripture uniformly enjoins us to look with expectation for the advent of Christ," does not mean he believed in *imminence*. He was "looking" for the return of Jesus, as all Christians are commanded to do (Titus 2.13). He was doing what the early Church fathers did, and what the other Reformers were doing – "looking" for the fulfillment of the *warning signs* of the Lord's return. They were not experts in eschatology, and they mistakenly thought that many of the *warning signs* had been fulfilled.

John Knox
(1510-1572)

John Knox, considered to be the founder of the Presbyterian denomination, joined the Reformation to reform the Scottish church. He wrote numerous volumes on religion, the last being, *The Historie of the Reformation in Scotland.* The return of Christ was foremost in his thoughts:

> The Lord Jesus shall return, and that with expedition. What were this else but to reform the face of the whole earth, which never was nor yet shall be, till that righteous King and Judge appear for the restoration of all things. (*Systematic Theology*, vol. 4, p. 279)

Knox believed Christ would return with "expedition" (promptness in doing something), because he mistakenly thought that he was living in the last days.

None of the Reformers that Dr. Chafer cited believed in the doctrine of *imminence*. They "watched" for *signs* of the return of Jesus. They were wrong in thinking that most of the *signs* had been fulfilled, and that Christ would return in their lifetimes.

Everyone who has taught that Christ would return in his lifetime believed it, because they thought the *warning signs* of His return had been fulfilled! The early Church fathers and the Reformers "watched" for the fulfillment of *warning signs* as all Christians should do today.

Conclusion

Some of the Reformers mistakenly thought that most of the *signs* of the return of Christ had been fulfilled in their lifetime just as some of the early Church fathers did. They were not given understanding concerning the "last days" because they were not living in them. We have far more knowledge and understanding about eschatology because we are living in the "end times." We know what major Bible prophecies will be fulfilled before the Tribulation starts. All we have to do is "watch" them be fulfilled. When the last few *warning signs* are about to be fulfilled we will know the Tribulation and the Rapture are upon us.

STUDY QUESTIONS

Chapter 7

1. Did Luther, Calvin, Latimer and Knox recognize there are *signs* of the return of Christ?

2. Why did some of the Reformers think the Tribulation and the Rapture were very near?

3. Why were the Reformers not given proper understanding concerning the fulfillment of "end times" prophecies?

4. Have Christians today been given the proper knowledge and understanding to know the approximate time of the Rapture and the start of the Tribulation?

5. How can we know when the approximate time of the Rapture has come?

6. Are you diligently *"watching"* for the remaining *warning signs* to be fulfilled?

EIGHT

MODERN ERA

A large number of the prophecy teachers of the Modern Era believe that specific *signs* would be fulfilled before the Rapture.

Morgan Edwards
(1722-1795)

Morgan Edwards was the first Protestant preacher of the Modern Era to teach the Rapture would take place before the Second Coming of Jesus Christ. He wrote only one essay concerning it, but it is clear from that writing that he believed there would be at least one *sign* before the return of Christ:

Another event previous to the millennium will be the appearing of the son of man in the clouds, coming to raise the dead saints and change the living, and to catch them up to himself, and then withdrawing with them, as observed before. This event will come to pass **when the antichrist be arrived at Jerusalem in his conquest of the world**; and about **three years and a half before his killing the witnesses**, and assumption of godhead. (*Two Academical Exercises on Subjects Bearing the Following Titles: Millennium, and Last-Novelties*, p. 21, emphasis mine)

Edwards believed the Rapture would take place before the Tribulation starts. Yet because he thought the Tribulation would last only 42 months he is considered to be a Mid-Tribulationist.

George Muller
(1805-1898)

George Muller was an evangelist and coordinator of orphanages in Bristol, England. Well-known for providing an education for children, he cared for more than 10,000 orphans in his lifetime. He was criticized for raising the poor above their natural station in life. Though not known for his teaching on eschatology, he nevertheless made a powerful statement concerning it shortly before he went home to be with the Lord:

I know that on this subject there is great diversity of judgment, and I do not wish to force on other persons the light that I have myself. The subject, however, is not new to me; for having been a careful diligent student of the Bible for nearly fifty years, my mind has long been settled on this point and I have not the shadow of a doubt about it. The Scripture declares plainly that the **Lord Jesus will not come until the Apostasy shall have taken place, the Man of Sin, the son of perdition shall have been revealed as seen in 2 Thessalonians 2:1-5**. Many other portions also of the Word of God distinctly teach that **certain events are to be fulfilled before the return of our Lord Jesus Christ**. It does not, however, alter the fact that the coming of Christ, and not death, is the great hope of the Church and, if in a right state of heart, we (as the Thessalonian believers did) shall 'serve the living and true God, and wait for his Son from heaven'. (Jones, Martyn-Lloyd, *Great Doctrines of the Bible*, Vol. 3, p. 140, emphasis mine)

Muller believed 2 Thessalonians 2.1-5 teaches "the Apostasy" must take place prior to the Rapture. He also believed, as some early Church fathers did, that the Antichrist would rise to power before the Rapture.

Cyrus Scofield
(1843-1921)

The notes in the original Scofield Bible say the Day of the Lord is preceded by seven *signs*:

The day of the LORD is preceded by seven signs: (1) The sending of Elijah (Mal. iv.5; Rev. xi.3-6); (2) cosmical disturbances (Joel ii.1-12; Mt. xxiv.29; Acts ii.19,20; Rev. vi.12-17); (3) the insensibility of the professing church (1 Thes. v.1-3); (4) the apostasy of the professing church, then becomes "Laodicea" (2 Thes. ii.3); (5) the rapture of the true church (I Thes. iv.17); (6) the manifestation of the "man of sin," the beast (I Thes. ii.1-8); (7) the apocalyptic judgments (Rev. xi.-xviii.). [The citation for #6 should be 2 Thes. ii.1-8, R.W.K.] (*First Scofield Study Bible*, p. 1349)

Scofield believed four things would take place before the Day of the Lord starts – Elijah would come, there would be cosmic disturbances, the professing church would become spiritually asleep and indifferent and the professing church would become apostate. He knew there are *signs* of the Tribulation.

(E. Schuyler English, chief editor of the New Scofield Bible, did not include the notes on the seven *signs* from the Old Scofield Bible in the New Scofield Bible. He may have understood the notes cited above destroy the doctrine of *imminence,* which he defended.)

Scofield also believed the seven churches of Revelation are symbolic of seven periods of the Church Age (Ibid., p. 1331). Therefore, he could not have reasonably believed the Rapture was an *imminent* event until the start of the Philadelphia period.

Arno Clemens Gaebelein
(1861-1945)

Dr. Arno Gaebelein was a Methodist minister, a teacher and a conference speaker. Being a dispensationalist, he was a developer of the movement in its early days. Two of his books, *Revelation, and Analysis and Exposition* and *Current Events in the Light of the Bible* explain the dispenstationalist view of eschatology. He was a consulting editor for the Scofield Bible and a close assistant of Cyrus Scofield. In his book, *Things to Come*, he listed six things that would take place before the Rapture. They were the denial of: faith, sound doctrine, the power of godliness, Jesus came in the flesh, Jesus Himself and the authority of the Bible. He commented on these 6 denials saying:

And now we come to the most solemn fact. We **behold about us** the **complete fulfillment of all these predictions**. Not one of them is unfulfilled. It is true in the past there have been false teachers, departures from the faith and delusive teachings, but never before has the fulfillment of these predictions been so intense, so persistent, so widespread as in our days. Nothing more remains to be fulfilled...

Again we say it is a most significant fact that we behold about us the **literal fulfillment of all these predictions concerning the last days**. What an evidence this is that the Bible is the Word of God... The next great event is nothing less than the Coming of the Lord for His Saints. (*Things to Come*, p. 8, citing Harold Lindsell, *The Gathering Storm*, p. 126, emphasis mine)

Gaebelein saw numerous prophecies concerning the "last days" fulfilled. He mistakenly thought the "next great event" was the return of Christ. He did not know that other prophecies would be fulfilled before the Rapture, such as the return of the Jews to Israel.

Lewis Sperry Chafer
(1871-1952)

Dr. Lewis Sperry Chafer, founder of Dallas Seminary, formed a traveling evangelistic music ministry with his new bride, Ella Case, in 1896. He sang and preached while she played the organ. He then became an evangelist in the Presbytery of Troy in Massachusetts and was mentored by Dr. Cyrus Scofield. Chafer became the pastor after Scofield's death in 1921. In 1924 he founded the Evangelical Theological College (Dallas Seminary), with help from William Henry Griffith Thomas. This is what he wrote in his monumental work, *Systematic Theology,* concerning the fact that the Bible teaches there are clear *signs* of the Pre-Tribulation Rapture:

THE ANTICIPATION OF THE ELEMENT OF TIME. It will be recognized that no prediction could be made of the events within this age without a veiled intimation that the element of time would intervene. The problem is not one engendered by man; it is wholly of God. Therefore, it is, as other problems of a like nature, solved only in the mind of God. Both things are true – the Lord has always been at hand; **yet certain times and events are predicted**. Peter would grow old and die (John 21:18). The nobleman would delay a long time in a far country (Luke 19:11) – which parable teaches more the requirement that service is to continue than that time intervenes. The gospel is to be preached to all the world; but had it been commanded to convert all nations the case would have been different. (Vol. IV, p. 368, emphasis mine)

Chafer understood that specific prophecies (*warning signs*) must be fulfilled before the Rapture can take place.

Henry "Harry" Ironside
(1876-1951)

Dr. Harry Ironside was a Canadian-American Bible teacher, preacher, pastor, and author of the late 19th- and early 20th centuries. He began preaching for the Salvation Army in Southern California at the age of 16. He moved to San Francisco and started preaching there 4 years later after taking 2 years off from preaching. He became associated with the Plymouth Brethren, and by 1929 he had preached to over 1 million people. In 1924 he began preaching under the direction of the Moody Bible Institute and in 1929 he became pastor of the Moody Church. He turned down a full-time faculty position at Dallas Theological Seminary in 1926. He was called the "archbishop of fundamentalism" and he firmly believed there were *signs* of Christ's return. He thought two of them were being fulfilled in his day:

Reader, let me press my point again. – The world-wide Gospel proclamation and world-wide apostasy at the same time are **clear proofs** that the **end is close upon us**. (*The Midnight Cry*, p. 28, citing Lindsell, p. 123, emphasis mine)

Laodicea is the closing period of the Church's history, and who can doubt that we have now reached the very time predicted? It behooves us to act as men who wait for their Lord, knowing that His coming cannot be much longer delayed (Ibid. p. 35, citing Lindsell, p. 124)

Dr. Ironside thought, in 1915 when he wrote the book cited, he was living in the "last days" because of the apostasy of the Church. It has been 94 years since he wrote that the return of Christ "cannot be much longer delayed." He saw some *warning signs*, but not all of them. No one can know the nearness of the Rapture without knowing all of the major *warning signs*.

Herbert Lockyer
(1886-1985)

Dr. Herbert Lockyer was a prominent pastor in England and Scotland who spent 20 years of ministry in America (1935-1955), and served Jesus faithfully for over 70 years. He was the author of *All the... of the Bible* series, *Seasons of the Lord*, and many more books. He taught the doctrine of *imminence* and firmly believed that Jesus Christ could return at *any moment*. When he returned to England he devoted himself to writing books about the Bible. He believed he was living in the *last days* because of the numerous *signs* he saw all around him. He listed several *signs* in a booklet published in 1979. By way of introduction he said:

> While we do not believe that the Church is to pass through the Great Tribulation, we do affirm that coming events have the power to cast their shadows beforehand. And, if we have any discernment of the **signs of the times**, we must see in them a preview of the terrible drama about to be unfolded. (*Rapture of the Saints*, p. 62, emphasis mine)

Lockyer then said the world was moving toward a consolidation of commerce, politics and religion. He saw a movement to create a world economy that would fulfill the prophecy in Revelation:

> *And that no man might buy or sell, save he that had the mark or the name of the beast or the number of his name* (Revelation 13:17). (Ibid., p. 63, KJV)

He believed there was a movement to unite all the nations of the world into a world government, and he saw a move to unite all of the religions of the world into "one universal Church, apostate and Romish in character that will control all things religious" (Ibid., p. 63).

Lockyer moved on to other *signs* that made him believe he was living in the "end times." He cited natural catastrophes, war, famine, pestilences, earthquakes, increasing worldliness, restrained lawlessness and Jewish activities. He noted *signs* within the Church – spiritual declension, powerless religion, apostate teaching and seductive doctrines (Ibid., pp. 64-69).

His conclusion was that he was "living in the closing period of the wonderful Church Age and signs abound that her translation is near." He believed in the *imminent* return of Jesus Christ, but also in *signs*:

> In all our study of Prophecy we must not forget that Christ may be here at any moment. It is within the range of possibility that the saints may be called away before another sunrise. The **troubled condition of the world indicates that the Lord is at hand**. We are living in the **closing period of the wonderful Church Age** and **signs abound that her translation is near**. While no man has any knowledge of the exact day of Christ's return,

all the saints believing such an evident New Testament truth, realize that the blissful event **cannot be far away.** (Ibid., p. 62, emphasis mine)

Lockyer believed that Christ could return at *any moment* yet he looked for *signs* of His return. Lockyer firmly believed he was living in the *end times* and that Jesus would return in his lifetime. Some of the early Church fathers and some of the Reformers believed the same thing. They saw general *signs* that made them think the end was near. Instead, they should have been looking for specific *warning signs*.

One of his last books, *All About the Second Coming,* was edited by his son, Herbert Lockyer, Jr. In the introduction he made a list of the order of events. He divided the period from the appearing of the Antichrist unto the Eternal Age. Here are the first two divisions:

1.   The present age will culminate in apostasy and a period of unprecedented trial. The "man of sin" will be fully manifested, will assume political supremacy, and will claim religious homage.

2.   The true church of Christ will be raptured to heaven, and the man of sin will establish a covenant with the Jews. But he will violate his agreement with the Jews, gather forces against them from other nations, and seek to destroy God's ancient people. (p. xxiv)

Lockyer not only showed that the "signs of the times" are all around us, he stated clearly that the Antichrist will rise to power and be "fully manifested" (identified as the Antichrist) before the Rapture. He agreed with the early Church fathers that the Antichrist would be revealed before the Rapture.

John Walvoord
(1910-2002)

Dr. John Walvoord believed Jesus could return at *any moment* since Pentecost. Yet he believed there are *signs* of the return of Christ. In his 1974 book, he had this to say about *signs*:

As **signs** that we may be moving into this period **multiply**, the **direction of present world events** also points to the conclusion that the coming of Christ for His Church, promised in John 14, may occur any day. (*Armageddon, Oil and the Middle East Crisis,* pp. 96-97, emphasis mine)

He then elaborated on the *warning signs* of the end times:

Prophesies about Israel, and especially Jerusalem, provide important reference points for all of prophecy. The **most significant prophetic event** in the twentieth century has been the **restoration of Israel**. All the prophecies of the end age indicate that at the time the Jews will be back in their land and in precisely the same situation in which they find themselves today.

All areas of prophecy combine in the united testimony that history is preparing **our generation for the end of the age**. In each area of prophecy a **chronological checklist of important prophetic events** can be compiled. In each list in regard to the church, the nations, or Israel, **the events of history clearly indicate that the world is poised and ready for the rapture of the church** and the beginning of the countdown to Armageddon. (Ibid., pp. 199-200, emphasis mine)

He then went through a "prophetic checklist for the Church," listing 13 signs. He gave 22 signs of a "prophetic checklist for the nations" and 17 signs of a "prophetic checklist for Israel" (Ibid., pp. 200-204). (See our chronological checklist of important prophetic events in Appendix A.)

In the conclusion of his book, *Armageddon, Oil and the Middle East Crisis*, Walvoord said that "all the necessary historical developments have already taken place." He noted the move for a world government and world church, that Israel is back in the Holy Land, that Russia is ready to attack and "Red China" can field an "army as large as that described in the book of Revelation" (pp. 206-207).

In another book, *The Church in Prophecy*, Walvoord recognized that there was a problem with the doctrine of *imminence*. He said the most important *sign* of the 20th century – the establishment of the nation of Israel – had to be fulfilled because "Israel had to be in their ancient land and had to be organized into a political unit" to be able to make the covenant with the Antichrist that Daniel prophesied (Daniel 9.27). He said this fulfillment of prophecy is "striking evidence that the rapture itself may be very near" (pp.173-174).

It is obvious that Israel had to be in existence before the Antichrist could make a covenant with her. This is the *super-sign* that all Pre-Tribulationists have talked and written about since May 14, 1948.

Harold Lindsell
(1913-1998)

Dr. Harold Lindsell firmly believed in *signs* of the return of Christ. In his book, *The Gathering Storm*, he explained why *signs* of the Tribulation are also *signs* of the Rapture. He noted that the "overwhelming verdict of those who hold to a pretribulation rapture is that this so-called *signless event* is followed immediately by the seven-year tribulation period." He went on to explain that "there could be no rapture until the Jews come back to Palestine and Jerusalem is in their hands so they can rebuild the temple." He concluded by saying that "it becomes plain that the signs having to do with the tribulation are pertinent to the rapture and that these signs make an any-moment rapture from the days of the apostles an invalid thesis" (p. 137).

J. Dwight Pentecost

Dr. J. Dwight Pentecost firmly believes in the doctrine of *imminence*, yet he believes that specific prophecies will be fulfilled before the Rapture takes place. The primary prophetic *sign* is a period of "peace and safety." Quoting from his best-known book, *Things to Come*:

> *The announcement of peace and safety.* In 1 Thessalonians 5:3 Paul tells the Thessalonian church that the Day of the Lord will come **after** the announcement of "peace and safety." This false security will lull many into a state of lethargy in relation to the Day of the Lord so that that day comes as a thief. This announcement that has produced this lethargy **precedes** the Day of the Lord. If the church were in the seventieth week there would be no possibility that, during the period when believers are being persecuted by the beast to an unprecedented degree, such a message could be preached and find acceptance so that men would be lulled into complacency. All the signs would point to the fact that they were not in a time of "peace and safety." The fact that the visitation of wrath, judgment and darkness is preceded by the announcement of such a message indicates that the church must be raptured before that period can begin. (pp. 209-210, emphasis mine)

Pentecost makes it clear that there must be a time of "peace and safety" before the Rapture. We must note that Pentecost does not believe in a *gap* between the Rapture and the start of the Tribulation (Chapter 10). Since this time of *"peace and safety"* takes place prior to the start of the Day of the Lord (Tribulation) it also precedes the Rapture, as he explained. This is what Paul taught:

> *When they are saying, Peace and safety, then sudden destruction comes upon them, as travail upon a woman with child; and they will in no wise escape.* (1 Thessalonians 5.3)

Paul told them, after saying that there will be a time of "peace and safety" before the Rapture, to not be caught by surprise by the Rapture:

> *But you, brethren, are not in darkness, that that day should overtake you as a thief: for you are all sons of light, and sons of the day: we are not of the night, nor of darkness; so then let us not sleep, as do the rest, but let us watch and be sober.* (1 Thessalonians 5.4-6)

Christians who do not know the **What** will be caught by surprise by the **When**. If you want to follow the advice of Paul, learn what the *warning signs* are, and then *"watch"* closely as they are fulfilled.

Jack Van Impe

Dr. Jack Van Impe believes in the doctrine of *imminence*, and that there are *signs* of the Second Coming of Jesus Christ. This is what he wrote in 1989:

These signs of Christ's Second Coming are in evidence worldwide, and increasing both in frequency and intensity. (*Your Future*, p. 120)

He went on to list numerous *sign* events that must take place before the Second Coming:

Old Testament Signs of the end times:
Horseless carriages or automobiles (Nahum 2:3-4)
Airplanes (Isaiah 31:5)
Desert blossoming as a rose (Isaiah 35:1)
Alignment of a ten nation western confederacy (Daniel 2, 7)
Knowledge explosion (Daniel 12:4)
Great Increases in travel (Daniel 12:4).

New Testament Signs of the end times:
False Christs and False Prophets (Matthew 24:5, 24; 2 Peter 2:1)
Wars and rumors of wars (Mark 13:7; Matthew 24:6)
Famines, earthquakes in divers places, pestilences (Luke 21:11)
Iniquity abounding (Matthew 24:12)
Gospel of the kingdom preached to all the world (Matthew 24:14)
Signs in the sun, moon, and stars, sea and waves roaring (Luke 17:26-30; 21:25-27)
Introduction of evil spirits which control cults and false religions (1 Timothy 4:1-2). (*Your Future*, p. 121)

Van Impe stated in his study Bible that *signs* were given to the nation of Israel concerning the return of Christ, but "no such signs were ever given to the Church concerning the Rapture" (p. 45). He understands there are *signs* of the return of Christ. He calls them *signs* of the Second Coming.

The importance of *signs* is emphasized in his book, *11:59 and Counting*. This is what he wrote in the introduction of that 1983 book:

Never in the annals of world history have we witnessed such a proliferation of the **signs** Jesus predicted to be in effect immediately prior to His return. No longer are the days of simultaneous war, famine, pestilence, earthquakes and cultic activity limited to the pages of Holy Writ. One need only pick up the evening newspaper or tune to his favorite news broadcast to realize that these **signs** of Christ's second coming are in evidence worldwide, and increasing both in frequency and intensity. No wonder the scientists who control the famed "doomsday clock" are moving its hands ever closer to midnight! (p. 5, emphasis mine)

On television show (Trinity Broadcasting Network 2.02.2009), he said 500 Rapture prophecies have been fulfilled. It is obvious that the fulfilled prophecies of the Rapture are *signs* of that blessed event. He also stated on his May 18, 2009, broadcast that the 7 final *signs* were – the creation of the European Union, development of the mark of the Beast technology, Israel being reborn, Jerusalem being retaken, and the prominence of Iran, Russia and China.

He implied in his 1990 video "A.D. 2000 – the End?" that crop circles appearing all over the world was a fulfillment of Bible prophecy. He believes it fulfills the "*signs in sun and moon and stars*" (Luke 21.25).

In that same video he argued vehemently that even though no one can know the "day or hour" of the Rapture Christians can know the "times and seasons" and "we will know when it's near."

Arnold Fruchtenbaum

Dr. Arnold Fruchtenbaum devoted Chapter 4 of his book, *The Footsteps of the Messiah* (1993 edition), to explain what events will take place prior to the start of the Tribulation. He also devoted Chapter 5 to "Other Pretribulational Events."

In Chapter 4 he said that the first two world wars were *signs* of the approaching Tribulation. He also said that the establishment of the nation of Israel and the taking of the holy city of Jerusalem were *signs*. The formation of the northern alliance that attacks Israel, the formation of a world government, the formation of 10 kingdoms, the rise of the Antichrist, a period of "peace and safety" and the signing of the seven-year covenant will be other Pre-Tribulation *warning signs*.

In Chapter 5 he argued that there will be 3 other Pre-Tribulation events: the sun will be blacked out (Joel 2.31), Elijah will appear (Malachi 4.5-6) and the third temple may be rebuilt (pp. 129-138).

Texe Marrs

Texe Marrs was a professor of aerospace studies, teaching American Defense Policy, strategic weapons systems and related subjects at the University of Texas at Austin from 1977 to 1982. He has also taught international affairs, political science, and psychology for two other universities. He is the founder of Power of Prophecy Ministries in Austin, Texas, and a frequent guest on radio and television talk shows throughout America and Canada. He understands there are *signs* of the Tribulation, and that Christians should look for the fulfillment of these *signs*. He explains the importance of looking for *signs* in an essay, "The Night Cometh!" In it he explains the rise of Mystery Babylon (the coming world church) and how it will martyr Christians in large numbers. He also touches on the subject of "A Great Falling Away":

When will all these things take place? Jesus told us that no man knows the day nor the hour, but He also said that when you see **certain signs**, you can look up because you know redemption is drawing near.

The whole purpose of Bible prophecy is to let us know that **the time is short** – to let us know that night cometh when no man can work. But some people today refuse to believe the prophecies of Scripture.

The apostle Peter wrote that in the last days scoffers would come walking after their own lusts, *"And saying, Where is the promise of his coming? For since the fathers fell asleep, all things continue as they were from the beginning of the creation"* (2 Pet.3:4).

My friends, when somebody mockingly asks you where is the sign of His coming – saying, in effect, I don't see these signs; I don't believe Jesus is coming again for His saints; I don't believe in the Rapture; I don't believe in Bible prophecy – they are in reality bringing to pass Peter's prophecy that in the last days scoffers would come on the scene.

Because this **sign** of prophecy – the scoffers – is so prevalent today, we know that **Jesus Christ is coming soon**. Where in the history of the Christian church has prophecy been so scoffed at and scorned? God warned us that this would be so. (James, William T., *Storming Toward Armageddon,* pp. 128-129, emphasis mine)

Chuck Smith

Chuck Smith, founder of the Calvary Chapel movement and author of numerous books on Bible prophecy, told a caller to his radio talk show "Pastor's Perspective" (December 18, 2008), who asked if it would be a good idea to compile a list of prophecies that will be fulfilled before the Tribulation starts, he said it should be done quickly. Co-hosts Brian Brodersen and Don Stewart also said it is a good idea. Here are some key statements by them:

Smith: I would think it would be **very fine to do it**. It sounds like a very interesting way to sort of create some sort of a **time-table,** and, of course, you better **do it fast** because, the way things are moving today, you know, we're still, we could be at an extremely critical point with Israel; and Iran and Israel…

Brodersen: Well, you know, I think that a lot of the, you know, books, Chuck, of course, has a couple of books out on essentially what has happened. You take the prophecies and lay them out, sort of, you know, systematically, and then you look at what is going on in the world, and you **see how close we are**.

Stewart: Right. The general themes that the Old Testament give, and the New Testament, about the coming of Christ, we can look at, and **we see these things happening today**. Chuck and I, again, we did the four-part series on His Channel on the signs of the coming of Christ. But basically, we just talked about **twelve signs** that, you know, fifteen hundred years ago were not signs, because they were not here yet. Now they're here. So now it's a **great idea** to look at that and say, here we are, and **check it off**. Now, there are no signs – now, let's make it clear...

Smith: The Rapture.

Stewart: The Rapture. Yes, we want to make it clear before the Rap...it could happen at any time. Before we finish this program, the Rapture of the Church could happen. But **the point is – the signs of the times are definitely there**.

Brodersen: And the **signs**, as you were saying, Don, the **signs** point to the Second Coming. And we know the Rapture precedes the Second Coming; so, Chuck, as you said so many times, if we're seeing the **signs** of the Second Coming...

Smith: Christmas and Thanksgiving, you know, at the malls and so forth, they have the Christmas decorations up; you can say, "Hey, Thanksgiving is getting close. Look at that, you know. That's Santa Claus." But we know that the Rapture precedes the Second Coming. So **signs** of the Second Coming only mean that the **Rapture is that much closer**.

Stewart: Alright, **great question there**. Appreciate it. (Pastor's Perspective, 12.18.2008, KWVE, emphasis mine)

Smith clearly taught that there are *signs* of the return of Christ in his book, *Snatched Away*. He partially quoted 1 Thessalonians 5.1-4, which says Christians of the Church Age should not be taken by surprise as the unsaved will when the Rapture takes place. He then wrote:

The Bible is saying that it shouldn't come to you as a surprise – "that day" shouldn't overtake you as a thief. Why? Because God has given to us the **signs** and the **evidences** that would **precede the coming of Jesus Christ**. (pp. 15-16, emphasis mine)

Smith also noted in his "Pastor's Perspective" radio program that there could be a period of *"peace and safety"* before the Rapture:

But if indeed they are successful that will surely be the time when we really you know, the Bible says when they say *"peace and safety"* then comes sudden destruction. So you're sort of concerned if they are able to force a peace treaty... (1.20.2010)

That is one of the last *warning signs* that all students of Bible prophecy should look for just as Paul commanded (1 Thessalonians 5.3-4).

John MacArthur, Jr.

Dr. John MacArthur, Jr. is certain that "nothing in the New Testament ever suggests we should defer our expectation of Christ's appearing until other preliminary events occur" (*The Second Coming*, p. 54). Yet he notes that there is an exception:

> The one **apparent exception** is 2 Thessalonians 2:1-3, which says, "that Day [the Day of the Lord] will not come unless the falling away comes first, and the man of sin is revealed." (Ibid., emphasis mine)

MacArthur realizes the passage teaches that prior to the Rapture two *signs* will be fulfilled – the "*falling away*" of the Church from the faith, and the revealing of the "*man of sin*." He says that the day Paul was speaking of is the "Day of the Lord and its apocalyptic judgment, not the Rapture" (Ibid., p. 56). He concluded his argument on this point saying:

> So the consistent teaching of the New Testament is that Christians should be looking for the imminent coming of Christ for His church, and 2 Thessalonians 2:1-4 is no exception. (Ibid.)

Dave Hunt

Dave Hunt says there are *signs* of the approaching Second Coming of Christ, but says those *signs* are not *signs* of the Rapture. The reason why *signs* are not for us are given in his book, *How Close Are We?* He believes that, since the Rapture takes place 7 years prior to the Second Coming, they are "not for us." Yet he understands that Jesus "commanded His own to watch for His coming and warned against being caught by surprise at His return – and surprise could only apply to the Rapture." He emphasized the importance of not ignoring "Christ's warnings about being caught by surprise. We are responsible, as every generation before us has been, to know the signs of His coming and to determine whether they are applicable to our day. No matter that others have misinterpreted Scripture and mistakenly set a time for Christ's return, only to be proved wrong. We are responsible to know the signs and to apply that knowledge biblically" (p. 116).

Hunt is correct in stating that Christians are "responsible to know the signs." The following statement by him is very insightful:

> Though past generations have so consistently misinterpreted the Scriptures, is it possible that we now possess the insight they lacked? Isn't such a suggestion the very height of conceit? It could be, except for one obvious but overlooked fact, which we will also discuss later. As we shall see, **ours is the first generation to whom certain special signs Christ foretold could possibly apply!** (*How Close Are We?*, p. 116, emphasis mine)

It is significant that he believes there are "definite signs" that will "herald the nearness" of the return of Christ:

> One cannot escape the fact that Christ and His apostles gave **definite signs to watch for** that would herald the **nearness of His return**. Why give these **signs** if some generation at some time in the future was not expected to recognize them and know that His Second Coming was, as He Himself said, "near, even at the doors"?
>
> Yes, but if the **Rapture occurs seven years prior to the Second Coming**, then those signs are not for us. So it would seem. Yet Christ commanded His own to watch for His coming and warned against being caught by surprise at His return – and surprise could only apply to the Rapture.. Are we faced again with a contradiction, and this time one that cannot be resolved?
>
> We may be certain that the answers are to be found if we desire to know them and diligently search His Word. Jesus also said, "*And when these things begin to come to pass, then look up, and lift up your heads; your redemption draweth nigh*" (Luke 21:28). When these things *begin .... look up*. The commencement of the **signs** cannot herald the Second Coming, for that event cannot occur until the signs are all complete. Therefore, with this statement, **Christ can only be referring to the Rapture**. (*How Close Are We?*, p. 115, emphasis mine)

He argues that those "definite signs" are not for Christians, but for those who go into the Tribulation. Yet he made a startling confession that when the *signs* of the Rapture begin to take place Christians are to "*look up*" because their redemption "*draweth nigh*."

Hunt also made another stunning admission about a significant *sign* that will be fulfilled before the Rapture:

> The **Rapture comes in the midst of peace** (I Thessalonians 5:3); the Second Coming in the midst of war (Revelation 19:11-21). (Ibid., p. 204, emphasis mine)

This time of "peace" is a *super-sign*. It is one of the last *warning signs* before the Rapture/Tribulation, and it will be unmistakable. It must be a special period of peace never seen before. If Hunt is correct Christians will see this period of false "*peace and safety*" just prior to the Rapture.

In Chapter 11 of *How Close Are We?*, he says there are *signs* of the return of Christ. He noted that wars, famines and earthquakes would precede the Second Coming, and that "Jesus is apparently revealing that these signs will begin to occur substantially ahead of the Second Coming" (p. 116). "It would seem that these signs *begin* prior to the Rapture" (p. 116). He also said that every generation is responsible "to know the signs of His coming" and that "we are responsible" to "apply that knowledge biblically" (p. 116).

All students of Bible prophecy should learn what the *warning signs* are so they can know nearness of the Tribulation, and therefore the nearness of the Rapture.

Timothy LaHaye

Dr. Timothy LaHaye believes in the doctrine of *imminence*. Yet he also believes there are *signs* that prove we are living in the "last days."

In his first book on prophecy, *The Beginning of the End* (1972), he said a primary sign of the "last days" was the fulfillment of Matthew 24.7:

For nation will rise against nation, and kingdom against kingdom; and there will be famines, and pestilences, and earthquakes, in various places. (NKJV)

What war was the fulfillment of that prophecy? LaHaye went on to write:

Now we are ready to ask: Has there ever been a war, started by two nations, which grew into a worldwide war by the kingdoms of the world, followed by unprecedented famines, pestilences, and earthquakes in various places (perhaps simultaneously)? I am of the opinion that we can discern such. Though reluctant to be dogmatic on the subject, I believe there is one event that fulfills all four parts of this prophecy. That terrible event has been labeled by historians as World War I, which took place between 1914 and 1918. (*The Beginning of the End,* pp. 35-36)

In this book, he devoted Chapter 4 to the "Infallible Sign." This "infallible sign" was the re-establishment of the nation of Israel in its ancient homeland. The opening paragraph of that chapter reads thus:

On May 14, 1948, an historical phenomenon appeared which traces its beginning to World War I. Against all human reasoning, a nation that had been dead for nineteen hundred years suddenly came to life. On that day the world unknowingly took a giant step closer to the end of the age, for Israel became a self-governing nation just as the prophets had foretold. (Ibid., p. 43)

He believes a third significant *sign* was the taking of the ancient city of Jerusalem by the Israeli army on June 8, 1967:

The hands on Israel's prophecy clock leaped forward on June 8, 1967, when the Israeli troops marched into the Old City of Jerusalem and took it with little or no destruction. For the first time in 2,500 years the Jews had gained complete control over the most important area in the entire world. Suddenly the world was aware of what Bible teachers have been saying for centuries, that Mount Moriah, the site of then Temple of Jesus' day, was to the Jews the most coveted ground in the world. For the first time in nineteen centuries Israel controlled the site of the old – and new – temple! (*The Beginning of the End,* p. 50)

LaHaye listed the 12 most important *signs* of the Second Coming and signified how close we are to it by giving the time of the night for each *sign*:

1-World War I (10:30pm)
2-Rebirth of Israel (10:35pm)
3-Russia and the Middle East (10:40pm)
4-Capital and Labor Conflicts (10:45pm)
5-Skyrocketing Travel (10:50pm) & Knowledge (11:00pm)
6-Apostasy (11:15pm)
7-Occult Shadows and Realities (11:20pm)
8-Perilous Times (11:30pm)
9-A Flood of Wickedness (11:30pm)
10-Scoffers Have Come (11:40pm)
11-The Ecumenical Church 11:50pm)
12-The Disunited Nations/World Government (11:58pm). (Ibid., pp. 162-163)

In the essay, "The Signs of the Times Imply His Coming," published in, *Ten Reasons Why Jesus Is Coming Soon* (Van Diest), he explained why *signs* are important (p. 192). Since the disciples equated *signs* with "the end of the age" (Matthew 24:3), he said, "it is equally legitimate today" for Christians to look for them. "Many wild speculators have sensationalized signs, and so brought confusion to the church," yet this should "not prohibit us from using them at all." Instead, "it should make us more careful in '*rightly dividing the Word of Truth,*' so we do not add to the confusion."

He believes there are clear *signs* of the "last days." He also sees the danger of date-setting, citing the mistake of Edgar Whisenant, who thought Jesus Christ would return in 1988, and Harold Camping, who predicted that Jesus would return in 1994 (and now May 21, 2011). He understands that date-setting can cause many to become disillusioned. Yet, even though he does not believe a date can be set, he thinks his generation will be the one that sees the Rapture. He bases this belief on the 12 *signs* that signal the soon return of Jesus Christ:

Together, they give us a basis for concluding that this generation has more reason to believe that Christ could come in our lifetime than at any time before it. (*The Beginning of the End,* p. 196)

In his essay, "The Signs of the Times Imply His Coming," he mentions other *signs* of the "soon at hand" coming of Jesus Christ. He noted that in the Olivet Discourse Jesus said, "*And this gospel of the kingdom will be preached in all the world as a witness to all the nations, and then the end will come*"

(Matthew 24.14). He believes that this prophecy will be fulfilled by the 144,000 during the Tribulation, but it is very close to being fulfilled by the Church around the year 2000. In 1998 he wrote:

> While we know this prophecy will be fulfilled during the Tribulation, the fact that so many effective groups are working for the same target date, at a time when such an effort is technologically possible, does indeed suggest **the coming of Christ for His church may soon be at hand.**
>
> It is safe to say that Matthew 24:14 will **soon be fulfilled**, which means, **the coming of Christ could be at hand.** (Van Diest, John, *Ten Reasons why Jesus is Coming Soon*, pp. 201-202, emphasis mine)

Several other *signs* made him believe we may be the last generation: the implantable computer chip being the mark of the beast (in his opinion); the Revelation-type plagues that already exist (AIDS, STDs); unprecedented earthquakes and natural disasters and worldwide satellite television.

Another proof that he gives is the 6-day, 6000-year theory that says Jesus Christ will return to set up His Millennial Kingdom (the day of rest) after 6000 years of human history. There were about 4000 years from Adam to Christ, so Jesus should return about 2000 years after His birth. (The 6000-year theory destroys the doctrine of *imminence*.)

In their 1999 book, *Are We Living in the End Times?*, Timothy LaHaye, and co-author Jerry Jenkins, continued to emphasize the importance of *signs*. In the opening of their book they write:

> We are **surrounded by so many obvious signs** that one would have to be blind not to see them – yet some fail to recognize them even when they are called to their attention. So many **signs** exist today that you could write a book about them. In fact, I did (LaHaye), *The Beginning of the End*, first published in 1972 and then again in 1991. Many changes in the twenty-seven years since that book's first publication have only brought further confirmation that we are indeed living in **"the times of the signs."** Never in history have so many **legitimate signs** of Christ's return existed. (pp. 26-27, emphasis mine)

LaHaye made a very interesting statement in his study Bible concerning the timing of the Rapture. In his note on 1 Thessalonians 5.3 he stated:

> The sudden destruction or Tribulation which follows the Rapture will occur at a time when the world is obsessed with a false sense of "peace and safety." Paul is reiterating Jesus' teaching to "watch and be ready" lest **that day [Tribulation]** should overtake them "as a thief" (v. 4). (*Tim LaHaye Prophecy Study Bible*, p. 1287, emphasis mine)

He noted there is no *gap* between the Rapture and Tribulation, and that the Rapture/Tribulation event takes place during a time of *"peace and safety."* From other statements and writings he thinks Christians will not be here on the day that the Tribulation starts. 1 Thessalonians 5.4 clearly teaches that Christians of the Church Age will be on Earth when the unsaved think they have achieved a time of *"peace and safety"*:

> When they are saying, Peace and safety, then sudden destruction comes upon them [Tribulation], as travail upon a woman with child; and they will in no wise escape. But ye, brethren, are not in darkness, that that day should overtake you as a thief. (1 Thessalonians 5.3-4)

Paul warns Christians to not be caught by surprise like the unsaved will be when *"that day"* (the Tribulation) breaks the period of *"peace and safety."*

LaHaye continues to teach that Christians should be watching for *signs* of the return of the Lord. He emphasized this in his monthly newsletter:

> Some would have us believe it is wrong for Christians to pay heed to the "Signs of the Times," particularly those that herald (or proclaim) the **soon** coming of our Lord. Admittedly, there are some in the past that have made a fetish out of the subject and see "signs" in Scripture that really do not exist. The truth is the disciples asked such a question of the Lord Himself just before He died for our sins and rose again, and He did not rebuke them! This leads us to believe that it is **good for us to examine the signs** to spiritually motivate us and those we would lead to Christ to help them hasten their decision to accept Him and thus prepare for His coming. (Pre-Trib Perspectives, Vol. VIII, Number 70, October 2009, emphasis mine)

All Christians should be *"looking"* for the *warning signs* that the Old Testament prophets, Jesus Christ and the Apostles gave us. To fail to *"watch"* for those *warning signs* is an act of disobedience because our Savior commanded us to *"watch," "be ready," "watch"* and be *"looking"* for His return (Matthew 24.42, 44; 25.13 Titus 2.13).

Hal Lindsey

Hal Lindsey firmly believes there are *signs* of the Rapture even though he believes in the doctrine of *imminence*. In his first book on prophecy he says this about three important "signs of the time":

> To be specific about Israel's great significance as a **sign of the time**, there are three things that were to happen. First, the Jewish nation would be reborn in the land of Palestine. Secondly, the Jews would repossess old Jerusalem and the sacred sites. Thirdly, they would rebuild their ancient temple of worship upon its historic site. (*The Late Great Planet Earth*, pp. 50-51, emphasis mine)

He then explained how one can pinpoint the *time of this restoration*, using a verse from the book of Ezekiel:

"After many days you shall be visited and mustered for service; in the latter years you shall go against the land that is restored from the ravages of the sword, where people are gathered out of many nations upon the mountains of Israel, which had been a continual waste; but its people are brought forth out of the nations..." (Ezekiel 38:8 Amplified).

The clues are that the restoration comes in the "latter years," the land had been "a continual waste," and the Jewish people return from exile "out of the nations" (*The Late Great Planet Earth*, p. 51).

Lindsey summarized his understanding of the return of the Jews to their ancient homeland:

It cannot be emphasized enough. This restoration would take place after a world-wide dispersion and long-term desolation of the land of Israel. However, it would occur shortly before the events which will culminate with the personal, visible return of the Messiah, Jesus Christ, to set up an everlasting Kingdom and bring about the spiritual conversion of Israel. (Ibid., p. 52)

Lindsey realizes the Bible teaches the Jews would be dispersed and that the land of Israel would be desolate for a "long time." We now know that this "long-term desolation" was nearly 1900 years. Therefore, it is impossible for the Rapture to take place at *any moment* since Pentecost. He then asked what generation would see the return of the Lord?:

Obviously, in context, the generation that would see the **signs** – chief among them the rebirth of Israel. A generation in the Bible is something like **forty years**. If this is a correct deduction, then within forty years or so of 1948, **all these things could take place.** Many scholars who have studied Bible prophecy all their lives believe that this is so. (Ibid., p. 54, emphasis mine)

Lindsey makes it clear that the generation that sees the "signs – chief among them the rebirth of Israel" – will see the return of the Lord.

In his second book on prophecy, *The 1980's: Countdown to Armageddon*, Lindsey described 7 *signs,* which he called "birth pains" – "religious deception, international revolution, war, famines, earthquakes, plagues and strange events in the skies" (pp. 19-33). This is what he had to say about these "birth pain" *signs*:

Over the past 10 years the appearance of Jesus's **signs** has accelerated, and today, we find them occurring one on top of the other. Let me report on the **signs** I see and maybe we can learn what is in store for us. (Ibid., p. 20, emphasis mine)

Lindsey has continued to emphasize the importance of *signs* throughout his writing career. He did so in an essay entitled, "The Armageddon Scenario," which was published in the 1995 book, *Steeling the Mind of America* (Perkins, Bill). He is convinced that we are living in the *general time* of the return of Jesus, and forcefully explained why:

> I'm not a date setter because I don't know the day or the hour when Christ is coming back, but I know He commanded us to **know** the **general time of His return** and **we are in it**. We are drawing **very near** to the time when we'll hear the footsteps of Christ at the very threshold of heaven, ready to return for us. And so much has happened since I wrote *The Late Great Planet Earth* that I feel an update is in order. (pp. 103-104, emphasis mine)

Lindsey then took several pages to explain how the *signs* that Jesus told His disciples to look for in the Olivet Discourse were being fulfilled in the 20th Century and concluded:

> As I look at these things, it's unmistakable I believe that **Christ's coming must be very near** because we see these things in an advanced state of fulfillment. But these are **general signs**. (Perkins, Bill, *Steeling the Mind of America*, p. 111, emphasis mine)

He continued to deal with *signs,* and went from general *signs* to specific *signs* that could only be fulfilled in our generation due to technological advances. This is what he said about the mark of the beast:

> There are some technical realities hidden in prophecy that **couldn't be possible until this present time**... In Revelation 13:7, it talks about the whole world being brought under control of this person. Those in past generations who looked at this must have wondered, "How could one man cause every person – man, woman, and child – on the face of this planet to be numbered and then be able to keep track of them." It was impossible in other generations, but now, just at the time when **all of the other predicted events are happening**, we have the technical ability for this Antichrist to come in and number every person on earth and have instant access to those that have violated it. We're talking about a total control of the world through economics... and it's child's play. With today's technology it is now easy for computers to not only identify every person on earth, but to also keep a dossier, a history, on every person. Technically, a chip can be placed under the skin of the forehead or the forehand, and it will have much more than a number. (Ibid., pp. 111-112, emphasis mine)

If Lindsey is correct, that our generation is the first one with the technology that will enable the Antichrist to force everyone on Earth to take his mark, then the Rapture could not possibly have been an *imminent* event since Pentecost. He made a strong argument against the hypothesis that Christ could return at *any moment*, and a powerful argument that there are *warning signs* of the return of Christ.

Lindsey was certain, in 1995, when he wrote the essay "The Armageddon Scenario," that the Antichrist was alive:

When the Antichrist comes on the scene (and **he's already alive somewhere in Europe**; I'm sure of it), you will have to swear allegiance to him as the supreme ruler and deity in order to buy, sell, or hold a job. (Ibid., p. 112, emphasis mine)

If the Antichrist was alive in 1995, then, according to Lindsey, our generation is the last generation. After giving several other reasons why he is convinced that we are the terminal generation, he quoted the parable of the fig tree, and commented on it:

Now from the fig tree learn her parable: when her branch is now become tender, and putteth forth its leaves, ye know that the summer is nigh; even so ye also, when ye see all these things, know ye that he is nigh, even at the doors. Verily I say unto you, This generation shall not pass away, till all these things be accomplished. (Matthew 24:32-34, KJV)
We are that generation without a shadow of a doubt. The leaves on the fig tree were symbolic of the events of prophecy that I've just described to you. (Ibid., p. 129)

In this essay he made a powerful argument that numerous *warning signs* of the return of Christ have been fulfilled, and that we are the "terminal generation" that will see the return of the Lord. He also argued forcefully that Jesus could not have returned at *any moment* since Pentecost because the mark of the beast technology had only recently been invented.

In his book, *Vanished Into Thin Air*, published in 1999, Lindsey taught that the Antichrist must rise to power prior to the start of the Tribulation, just as the early Church fathers did:

Events Just before the Tribulation

It is apparent that **sometime before the seven-year Tribulation begins, the Antichrist will receive a mortal wound**, be miraculously healed, be indwelt by Satan, and take over the ten nations out of what we now know as the European Union (Revelation 13:3). These things must first occur in order to give him the political position and power base from which to sign the protection treaty with Israel, which officially begins the Tribulation.

A **False Prophet**, or pseudo-Messiah to Israel (Revelation 13:11-17), **will be manifested before the Tribulation begins,** for he is the leader of Israel who will make the covenant with the Roman Dictator (the Antichrist).

The great falling away or **apostasy of the professing false church also takes place before the beginning of the Tribulation** which is sometimes called *"the Day of the Lord"* (2 Thessalonians 2:3). (p. 214, emphasis mine)

Lindsey agrees with the apostles and early Church fathers that the Antichrist must rise to power before the Tribulation. It is unlikely the Antichrist will receive a mortal wound before the Tribulation. The Bible says he receives the mortal wound at the mid-point of the Tribulation, and then he rules under the power of the devil for 42 months (Revelation 13.3-5).

The False Prophet must rise to power, and the apostasy (2 Thessalonians 2.3) must also take place before the Tribulation. Lindsey speculates there will be a *gap* of "several weeks" between the Rapture and the Tribulation (*Vanished Into Thin Air*, p. 387), but if there is no *gap*, the rise of the Antichrist and False Prophet are important *warning signs* for Christians to "watch" for just as the early Church fathers taught. (The question about a gap between the Rapture and the start of the Tribulation is explained in Chapter 10.)

Another significant *sign* that Lindsey says occurs before the Tribulation is the time of "peace and security":

> Throughout Europe and the rest of the world there is a kind of euphoria of peace. So what's the prophetic connection? It's interesting that in I Thessalonians, Chapter 5:1-3, it talks about a time *"When people say, 'There is peace and security.' then sudden destruction will come upon them... and there will be no escape."*
> The Bible is very clear that there will be a **period of time** in the **last days** when the **whole world lets down its guard**. It will be a time of great hope, but it will be a very **false hope and false peace**. (*Planet Earth-2000 A.D.*, p. 241, emphasis mine)

The people of the world will think they have entered a time of world-wide *"peace and security"* just before the start of the Tribulation. It is during this time of false peace that the Rapture takes place, as Dave Hunt noted. This means there will be a period of so-called universal *"peace and safety"* before the Rapture. It is one of the last *warning signs* for which we are to "look."

It is significant that Lindsey says there are four major *warning signs* that will take place before the Tribulation: the rise of the Antichrist, the rise of the False prophet, the great apostasy and the time of false "peace and security."

Peter Lalonde

Peter Lalonde, a Canadian televangelist and author of several books on prophecy, founded Cloud Ten Pictures in 1994. Along with his brother, Paul, they have produced several Christian films, including three "Left Behind" films. He believes that "end times" prophecies have been fulfilled: Israel in her homeland, Jerusalem retaken, revived Roman Empire, rise to power of the Soviet Union, mark-of-the-beast technology, earthquakes, pestilences and hatred of Christians (*One World Under Antichrist*, pp. 259-276; 291-300). He also sees a move to create a "New World Order." In his book noted above, he explained in two chapters entitled, "Toward the New World Order" and "The Blueprint" why he believes the new world order described in the Bible is being established.

John Hagee

John Hagee is founder and senior pastor of Cornerstone Church in San Antonio, Texas, a non-denominational charismatic church with more than 19,000 members. He is the chief executive officer of his non-profit corporation, Global Evangelism Television (GETV). He believes that Jesus can return at *any moment,* yet he believes there are specific *signs* that prove we are living in the "end times." In his 1996 book, *Beginning of the End*, he gave several significant *signs*:

1. Explosion of knowledge
2. Plague in the Middle East
3. Rebirth of Israel
4. The Jews will return home
5. Jerusalem no longer under Gentile rule
6. International instant communication
7. Days of deception
8. Famines and pestilence
9. Earthquakes
10. As in the days of Noah. (pp. 85-100)

Hagee, like many prophecy teachers, did not see all the Biblical *signs* of the *last days.* (We do not agree with his doctrines, some are unusual, but cite him to show what some of the leading prophecy preachers in America teach.)

David Webber and Noah Hutchings

David Webber, son of Dr. E.F. Webber, founder of the Southwest Radio Church (SWRC), published a booklet in 1978 with Noah Hutchings, the current president of SWRC. They speculated that the Second Coming of Jesus Christ might be in 2001. They based their belief of the timing of the Second Coming upon *signs*. Even though they have taught the doctrine of *imminence* for a few decades, they believe in the importance of looking for *signs*. This is what they wrote in 1978:

A vital question that affects every man, woman and child living today is: "Will Christ come by 2001?" This impending possibility looms ominously on the human horizon and confronts each of the nearly 4.5 billion people on this planet. A time of unparalleled affliction, tyranny, and destruction must occur before the most shattering event in all history of man – the physical return of Christ to the earth, in real, visible, and overwhelming power.

The irrefutable evidence of prophetic Scripture indicates that Jesus Christ may very well be here by 2001! The **general signs** in the heavens and on earth, plus the **specific signs** occurring in Israel (God's dramatic timepiece), all point to **His soon return**. (*Will Christ Come by 2001?*, p. 2, emphasis mine)

Webber and Hutchings went on to point out specific *signs* that made them believe that Jesus would soon return:

With the first non-Italian Pope in 455 years now at the helm in Rome, and the first peace treaty between Egypt and Israel in 3300 years in the offing, the world is **swiftly moving toward its rendezvous with destiny**; the coming of Israel's Messiah to smash the Antichrist, roll back the Tribulation tides of evil, and establish His righteous rule from Jerusalem, the future capital of the world. (*Will Christ Come by 2001?*, p. 2, emphasis mine)

The two *signs* they gave in the "Foreword" are not Biblical *signs*. A non-Italian Pope and a treaty between Egypt and Israel are not found in the Bible. They began the first chapter with a chart of past and future dates:

A.D. 1917-1921 - Balfour Declaration
A.D. 1918-1922 - The Beginning of Sorrows
A.D. 1948-1952 – Israel's Rebirth After the Flesh
A.D. 1967-1971 - Jerusalem Restored
A.D. 1974-1978 - Jewish Temple Rebuilt?
A.D. 1981-1985 - Beginning of the Tribulation
A.D. 1985-1989 - Middle of Tribulation
A.D. 1988-1992 - End of the Tribulation
A.D. 1995-1999 - Completion of Millennial Temple
A.D. 1996-2000 - The Jubilee, a rest
A.D. 1997-2001 - Beginning of the Kingdom Age. (Ibid., p. 3)

Even though no man can know the "*day or hour*" of the return of Christ, they say Christians will be able to determine how near the Rapture is:

The Prophetic Word is clear and forthright. The nearer the time for Christ's return, the more evident the **fulfilling of prophetic signs**, until Christians can be sure that **His coming is not only near, but at hand**. (Ibid., p. 5, emphasis mine)

There are many *prophetic signs* that we should look for, but we disagree with their date-setting. As *signs* are fulfilled, we can know that the Rapture is getting closer, but we cannot predict years in advance when the Rapture will take place. They were looking at some events that were not true *warning signs*, and they were making predictions based on intuition.

They noted that Jesus rebuked the hypocrisy of the Pharisees for not knowing the *"signs of the times"* of their day (Matthew 16.3). Then they accuse people today, who have no interest in the Second Coming, of being hypocrites. The "self-righteous hypocrites of our day scoff at the message of His soon return" (*Will Christ Come by 2001?*, p. 5).

(Many Christians have no interest in Bible prophecy because of the men who have claimed that the return of Jesus Christ is "very near" and "at hand" for the past 40 years.)

Webber and Hutchings went on to emphasize the importance of looking for *signs* by writing:

> But He indicated that when the **signs** that He gave began to come to pass, then believers in those days could know by way of investigation that **His coming was near, even at the doors**. Today, if you were to ask any number of well known prophetic scholars if Christ would **come by the year 2000 A.D.**, most would reply that it was not only possible, **but probable**. The closer we get to the time of Christ's return, the nearer prophetic observers can come to arriving at the **approximate date**. (Ibid., p. 6, emphasis mine)

They concluded their chapter on the *signs* of the times by writing this harsh statement:

> Scripture indicts ministers and pastors who refuse to investigate the **signs of the time** leading to Christ's return, and warn the unsaved to prepare, as being ignorant, hypocrites, and false prophets (Matthew 16:3; II Peter 3:3-5). (Ibid., p. 6, emphasis mine)

Most pastors who ignore prophecy are not false prophets or hypocrites. They do not teach Bible prophecy because they have been turned off by the teachers of *imminence*. The myriad false predictions of the return of Christ have diminished their interest in prophecy. The majority of Christians have no interest in prophecy, and many do not want their pastors to teach it.

Later in the booklet, Webber and Hutchings describe general *signs* that make them believe the Rapture is just over the event horizon – apostasy within the Church, Satanic infiltration of the Church, spiritual impotence of the Church, the rise of humanism and materialism in Christendom, ecumenism in the Church, the Roman Catholic Church, the world church headquarters, and the rise of scoffers within the Church (Ibid., pp. 32-36).

None of these *signs* that they were looking at were specific *signs* of the return of Christ (Appendix A). If they knew the right *warning signs* to "look" for, they most likely would not have thought the Rapture might take place by 2001. They focused on general *signs*, rather than on specific *signs*.

The most interesting *signs* that Webber and Hutchings gave to prove that we are living in the "end times*"* were the invention of the automobile, the airplane, space vehicles, the computer, radio and television. They cited Scripture for each of them and then concluded their booklet by writing:

We would ask, ARE YOU READY FOR THE COMING OF JESUS CHRIST? **It's almost here, according to the signs of our time. The Word of God admonishes us to be observing the signs of the time** for the return of Jesus Christ (Matthew 24:33). (Ibid., p. 84, emphasis mine)

Noah Hutchings has continued to teach that there are numerous *signs* of the Rapture. In his annual prophecy calendar for 2009 entitled, "Signs that Jesus May Come Today" he listed several signs – economic upheaval, rapid travel, increase of knowledge, the re-founding of the nation of Israel, alignment of nations, modern inventions, Jewish and Christian numerics, the days of Noah, the great falling away, wars, rumor of wars, famines, earthquakes, pestilences and delusions.

Believers should be "watching" the *signs* of the *end times* that we are living in to know how near the Rapture is, but we need to know what those *signs* are.

Grant Jeffrey

Grant Jeffrey believes there are dozens of *signs* of the Second Coming. He devoted an entire book, *Final Warning*, to these *signs*:

FINAL WARNING will explore the economic agenda of the elite globalist groups that are conspiring to force America and Canada to join the coming one-world government. We will examine the financial strategies that will allow us to survive the economic roller coaster awaiting us in the years ahead. FINAL WARNING reveals the fascinating biblical prophecies that warn us about a series of breathtaking political, economic, and military crises that will unfold as we rush toward the new Millennium. (p. 7)

Jeffrey explained in detail how the elitists have been working to establish a world government, economy and church. He even named a few of the financial organizations that are being used to create a world economic system: the World Trade Organization, the World Bank and the International Monetary Fund (Ibid., pp. 219-224). Organizations that he says are working to create a world government are: the Federal Reserve Corporation, the Council on Foreign Relations, the Trilateral Commission, the Bilderbergers, the Council of Europe, the Club of Rome, the World Federalist Movement and the Asian Pacific Economic Community (*Final Warning*, pp. 74-88).

(Some other organizations that should be included are: the Bohemian Club, the Fabian Society, the Freemasons, the Illuminati Order, the Knights of Malta, the Knights Templar, the Royal Institute of International Affairs, the Skull and Bones Order, the Theosophical Society and the Thule Society.)

Jeffrey explained that the Antichrist will need some recently developed technology to compel everyone to take his "mark" to be able to buy or sell (Revelation 13.16-17). Some of these technologies are: computers, the Society for Worldwide Interbank Financial Transmission and smart cards.

Since we understand that these developments must be in place before the Antichrist can take absolute control of the world, how could the return of Jesus Christ have been *imminent* for the last 1900 years? It would not be possible.

In his 2001 book, *Triumphant Return*, Jeffrey devoted Chapter 9 to *general signs*), and Chapter 10 to *unique signs* of the Second Coming. The *general signs* are: false messiahs, wars and rumors of wars, famines, pestilences, the AIDS plague, the preaching of the gospel and perilous times (pp. 201-216).

The *unique signs* that he listed are:

The rebirth of Israel, the restoration of the Hebrew language, the Arab-Israeli conflict, the return of Ethiopian Jews, the astonishing fertility of Israel, the rebuilding of Jerusalem, the plan to rebuild the temple, the rediscovery of the "oil of anointing," the revived Roman Empire, the massive increase of the male population in Asia, the building of a highway from China to the Middle East, the damming of the Euphrates River, the plan to rebuild the ancient city of Babylon, the plans for global government, the mark of the beast technology, satellite television, and the increase in knowledge. (Ibid., pp. 219-263)

Jeffrey has found many *unique signs*. These *signs* that point to the nearness of the Tribulation are also *signs* of the approaching Rapture. He says these *signs* are for the generation of the "last days":

The Scriptures teach that the final last days' generation, the population who are living when Christ returns, will witness the **fulfillment of numerous prophecies pointing to the soon return of the promised Messiah**. Our generation of Christians has **witnessed more fulfilled prophecies than any other generation** in the two-thousand-year history of the Church. The visions of the Old Testament prophets, together with the New Testament's prophetic words of Jesus and His apostles, testify with one united voice that the generation that sees the fulfillment of these prophecies will also witness the triumphant victory of Jesus the Messiah over Satan. The establishment of the long-awaited Kingdom of God is **at hand**. In light of the **incredible fulfillment of so many prophecies in our lifetime**, we need to heed the prophetic words of Jesus Christ that speak especially to our generation. "*And when these things begin to come to pass, then look up, and lift up your heads; for your redemption draweth nigh*" (Luke 21:28, KJV). (Ibid., pp. 262-263, emphasis mine)

Jeffrey also believes that students of Bible prophecy will know the approximate time of the Second Coming and the Rapture:

The Lord has not left us in spiritual darkness concerning the **approximate time** of Christ's Second Coming. Although we are specifically warned that we cannot know "*the day nor the hour wherein the Son of Man cometh*" (Matthew 25:13), the **fulfillment of dozens of specific prophecies in our**

generation strongly suggests that Jesus Christ's Second Coming will occur in our lifetime. (Ibid., p. 263, emphasis mine)

The prophecies should come to pass in the lifetime of those who saw the first fulfilled prophecy, the re-birth of Israel (Matthew 24.34). Jeffrey is correct that Christians do not live in spiritual darkness. If believers know the **What** (*warning signs*) they can know the **When** (approximate time of the start of the Tribulation).

Conclusion

The men who teach *imminence* also teach there are *signs* of the return of Christ agree with Scripture that several *warning signs* of His return have been fulfilled. Scripture says that many more will be fulfilled. We urge all Christians to learn what those *warning signs* are (Appendix A), and then "*watch*" for their fulfillment, just as our Savior commanded us to (Matthew 24.42-44).

STUDY QUESTIONS

Chapter 8

1. Did Cyrus Scofield, Lewis Sperry Chafer and John Walvoord, and do J. Dwight Pentecost, Jack van Impe, Chuck Smith, Dave Hunt, Tim LaHaye, Hal Lindsey and Grant Jeffrey see *signs* of the return of Christ?

2. Are disciples of Jesus Christ commanded to "*watch*" for His return?

3. How do they "*watch*" for the return of Christ?

4. Are *signs* of the Tribulation also *signs* of the Rapture?

5. Was all of the information about the Antichrist placed in the Bible so Christians would be able to identify him before the Rapture or was it given for the unsaved to identify him after the Rapture?

6. Will the False Prophet rise to power before the Tribulation?

7. Will the Antichrist rise to power before the Tribulation?

8. List some of the *warning signs* that will be fulfilled before the Tribulation.

9. Did the following eschatologians believe and teach that there are *signs* of the Tribulation and also of the Rapture? – George Muller, Cyrus Scofield, Arno Gaebelein, Lewis Sperry Chafer, Henry Ironside, Herbert Lockyer, John Walvoord, Harold Lindsell, J. Dwight Pentecost, Jack Van Impe, Arnold Fruchtenbaum, Texe Marrs, Chuck Smith, John MacArthur, Jr., Dave Hunt, Timothy LaHaye, Hal Lindsey, Paul LaLonde, John Hagee, David Webber, Noah Hutchings and Grant Jeffrey.

PART IV

WHEN WILL THE RAPTURE TAKE PLACE?

*But concerning the **times and the seasons**, brethren, ye have no need that aught be written unto you. For yourselves know perfectly that the **day of the Lord** [Tribulation] so cometh as a thief in the night. When they are saying, **Peace and safety**, then sudden destruction cometh upon them, as travail upon a woman with child; and they shall in no wise escape. But ye, **brethren**, are not in darkness, **that that day should overtake you as a thief.*** (1 Thessalonians 5.1-4)

*Now we beseech you, brethren, touching the **coming of our Lord Jesus Christ**, and **our gathering together unto him**; to the end that ye be not quickly shaken from your mind, nor yet be troubled, either by spirit, or by word, or by epistle as from us, as that the day of the Lord is just at hand; let no man beguile you in any wise: for **it will not be, except the falling away come first**, and **the man of sin be revealed***, the son of perdition. (2 Thessalonians 2.1-3)

NINE

COMMANDS TO BE ALERT

Christians are commanded to *"watch,"* to be *"alert"* and to be spiritually *"awake"* for the Rapture by Jesus, Paul and Peter. Their commands and admonishments were not given to make Christians think Jesus Christ could return at *any moment*. They were given to motivate Christians to *"watch"* for the *warning signs* of His return.

The commands by Jesus to be alert

Jesus gave a few commands to His disciples, and to all Christians of the Church Age, to be *"alert"* and *"ready"* when He returns.

Matthew 24.42-44

A command by Jesus to *"watch"* and to be *"ready"* was given at the conclusion of the Olivet Discourse:

Watch therefore: for ye know not on what day your Lord cometh. But know this, that if the master of the house had known in what watch the thief was coming, he would have watched, and would not have suffered his house to be broken through. Therefore be ye also ready; for in an hour that ye think not the Son of man cometh.

This command was given to all Christians, but it has greater meaning to us who are living in the "last days" of the "end times." The "last days" started with the taking back of the holy city of Jerusalem from the Arabs in 1967. That event marked the start of the "end times" (Luke 21.24). We must *"watch"* the *warning signs* to know when Christ will return so we are not caught by surprise as Jesus commanded.

Many prophecy teachers argue that this one command implies that Christ can return at *any moment* since Pentecost. We know this is not what He wanted Christians to believe. Why? He commands all Christians to be *"ready"* and to *"watch"* so we will not be caught by surprise when He returns. How can we be *"ready"* and what do we *"watch"* for to not be caught by surprise? There are only two things we can do – live holy lives and *"watch"* for the *warning signs* that precede the return of Christ. If there is nothing to *"watch"* for how can we *"watch"*?

Matthew 25.13

Jesus told two parables in the Olivet Discourse after giving a detailed description of what would take place before and during the Tribulation. The first was the parable of the ten virgins (Matthew 25.1-13). Five of the virgins were waiting and ready when the bridegroom returned, and five were not. The virgins who were not ready were not allowed into the wedding feast. At the conclusion of the parable He warned:

Watch therefore, for ye know not the day nor the hour.

The bridegroom was delaying his return; that is why all of the virgins fell asleep. The question of how long the delay will be is obvious. It will be nearly 2000 years, because He has not yet returned. All of the virgins fell asleep, but five were prepared when the bridegroom returned. They had oil in their lamps. Christians today who *"watch"* the *warning signs* are prepared for the return of Christ. Those who are not "watching" the *warning signs* are not prepared for His return.

The second parable concerns a man who goes on a journey and gives his servants money to invest while he is gone (Matthew 25.14-30). He was away for a *long time* (Matthew 25.19). We know that the duration between the ascension of Jesus and His return will be about 2000 years. It is obvious that He could not return at *any moment* since His ascension, because He has not returned.

Mark 13.33-37

Jesus gave a command in the Olivet Discourse that is similar to the command that Matthew recorded. We know it is a different command because of the wording.

Take ye heed, watch and pray: for ye know not when the time is. It is as when a man, sojourning in another country, having left his house, and given authority to his servants, to each one his work, commanded also the porter to watch. Watch therefore: for ye know not when the lord of the house cometh, whether at even, or at midnight, or at cockcrowing, or in the morning; lest coming suddenly he find you sleeping. And what I say unto you I say unto all, Watch.

The only things that we can *"watch"* for are the prophetic *warning signs* that the Old Testament prophets, Jesus, Paul and Peter gave us to *"watch"* for so we would know the approximate time of the Rapture.

Luke 12.40

Jesus gave a similar command earlier in His ministry, after admonishing His followers to seek the kingdom of God rather than the riches of the world (Luke 12.35-40). He concluded by saying:

Be ye also ready: for in an hour that ye think not the Son of man cometh.

It appears to some that Jesus taught the doctrine of *imminence*, but this statement, as you will see, and all similar statements do not have to do with His *imminent* return. The commands to believers to be *"ready"* and to eagerly *"wait"* for the return of Jesus were given specifically for the "generation" living in the "last days." It was also given in a general manner for all generations to keep their minds on the things above rather than the things on Earth (Colossians 3.1-2). Christians who *"watch"* for the *warning signs* of the return of Christ, rather than seek after the riches and the pleasures of this sinful world, are the obedient and faithful servants.

One may also consider that this statement is referring to a Christian who is not actively *"watching"* for the return of Christ by *"looking"* for *warning signs* to be fulfilled. Christ will return when those who are not *"watching"* do not think He will return. Those who are *"watching"* the *warning signs* will know the approximate time of His return (1 Thessalonians 5.4).

The admonishments by Paul to be alert

Paul gave several admonishments to the churches that he founded to "wait" for the return of Jesus Christ. As we will see, he did not imply that Christ could return at *any moment*.

1 Corinthians 1.7-8

Paul gave this admonishment to the church in Corinth to wait the return of the Lord:

So that ye come behind in no gift; waiting for the revelation of our Lord Jesus Christ; who shall also confirm you unto the end, that ye be unreproveable in the day of our Lord Jesus Christ.

It was given specifically for those living in the "end times" and generally to all believers throughout the Church Age, just as the commands by Jesus were given. If Christians keep their eyes on Jesus, each and every day, they are less likely to be carried away by the temptations of the world. One way a Christian keeps his eyes on Jesus is by "waiting" for the fulfillment of the prophecies (*warning signs*) that will take place before Christ returns. Other ways are through daily prayer (Ephesians 6.18; 1 Thessalonians 5.17), study of

Scripture (Acts 17.11; 2 Timothy 2.15), and regular fellowship with fellow Christians (Hebrews 10.24-25).

Philippians 3.20

In his letter to the Philippians, Paul stated that all believers are to *"wait"* for the return of Christ:

For our citizenship is in heaven; whence also we wait for a Saviour, the Lord Jesus Christ.

Prior to this statement Paul exhorted his readers to press on toward the goal, be complete, live by the same standard he does and to follow his example (Philippians 3.14-17). He also warned them that there were some people who claimed to be saved, yet they were *"enemies of the cross of Christ, whose end is destruction, whose god is their appetite, and whose glory is in their shame, who set their minds on earthly things"* (Philippians 3.18-19). In this admonishment, Paul is reminding all believers throughout the Church Age to remember that our home is Heaven, and that they should *"wait"* for their Savior and Lord, Jesus Christ.

1 Thessalonians 1.9-10

In his first letter to the Thessalonians, Paul praised them for turning from idols to the living and true God. He then told them to *"wait"* for His Son Jesus, who will come from Heaven to deliver them from the wrath (Tribulation) to come:

For they themselves report concerning us what manner of entering in we had unto you; and how ye turned unto God from idols, to serve a living and true God, and to wait for his Son from heaven, whom he raised from the dead, even Jesus, who delivereth us from the wrath to come.

This command was given to newly-born believers who had turned away from *"idols"* to live holy lives. He added to that command the admonishment to *"wait"* for the return of Jesus. The context of this passage is holiness, and Paul added the promise that Jesus would return someday and keep Christians from going through the Tribulation. The *"wrath to come"* is the Tribulation. When one lives a holy life he will patiently *"wait"* for the return of Christ by *"watching"* the *warning signs.*

All believers from the apostles to the last generation are commanded to *"wait"* for the return of Christ. When one considers the parables of Jesus (Matthew 25.14-30; Luke 19.11-27), where He made it explicitly clear that He would be gone a *"long time"* (Matthew 25.19), it becomes obvious that *"waiting"* for Him does not mean He could return at *any moment* since

Pentecost. It means one must be *"patient,"* as James wrote (5.7-8), and *"wait"* for His return by *"looking"* for the *warning signs.*

This conclusion is supported by the fact that Jesus made several prophecies which must be fulfilled prior to His return. He prophesied the Temple would be destroyed (Matthew 24.2), the city of Jerusalem would be taken and controlled by the Gentiles until the *"times of the Gentiles"* was fulfilled (Luke 21.24), and Peter would be martyred in his old age (John 21.18-19).

1 Thessalonians 5.1-9

Later, in his first letter to the Thessalonians, Paul gave another warning to them to *"watch"* for the return of Christ. He described the Rapture (4.13-17), and then commanded them to *"comfort one another with these words"* (v. 18). He continued to explain that they do not need anyone to teach them what will happen just before the Rapture takes place. (There are no chapter breaks in the original text.):

But concerning the times and the seasons, brethren, ye have no need that aught be written unto you. For yourselves know perfectly that the day of the Lord so cometh as a thief in the night. When they are saying, Peace and safety, then sudden destruction cometh upon them, as travail upon a woman with child; and they shall in no wise escape. (vs. 1-3)

Paul then warned his readers in verses 4-9 to be spiritually alert and sober:

But ye, brethren, are not in darkness, that that day should overtake you as a thief: for ye are all sons of light, and sons of the day: we are not of the night, nor of darkness; so then let us not sleep, as do the rest, but let us watch and be sober. For they that sleep sleep in the night: and they that are drunken are drunken in the night. But let us, since we are of the day, be sober, putting on the breastplate of faith and love; and for a helmet, the hope of salvation. For God appointed us not into wrath, but unto the obtaining of salvation through our Lord Jesus Christ.

In verse one, Paul told his readers they had no need for someone to explain to them how they would know when the Rapture would be an *imminent* event. He had already taught them about it when he founded the church. Yet he summarized that teaching in verses 2 and 3. The Rapture/Tribulation will catch the unsaved by surprise, as a *"thief"* does when he comes to steal in the dead of night. They will be cheering when there is a time of so-called *"peace and safety"* in the world. It is just after this period of peace that the Rapture will take place and the Tribulation will start.

The lost will be caught by surprise, but believers who are awake will not be caught by surprise by the return of Christ. They will know the **When** because they will know **What** to look for – a period of false *"peace and safety"* throughout the world.

2 Thessalonians 2.1-3

In his second letter to the church in Thessalonica Paul commanded them to not be deceived about the return of the Lord:

> *Now we beseech you, brethren, touching the coming of our Lord Jesus Christ, and our gathering together unto him; to the end that ye be not quickly shaken from your mind, nor yet be troubled, either by spirit, or by word, or by epistle as from us, as that the day of the Lord is just at hand; let no man beguile you in any wise: for it will not be, except the falling away come first, and the man of sin be revealed, the son of perdition.*

Someone had forged a letter claiming that the *"Day of the Lord,"* which starts with the Tribulation, was *"just at hand."* Paul cleared up the confusion by explaining that two things had to take place before the Tribulation could start – the *"falling away"* and the revealing of the *"man of sin."*

The only way to keep from being deceived is to know what must take place prior to the start of the Tribulation. Paul had told them in his first letter that there will be a period of *"peace and safety"* before the Tribulation (1 Thessalonians 5.3). In his second letter he gave two more signs – the *"falling away"* of the Church from the faith, and the revealing of the *"man of sin."* As noted previously we are living in the time of the *"falling away."* The next two super-signs are the rise of the *"man of sin"* (Antichrist) and a period of false *"peace and safety."*

Titus 2.11-13

Paul also exhorted Titus to warn his flock to live holy lives by *"looking"* for the return of Christ:

> *For the grace of God hath appeared, bringing salvation to all men, instructing us, to the intent that, denying ungodliness and worldly lusts, we should live soberly and righteously and godly in this present world; looking for the blessed hope and appearing of the glory of the great God and our Saviour Jesus Christ.*

This is an exhortation to live a holy life. All Christians should be *"looking for the blessed hope and appearing"* of Christ. It is holy living that leads a person to look for the return of Jesus Christ, and one does that by knowing what the *warning signs* are.

The statement by Jesus to, *"Watch therefore, for ye know not the day or the hour"* of His return (Matthew 25.13), complements the statements by Paul cited above. One cannot know the exact *"day or hour"* of the return of Christ years ahead of time (Matthew 24.36), but when the prophecies leading up to the Tribulation are fulfilled we will be in a much better position to recognize the approximate time of the start of Tribulation. Alert Christians can know the

Tribulation is extremely close when there is a worldwide period of false *"peace and safety"* (1 Thessalonians 5.3), and the Antichrist has been revealed (2 Thessalonians 2.3). A Christian can know the approximate time of the **When**, because the **What** has taken place.

The admonishment by Peter to look for the Rapture

Peter also admonished his readers to be *"looking"* for the return of Jesus Christ.

2 Peter 3.10-12

Peter wrote this after saying that the world would be destroyed by fire:

But the day of the Lord will come as a thief; in the which the heavens shall pass away with a great noise, and the elements shall be dissolved with fervent heat, and the earth and the works that are therein shall be burned up. Seeing that these things are thus all to be dissolved, what manner of persons ought ye to be in all holy living and godliness looking for and earnestly desiring the coming of the day of God, by reason of which the heavens being on fire shall be dissolved, and the elements shall melt with fervent heat?

The context of this passage is holiness. Peter explains that, because this present world and universe will be destroyed by fire some day, Christians should live holy lives. While a believer is living a holy life he should be *"looking"* for the Rapture. Again, holiness precedes *"looking"* for the return of Christ. If one is living a holy life, he will then *"watch"* for Christ's return.

Conclusion

The context of the commands and warnings by Jesus, Paul and Peter to be *"alert"* is holiness. Christians are commanded to live holy lives, and *"looking"* for the return of Christ is an important aspect of holy living. They were not theological truths on which to base a doctrine. Christ cannot return at *any moment*, because numerous prophetic *signs* have to be fulfilled before the start of the Tribulation. If there is no *gap* between the Rapture and the Tribulation those *warning signs* will be fulfilled before we make our exit. The two most important *warning signs* are the time of false *"peace and safety"* (1 Thessalonians 5.3), and the revealing of the *"man of sin,"* the Antichrist (2 Thessalonians 2.1-3).

Christians who believe in the false doctrines of Preterism, Amillennialism, Postmillennialism and Dominion Theology are not obeying the commands of Jesus to *"watch"* for His return by actively *"looking"* for prophecies to be fulfilled before that blessed event. One radio talk show host said that

Christians are to "wait for the Second Coming," but not to look for prophecies to be fulfilled beforehand because there are none ("Bible Answer Man" radio program, 6.22.2009).

The commands to be "*alert*" were not given to make Christians think Christ could return at *any moment*. The Holy Spirit, who inspired Paul and Peter to write all of their letters, knew that Christ would not return in their lifetime, nor would He return for nearly 2000 years! It would be an act of deception by the Holy Spirit, the Father and the Son to give us commands to eagerly "*wait*" for Christ to return at *any moment* when They knew He would not return for 2000 or more years! The end (holy living) can never justify the means (doctrine of *imminence*)! We should all eagerly "look" for the **What** (*warning signs*) to know the time of the **When** (the Rapture).

STUDY QUESTIONS

Chapter 9

1. Jesus and Paul commanded Christians to be "*alert*" for the Rapture. How do Christians stay "*alert*?"

2. Does the command to "*wait*" for the return of Jesus Christ mean He can return at *any moment*?

3. What does the word "*wait*" imply concerning the length of time of the return of Christ?

4. Are Christians commanded to be "*patient*" while they "*wait*" for Christ to return?

5. Should Bible students know the *"times and seasons"* of the return of Christ, and how do they determine what the *"times and seasons"* are?

6. Will the Rapture and the start of the Tribulation catch the unsaved by surprise?

7. Will some Christians be caught by surprise by the Rapture?

8. What is the *super-sign* that Paul says will take place just prior to the Rapture in his first letter to the Thessalonians?

9. What are the other *super-signs* that Paul wrote about in his second letter to the Thessalonians?

10. If one is living a holy life, will he be *"looking"* for the return of Christ?

11. Can the end ever justify the means?

TEN

THE GAP

Most Pre-Tribulation eschatologians do not teach that there is a *gap* between the Rapture and the start of the Tribulation, yet some argue that there is a *gap* of a few days, weeks or months. Some even argue that there could be years or decades between these two events. A few prophecy teachers who have held to this hypothesis are – Clarence Larkin, Timothy LaHaye, Hal Lindsey, Chuck Smith, Chuck Missler, Jimmy Swaggart and Earl Radmacher.

Arguments against a Gap

Morgan Edwards
(1722-1795)

Morgan Edwards, a Welsh historian of religion and Baptist preacher, pastored several churches in England, Ireland and America. He was the second person in the Modern Era to publish a writing concerning the timing of the Rapture. During his studies at Bristol Baptist Seminary in England (1742-44), he wrote a 56 page essay for eschatology class that was later published in Philadelphia in 1788 under the title: *Two Academical Exercises on Subjects Bearing the following Titles; Millennium, Last-Novelties.* He said the Rapture would take place 3½ years before the Second Advent of Jesus Christ:

> I say, *somewhat more --;* because the dead saints will be raised, and the living changed at Christ's "appearing in the air" (I Thes. iv. 17); and **this will be about three years and a half before the millennium,** as we shall see hereafter: but will he and they abide in the air all that time? No: they will ascend to paradise, or to some one of those many "mansions in the father's house" (John xiv. 2), and so disappear during the foresaid period of time. The design of this retreat and disappearing will be to judge the risen and changed saints; for "now the time is come that judgment must begin," and that will be "at the house of God" (I Pet. iv. 17) (Ibid., p. 7, emphasis mine)

Edwards believed the Rapture would take place 3½ years before the Second Coming. That would make him a Mid-Tribulationist. He obviously did not believe in a *gap* between the Rapture and the start of the Tribulation.

Edwards wrote of a Rapture almost 90 years before John Darby made public his belief in a Pre-tribulation Rapture. He also pre-dated the work of the Jesuit priest Manuel de Lacunza (1731-1801), *The Coming of the Messiah in*

Glory and Majesty, published in 1812, by 70 years. It was later published in English in 1827. It is possible that Edwards was influenced by the commentary that Jesuit priest Francisco Ribera (1537-1591) wrote on the book of Revelation, published in 1590. He said the Tribulation would last 3½ years.

John Nelson Darby
(1800-1882)

John Darby was an Anglo-Irish evangelist, and a co-founder of the Plymouth Brethren. He is considered to be the father of modern Dispensationalism, and the Pre-Tribulation Rapture doctrine. He did not believe in a *gap* between the Rapture and the start of the Tribulation:

In 1 Thessalonians 5: 1-4, after speaking of the day of the Lord coming on the world as a thief in the night, the apostle adds, *"But ye, brethren, are not in darkness that that day should overtake you as a thief."* The natural inference being, that the day of the Lord will come **simultaneously** upon the world and the church; only it will find the latter prepared for it, while it will be destruction to the former.[1] (The Coming of the Lord and the Translation of the Church, emphasis mine)

He said the "day of the Lord" (Tribulation) will come upon the righteous and the unsaved "simultaneously." He does not leave room for a *gap* just as the Bible does not.

J. Vernon McGee
(1904-1988)

Dr. J. Vernon McGee, an ordained Presbyterian minister who later pastored the interdenominational Open Door Church in Los Angeles, was a well-loved Bible teacher (Bible Institute of Los Angeles), noted graduate of Dallas Theological Seminary, theologian and radio preacher (Thru the Bible Radio program). He emphatically taught that there is no *gap* between the Rapture and the start of the Tribulation. He said the rapture of the church actually does two things:

"It **ends this day of grace**" and "it **begins the day of the Lord**. The great tribulation will get under way when the church leaves the earth. The **one event** of the **rapture** will **end the day of grace and begin the day of the Lord**. It **closes one day** and **opens another**." (*1 and II Thessalonians*, p. 86, emphasis mine)

John Walvoord
(1910-2002)

John Walvoord, who succeeded Dr. Lewis Sperry Chafer as president of Dallas Seminary in 1952, was the author of over 30 books. His expertise was prophecy, and he did not teach a *gap* between the Rapture and Tribulation:

> The **first thing** that's going to happen **after the Rapture** is that we're entering a new period called the "Day of the Lord"... This is a day of grace, God's withholding judgment. **Once the Rapture occurs it changes immediately.** It's the "Day of the Lord"... Now the **"Day of the Lord" is going to begin at the time of the Rapture** according to 1 Thessalonians 5,... **So that's going to be the beginning.** ("The Second Coming" audio tape, date unknown, recording available, emphasis mine)

> There seems some evidence that the Day of the Lord begins **at once** at the time of the translation of the church (cf. 1 Thess. 5.1-9). The **same event** which translates the church begins the Day of the Lord. The events of the Day of the Lord begin thereafter to unfold: first the preparatory period, the first half of Daniel's last seven years of Israel's program preceding the second advent. (*The Rapture Question*, p. 163)

> In a word, the Day of the Lord begins *before* the great tribulation. When the day of grace ends with the translation of the church, the Day of the Lord begins **at once**. (Ibid.)

Walvoord clearly taught that there will be no *gap* between the Rapture and the start of the Tribulation.

Harold Lindsell
(1913-1998)

Dr. Harold Lindsell, former associate editor of *Christianity Today* magazine, and co-founder of Fuller Seminary, believed there is no *gap* between the Rapture and the start of the Tribulation. We quote him again because of his clear statement concerning the *gap* theory:

> The overwhelming verdict of those who hold to a pretribulation rapture is that this so-called *signless event* is **followed immediately by the seven-year tribulation period.** Thus, immediately following the rapture of the Church, Israel and the Antichrist will enter into a covenant. (*The Gathering Storm*, p. 137, emphasis mine)

Oliver Greene
(1915-1976)

Oliver Greene, independent fundamental Baptist evangelist, author of over 100 books and booklets and founder of the Gospel Hour radio ministry, left no room for a *gap* between the Rapture and the start of the Tribulation in his theology:

Immediately after the Rapture, the false Messiah will make his appearance. He will be riding upon a white horse (a symbol of peace) with a bow – but no arrow – in his hand (another symbol of peace). (*The Epistles of Paul the Apostle to the Thessalonians*, p. 157, emphasis mine)

Dave Breese
(1926-2002)

Dave Breese, a notable televangelist and pastor, founded Christian Destiny Ministry, helped form the AWANA Youth Association and served with Youth for Christ for 13 years. He taught the Pre-Tribulation Rapture during his distinguished ministry, yet he did not believe there would be a *gap* between the Rapture and the Tribulation. In his essay, "The Rapture," he explains:

The Tribulation is the beginning of "the day of the Lord." As we have seen, the Christians were conscious – because they read about it in the Old Testament – that there was a time of fearful judgment coming upon the world called the day of the Lord. The churches, however, needed instruction as to how to discern the presence of the day of the Lord and the way to know that the day of grace was finished. Concerning this, the apostle Paul wrote to the Thessalonians, saying, *"Now we beseech you brethren, by the coming of our Lord Jesus Christ, and our gathering together unto him, That ye be not soon shaken in mind, or be troubled, neither by spirit, nor by letter as from us, as that the day of the Christ is at hand"* (2 Thess. 2:1-2).

The apostle Paul is, therefore, saying that the **rapture** of the Church, concerning which he had carefully instructed the Thessalonians, was the **watershed point ending the day of grace and beginning the day of the Lord.** In that the Rapture had not taken place, the day of the Lord was not yet present.

Here, the apostle Paul gives us a **clear line of demarcation** between the Church Age, the day of grace, and the day of the Lord, which is the day of divine judgment. That **line of demarcation is the rapture of the Church.** (James, William T., *Storming Toward Armageddon*, pp. 298-299, emphasis mine)

The Rapture is the event that separates the "Day of Grace" (Church Age) from the "Day of the Lord" (Tribulation). Some Pre-Tribulationists understand this, and do not allow for a *gap* between those events.

J. Dwight Pentecost

Dr. J. Dwight Pentecost, a theologian best known for his book *Things to Come*, is the Distinguished Professor of Bible Exposition, Emeritus, at Dallas Theological Seminary, one of only two so honored. During his academic career he has taught biblical subjects for 6 decades (Philadelphia College of Bible, 1948-55; Dallas Theological Seminary, 1955-present). He is a leading Pre-Tribulationist who does not allow room for a *gap*. His book, *Things to Come*, states that the Tribulation begins immediately after the Rapture:

> The only way this day could break unexpectedly upon the world is to have it begin **immediately after the rapture of the church**. It is thus concluded that the Day of the Lord is that extended period of time beginning with God's dealing with Israel after the **rapture at the beginning of the tribulation period** and extending through the second advent and the millennial age unto the creation of the new heavens and new earth after the millennium. (*Things to Come*, pp. 230-231, emphasis mine)

Jack Van Impe

Dr. Jack Van Impe, a noted televangelist, host of the "Jack Van Impe Presents" television show and an avid teacher of the Pre-Tribulation Rapture for over 50 years, teaches the doctrine of *imminence*, yet he makes no allowance for a *gap* between the Rapture and the start of the Tribulation:

> Multitudes today are unaware of the fact that there are two stages or phases within the process of the second coming – the Rapture and the Revelation – and that these events are **separated by a seven-year** period of time. (*11:59 and Counting*, p. 8, emphasis mine)

> The Rapture is not Christ's appearance upon earth, but a meeting in the heavenlies – an intermediary evacuation of believers from earth before the storm. **Seven years later**, Christ does come to earth, touching down on the Mount of Olives (Zechariah 14:4). (Ibid., pp. 16-17, emphasis mine)

> The Day of the Lord begins as the Tribulation period commences. It continues through the 1,000-year reign of Christ because the destruction of the world by fire afterward is still called the Day of the Lord (2 Peter 3:10). Some try to make this the Rapture, causing confusion. It begins immediately *after* the Rapture. This is the reason that the Day of the Lord comes *as a thief in the night* (1 Thessalonians 5:2). (*Jack Van Impe Study Bible*, pp. 28-29, emphasis added, JVI)

There are two stages or phases within the process of the Second Coming – the Rapture and the Revelation – and these are **separated by a seven-year period of time... This event ends the Church Age** and ushers in the **Tribulation period**. (Ibid., p. 81, emphasis mine)

Van Impe says there is a time of just 7 years between the Rapture and the Second Coming. Therefore, there could not be a *gap* between the Rapture and the beginning of the 7-year Tribulation. In his television show that aired on the Trinity Broadcasting Network (April 20, 2009), clarified his position:

The **first night** of the **New World Order** is when a leader goes to Israel and makes peace between the Arabs and the Jews; **that is the night we're gone**. Then that government **lasts for 7 years**, then Christ comes back to stop the New World Order, and set up His kingdom here. That's how near it is.

Remember, we'll not know who he (**Antichrist**) is because the **Rapture takes place the night before this one comes to power**. That's how near it is. (Emphasis mine)

Salem Kirban

Salem Kirban has been writing prophecy books for over 40 years, and firmly believing in the Pre-Tribulation Rapture and in *imminence*, yet he does not see a *gap* between the Rapture and the start of the Tribulation. Concerning the concept that human history will last 7000 years, he wrote in 1978:

The 6th day then, according to this suggestion would end at about the year 1996. The Millennium would then be ushered in and the thousand year reign of the saints with Christ would begin. If this assumption was correct, then the **Rapture** would take place at **seven years before the Millennium**. (*Guide to Survival*, pp. 136-137, emphasis mine)

Timothy LaHaye

Dr. Timothy LaHaye teaches that there may be a *gap* between the Rapture and start of the Tribulation, but in a chart in his prophecy Bible he does not show there is a *gap*.[2]

Thomas Ice

Dr. Thomas Ice, Executive Director of the Pre-Trib Research Center that was founded by Dr. Timothy LaHaye in 1994, Associate Professor of Religion at Liberty University and author of several books on Bible prophecy, does not believe there is a *gap*. From his website, in an essay concerning the *signs* of the times, he tells us:

> The present church age is not a time in which Bible prophecy is being fulfilled. Bible prophecy relates to a time after the rapture (the seven-year tribulation period). However, this does not mean that God is not preparing the world for that future time during the present church age – in fact, He is. But this is not "fulfillment" of Bible prophecy. So while prophecy is not being fulfilled in our day, it does not follow that we cannot track "general trends" in current preparation for the coming tribulation, **especially since it immediately follows the rapture.**[3] ("Signs of the times and Prophetic Fulfillment," emphasis mine)

Perry Stone

Perry Stone, televangelist and host of the "Manna-Fest" television program, said there is no *gap* between the Rapture and the Tribulation:

> Everything changes in **one day**. In **one day's time** the **Rapture happens**. In that **same time** when the Rapture happens, in that **same hour**, it **introduces the day of the Lord**, the day of God's judgment, the day of God's wrath.
> We have the Rapture which is the day of Christ. It's the gathering together unto the Lord the Bible talks about. But that **Rapture**, day of Christ, **introduces the beginning of the day of the Lord**. The day of the Lord then goes for **7 years**, the great **Tribulation period**. The first part is the wrath of the Lamb, the second half, the second 42 months, is the wrath of God poured out on the Earth. ("Manna-Fest" TV program, 3.09.2009, emphasis mine)

Dave Hunt

Dave Hunt, a Christian apologist, speaker, radio commentator and author, began full-time ministry in 1973, and founded the Berean Call in 1990. He has written several books on theology, prophecy and the cults. He stated that the Rapture takes place 7 years before the Second Coming of Jesus Christ:

> One cannot escape the fact that Christ and His apostles gave definite signs to watch for that would herald the nearness of His return. Why give these signs if some generation at some time in the future was not expected to recognize them and know that His Second Coming was, as He Himself said, "near, even at the doors"?
> Yes, but if the **Rapture occurs seven years prior to the Second Coming**, then those signs are not for us. (*How Close Are We?*, p. 115, emphasis mine)

Hilton Sutton

Hilton Sutton, founder of Hilton Sutton World Ministries, and author of numerous books about the Bible, has been teaching Bible prophecy for over 50 years. He does not believe in a *gap*:

> The return of Jesus is in two stages **separated by seven years**: Rapture before the Tribulation and return at the end of the Tribulation.[4] (Emphasis mine.)

Chuck Smith

Chuck Smith has stated a few times that he does not believe there is a *gap* between the Rapture and the start of the Tribulation. In his 1976 book, *Snatched Away*, he did not leave room for a *gap*:

> We'll be with the Lord in heaven for a **7-year period** during which time the earth will experience what's known as the Great Tribulation, when the judgment of God is being poured out upon the earth. (pp. 7-8, emphasis mine)

In his 1977 book, *What the World is Coming to*, he said:

> The Church will be transported into heaven for a **seven-year period** during which time there will be a Great Tribulation upon the earth. (pp. 39-40, emphasis mine)

When he was asked if he believes Daniel's 70th week begins immediately after the Rapture he said, "Yes, yes, we believe that. We definitely believe that." He also made the following comments during the same radio broadcast concerning the Rapture and the start of the Tribulation:

> Well, I believe that the **7-year period** will probably, pretty much take place **as soon as the Church is out**. As I see the events in the Bible, when Israel is invaded by this army, great army of combined Muslim nations in Ezekiel 38, and God then rises to their defense supernaturally, and destroys this army that is coming against Jerusalem, that in chapter 39 of Ezekiel in that day He is going to pour His Spirit again upon the nation of Israel. He'll no longer hide Himself from them, and that, I believe, will **correspond with the Lord taking His Church out of the Earth**. ("To Every Man an Answer" radio program, 4.01.2002, emphasis mine)

And I believe that the power of the Holy Spirit dwelling within the Church today is the only thing that is keeping the Antichrist from taking over the world at this very moment. And I do believe that **the moment the Church is taken out** that **the Antichrist will be revealed along with the False**

Prophet. ("To Every Man an Answer" radio program, 5.15.2003, emphasis mine)

Smith reinforced his belief that there is no *gap* between the Rapture and the Tribulation on the "Pastor's Perspective" radio program in 2010. A caller said he heard Timothy LaHaye say there was a *gap* between the Rapture and Tribulation, and asked Smith what his position was. He responded by saying:

I really **don't know** where Tim LaHaye would get the idea that there was a gap between the rapture of the Church and the Tribulation… **I don't see that there's necessarily a time gap there**. I would think that as soon as God destroys this invading army it would appear that the Church will already be gone or raptured. ("Pastor's Perspective" radio program, 1.19.2010, emphasis mine)

Although Smith has said a few times that he believes there is no *gap* he has stated a couple times that there is a *gap*. A caller asked him if he believed the Rapture and the start of the Tribulation would take place on the same day based on Luke 17.27, 29. He replied:

Well, well I still believe the judgment of God in the great Tribulation probably **won't be the moment the Church is taken** out because of the fact the Church, it seems that the Church would be taken out, I believe, at that time the Antichrist would be revealed. (KWVE, 107.9 FM, 12.10.2007, emphasis mine)

He made a confession concerning the example of judgment falling on Sodom the same day Lot departed the city:

And so **it would appear** that with, with Lot you know, that in **the day** that he went out that the **judgment came**. (Ibid., emphasis mine)

In conclusion he answered by saying it is "plausible" for the Rapture and the start of the Tribulation to take place on the same day:

So, I… I don't… you know, **it's a plausible thing**, but I don't quite see it that way myself. (Ibid., emphasis mine)

Brian Brodersen

Brian Brodersen, associate pastor of Calvary Chapel Costa Mesa, California, and son-in-law of Chuck Smith, said the Tribulation will start when the Rapture takes place. He first said the Day of the Lord begins with the Rapture, and the Rapture occurs simultaneously with the Tribulation. His last statement is that the Day of the Lord probably begins with the Rapture:

I think it **begins with the Rapture**... We believe that the **Rapture will occur and then the Antichrist will come to power**... ("To Everyman an Answer," radio program, 2002, emphasis mine)

The things that are building up to the Rapture or that Tribulation period of time, and we see the **Rapture as being simultaneous with the Tribulation beginning**. There is some guess work involved and sometimes we're close and sometimes we're not so close. ("To Everyman an Answer," radio program, 5.07.2002, emphasis mine)

The idea of the **Day of the Lord** is not restricted to one 24-hour day. It is a period of time, which probably, you know, it's a bit speculative, but it probably **begins with the Rapture**, because of course, Jesus speaks about His coming as a thief in the night, and He seems to indicate that that is going to be the time that what we call the **Tribulation** or the judgment **begins** to be poured out on the Earth. ("Pastor's Perspective," radio program, 10.02.2008, emphasis mine)

So of course the church being removed from the world is the Rapture, and **that would bring about the final seven-year period**. So we tend to see it more **simultaneously** that it would **happen concurrently**. ("Pastor's Perspective" radio program, 1.19.2010, emphasis mine)

Don Stewart

Don Stewart, associate pastor of Calvary Chapel in Costa Mesa, California, and co-host of "Pastor's Perspective" radio show does not believe there is a *gap*:

His coming is what we call His revelation; that's at His Second Coming, and that is what is in view here. The Rapture is an event that precedes it. Now the question, of course, is how long does it precede the revelation of Christ? Is it instantaneous or almost the same? Or is it like we believe here, we believe the Bible teaches, **7 years before**? ("To Every Man an Answer," 3.27.1998, emphasis mine)
The Second Coming is in two stages, first the Rapture of the Church and then **7 years later** the revelation of Christ. So Christ comes first for the Church, takes the Church back to Heaven, the Rapture, then the revelation comes **7 years later**. ("Pastor's Perspective," 5.12.2009, emphasis mine)

And the **day of the Lord** which is God's judgment on the Earth **begins** on the Earth **when the Rapture of the Church takes place**. We sort of set the stage, don't we Chuck? **Once we're out of here that's when the clock starts ticking again.** ("Pastor's Perspective," 8.27.2009, emphasis mine)

Smith answered Stewart's question by saying, "Yes, it opens the door." Stewart confirmed his belief that there is no gap in a radio call-in program that Chuck Smith and Brian Brodersen were part of:

Yeah, if there was a gap of time between the taking out of the Church, the beginning of the 70th week of Daniel you wonder who is God working with what people on the Earth because it's the Jews He is going to work with the last seven-year period, and if the Church isn't here He doesn't seem like He has anybody. So it seems almost it has to **happen simultaneously** there, Mel, and you know this is the Church Age, and when the **Church Age ends at the Rapture, at the same time that agreement will be confirmed or signed and that will begin the last seven-year period** culminating in the Second Coming of Christ. So again **we don't see a necessity of a gap** particularly with seven-year idea with the burning of the weapons and so it seems **one's going to follow directly after the other.** ("Pastor's Perspective" radio program, 1.19.2010)

The Days of Noah and Lot

Jesus taught the Rapture and the start of the Tribulation take place on the same 24-hour day:

And as it came to pass in the days of Noah, even so shall it be also in the days of the Son of man. They ate, they drank, they married, they were given in marriage, until the day that Noah entered into the ark, and the flood came, and destroyed them all. Likewise even as it came to pass in the days of Lot; they ate, they drank, they bought, they sold, they planted, they builded; but in the day that Lot went out from Sodom it rained fire and brimstone from heaven, and destroyed them all: after the same manner shall it be in the day that the Son of man is revealed. In that day, he that shall be on the housetop, and his goods in the house, let him not go down to take them away: and let him that is in the field likewise not return back. Remember Lot's wife. Whosoever shall seek to gain his life shall lose it: but whosoever shall lose his life shall preserve it. (Luke 17.26-33)

The flood began on the same 24-hour day that Noah entered the ark:

*In the **selfsame day** entered Noah, and Shem, and Ham, and Japheth, the sons of Noah, and Noah's wife, and the three wives of his sons with them, into the ark; And the flood was forty days upon the earth; and the waters increased, and bare up the ark, and it was lifted up above the earth.* (Genesis 7.13, 17, emphasis mine)

Jesus said that on the day that the Rapture takes place the Tribulation will start. On the day that Lot departed Sodom, God brought judgment upon it:

*And when the **morning arose**, then the angels hastened Lot, saying, Arise, take thy wife, and thy two daughters that are here, lest thou be consumed in the iniquity of the city. But he lingered; and the men laid hold upon his hand, and upon the hand of his wife, and upon the hand of his two daughters, Jehovah being merciful unto him; and they brought him forth, and set him without the city.* (Genesis 19.15-16, emphasis mine)

*The **sun was risen upon the earth** when Lot came unto Zoar. Then Jehovah rained upon Sodom and upon Gomorrah brimstone and fire from Jehovah out of heaven; and he overthrew those cities, and all the Plain, and all the inhabitants of the cities, and that which grew upon the ground.* (Genesis 19.23-25, emphasis mine)

The flood began on the very 24-hour day Noah and his family entered the ark. Sodom was destroyed on the same 24-hour day that Lot departed. Therefore, the Rapture should occur on the 24-hour day that the Tribulation starts. A "day" must be a normal 24-hour day or the statement about not going down from the rooftop or back to the house makes no sense (Luke 17.31).

Conclusion

Jesus said that on the very *"day that Noah entered into the ark, and the flood came, and destroyed them all"* (Luke 17.27), and *"in the day that Lot went out from Sodom it rained fire and brimstone from heaven, and destroyed them all"* (Luke 17.29). He then said, *"After the same manner shall it be in the day that the Son of man is revealed"* (Luke 17.30). This is the first revealing at the Rapture. If there is no *gap* between the Rapture and the Tribulation, all the prophecies that must be fulfilled before the Tribulation starts will be fulfilled before the Rapture. Therefore, the Rapture should not take place until all those prophecies (*warning signs*) have been fulfilled.

STUDY QUESTIONS

Chapter 10

1. Why do some eschatologians believe there is a *gap* between the Rapture and the start of the Tribulation?

2. Did judgment fall on the unsaved on the same 24-hour day that Noah and his family entered the ark?

3. Did judgment fall on the unsaved on the same 24-hour day that Lot and his family departed from Sodom?

4. Did Jesus say that *"as it came to pass in the days of Noah, even so shall it be also in the days of the Son of man,"* meaning judgment will fall on the world on the 24-hour day that He raptures the Church?

5. Is there any passage in the Bible that says there is a *gap* between the Rapture and the start of the Tribulation?

6. If a doctrine has no Scripture to support it, should it be taught as a biblical truth, or as an opinion?

7. Who do you think is right? Those who believe in **a** *gap,* or those who believe there is **no** *gap*:

No *gap*	*Gap*
Morgan Edwards	Clarence Larkin
John Nelson Darby	Timothy LaHaye
J. Vernon McGee	Hal Lindsey
John Walvoord	Chuck Smith
Harold Lindsell	Chuck Missler
Oliver Greene	Jimmy Swaggart
Dave Breese	Earl Radmacher
J. Dwight Pentecost	
Jack Van Impe	
Salem Kirban	
Thomas Ice	
Perry Stone	
Dave Hunt	
Hilton Sutton	
Chuck Smith (formerly believed in a gap)	
Brian Brodersen	
Don Stewart	

ELEVEN

SEVEN CHURCH PERIODS

Many Pre-Tribulationists believe that the seven churches mentioned in Revelation 2 and 3, are symbolic of seven periods in the Church Age. The promise of being kept from the *"hour of trial,"* which they interpret as a promise of the Pre-Tribulation Rapture, was made to the church of Philadelphia:

> *Because thou didst keep the word of my patience, I also will keep thee from the hour of trial, that hour which is to come upon the whole world, to try them that dwell upon the earth.* (Revelation 3.10)

They argue that we are living in the period of the last true church. Therefore, Christians will be raptured prior to the start of the Tribulation.

Arguments for the seven periods of the Church Age

Cyrus Scofield
(1843-1921)

Dr. Cyrus Scofield came under the influence of James H. Brookes, pastor of Walnut Street Presbyterian Church in St. Louis, Missouri, who was a prominent dispensational premillennialist. In 1883, Scofield was ordained as a Congregationalist minister. He became the pastor of a small mission church, the First Congregational Church in Dallas, Texas (now the Scofield Memorial Church). The church grew from 14 to over 500 members before he resigned in 1895 after being called to pastor Dwight L. Moody's church, the Trinitarian Congregational Church of East Northfield, Massachusetts, and head of Moody's Northfield Bible Training School. In 1903 he returned to his church in Dallas and worked on his Scofield Reference Bible which was published in 1909.

He believed the letters to the seven churches in the book of Revelation were symbolic of seven periods of the Church Age. He said the messages to the churches had a fourfold purpose. The fourth purpose is "prophetic, as disclosing seven phases of the spiritual history of the church from, say, A.D. 96 to the end" (*The First Scofield Study Bible*, p. 1331). He then explained what each church represented:

Again, these messages by their very terms go beyond the local assemblies mentioned. Most conclusively of all, these messages do present an exact foreview of the spiritual history of the church, and in this precise order. Ephesus gives the general state at the date of the writing; Smyrna, the period of the great persecutions; Pergamos, the church settled down in the world, "where Satan's throne is," after the conversion of Constantine, say, A.D. 316. Thyatira is the Papacy, developed out of the Pergamos state: Balaalism (worldliness) and Nicolaitanism (priestly assumption) having conquered. As Jezebel brought idolatry into Israel, so Romanism weds Christian doctrine to pagan ceremonies. Sardis is the Protestant Reformation, whose works were not "fulfilled." Philadelphia is whatever bears clear testimony to the Word and the Name in the time of self-satisfied profession represented by Laodicea. (Ibid., pp. 1331-1332)

Scofield did not believe in the doctrine of *imminence*. He believed that Christ could not return until the Philadelphia period of the Church Age started. He also believed that four *warning signs* would take place before the Rapture: the appearing of Elijah, cosmical disturbances, the insensibility of the professing church, and the apostasy of the professing church (Ibid., p. 1349).

Arnold Fruchtenbaum

Dr. Arnold Fruchtenbaum, founder and director of Ariel Ministries, an organization which specializes in the evangelization of Jews, gives 1648 as the date of the start of the sixth church period (*The Footsteps of the Messiah*, 1993, p. 48). If the *"hour of trial"* is the Tribulation, then the Lord could not have returned to rapture them (keep them from the hour of trial) until the Philadelphia church period started in 1649. (I believe the Philadelphia period began with the open door of missions, when William Cary sailed for India in 1792, F.K.B.)

Timothy LaHaye

Dr. Timothy LaHaye believes the seven churches of Revelation are symbolic of seven periods of the Church Age:

In my commentary on the Book of Revelation, I pointed out that the seven churches of Asia were selected out of the hundreds of young churches at that time because they were types of the seven church ages that would exist from the first century to the present. (*No Fear of the Storm*, p. 41)

LaHaye believes that the Philadelphia period of the Church Age began in 1750 and will continue until the Rapture. He takes the promise to the Philadelphia church that they would be kept from the *"hour of trial"*

(Revelation 3.10) as meaning that the Church in the last days would be kept from going through the Tribulation:

> This text represents Christ's message to one of His seven churches, the church of Philadelphia. It must transcend the one little church of Asia to which he wrote, for the church of Philadelphia is extinct and the hour "which shall come upon the whole world" has not yet come. (Ibid., p. 41)

According to LaHaye's own belief, the Rapture was not an *imminent* event until the Philadelphia period began in 1750.

Conclusion

The men who teach the doctrine of *imminence* should avoid writing and talking about the seven eras of the Church Age. Teachers of *imminence* who claim that the seven churches in Revelation symbolize seven eras of Church history destroy their argument for *imminence*. If the promise to keep the church of Philadelphia from the "*hour of trial*" (Tribulation) is a promise for us today, then the Rapture could not have taken place until at least the beginning of that era, around 1792. It is self-defeating for the teachers of the doctrine of *imminence* to teach this theory.

STUDY QUESTIONS

Chapter 11

1. If the seven churches in the book of Revelation are symbolic of seven periods of Church history, could Jesus Christ return at *any moment* since Pentecost?

2. Why could Christ not return before the period of the Philadelphia church?

3. Why should the men who teach the doctrine of *imminence* avoid writing and talking about the seven eras of the Church Age?

4. Does the doctrine of *imminence* contradict Scripture and also the command by Jesus to "*watch*" for His return?

TWELVE

THE DOCTRINE OF IMMINENCE

Ever since the disciples asked Jesus that all-important question, *"When will these things be, and what will be the sign of Your coming and of the end of the world?"* (Matthew 24.3), Bible students have tried to determine when Jesus Christ will return. Some have predicted His return would take place on specific dates while others have taught He can return at *any moment*. The Bible exhorts all Christians to *"look,"* *"watch"* and *"wait"* for His return.

Definition of Imminence

Dr. Thomas Ice gives a definition of this doctrine on his website:

What is the biblical definition of imminency? Four important elements contribute to a pretribulational understanding of imminency. First, imminency means that the rapture could take place at any moment. While other events may take place before the rapture, no event must precede it. If prior events are required before the rapture, then the rapture could not be described as imminent. Thus, if any event were required to occur before the rapture, then the concept of imminency would be destroyed.

Second, since the rapture is imminent and could happen at any moment, then it follows that one must be prepared for it to occur at any time, without sign or warning.

Third, imminency eliminates any attempt at date setting. Date setting is impossible since the rapture is signless (i.e., providing no basis for date setting) and if imminency is really true, the moment a date was fixed then Christ could not come at any moment, destroying imminency.

Fourth, Renold Showers says, "A person cannot legitimately say that an imminent event will happen soon. The term 'soon' implies that an event must take place 'within a short time (after a particular point of time specified or implied).' By contrast, an imminent event may take place within a short time, but it does not have to do so in order to be imminent. As I hope you can see by now, 'imminent' is not equal to 'soon.'" A. T. Pierson has noted that, "Imminence is the combination of two conditions, viz.,: certainty and uncertainty. By an imminent event we mean one which is certain to occur at some time, uncertain at what time." ("Imminency And The Any-Moment Rapture")[1]

The statement by Ice that teacher's of *imminence* cannot say that Christ is coming "soon" or "very soon" is correct. Unfortunately, some men who teach the doctrine of *imminence* frequently say the Rapture will take place "soon."

The doctrine of Imminence is not stated in the Bible

Dr. John Walvoord, who was an ardent Pre-Tribulationist, admitted that *imminence* is a doctrine that is not stated in the Bible:

Pretribulationalism is **an induction** rather than an explicit statement of the Bible. (*The Rapture Question*: Revised, 11th printing, 1973, p. 181, emphasis mine)

While pretribulationists have strained to find some specific reference in support of their views **most adherents concede** that there is no explicit reference... (Ibid, p. 182, emphasis mine)

The early church believed in the imminency of the Lord's return, which is an essential doctrine of pretribulationalism. (Ibid. p. 192)

If the doctrine of the Pre-Tribulation Rapture "is an induction rather than an explicit statement of the Bible," then the doctrine of *imminence* is also "an induction rather than an explicit statement." We disagree with Walvoord that *imminence* "is an essential doctrine of pretribulationalism." There is no need for it to defend the Pre-Tribulation doctrine as will be shown in the following chapter.

Arguments against Imminence

Sir Isaac Newton
(1642-1727)

Sir Isaac Newton was an English physicist, mathematician, astronomer, natural philosopher, alchemist and theologian. He was one of the most influential men in history, and is considered by some to have been the greatest scientist ever. The truth that the Jewish people must return to their ancient homeland before the Rapture has been known among some theologians throughout the Church Age. The most famous theologian who wrote about the physical return of the Jews to Israel was Newton. More than 300 years before the nation of Israel was re-established he made this insightful statement:

Since the commandment to return precedes the Messiah... it may perhaps come forth not from the Jews themselves, but from some other kingdom friendly to them, and precede their return from captivity and give occasion to it; and, lastly, that the rebuilding of Jerusalem and the waste places is predicted in Micah. vii. 11, Amos ix. 11, 14, Ezek. xxxvi. 33, 35, 36, 38,

Isa. liv. 3, 11, 12, lv. 12, lxi. 4, lxv. 18, 21.22...and thus the return from captivity and coming of the Messiah and his kingdom are described in Daniel vii, Rev. xix., Acts i., Mal. iv., Joel iii., Ezek. xxxvi., xxxvii., Isa. lx., lxii., lxiii., lxv., and lxvi., and many other places of Scripture. (Moore, Philip N., *The End of History Messiah Conspiracy*, p. 493; citing Franz Kobler, *Newton on the Restoration of the Jews*, 1943, pp. 22-23, citing *Yahudah Manuscript* 9.2)

Newton knew the Jews had to return to the Holy Land before Christ could return. He did not believe in *imminence* and understood specific prophecies had to be fulfilled before Christ could return to rapture the Church.

Harold Lindsell
(1913-1998)

Dr. Harold Lindsell rejected the doctrine of *imminence*. In his book, *The Gathering Storm*, he explains why *warning signs* of the Tribulation are also *warning signs* of the Rapture, and why this fact destroys the doctrine of *imminence*:

Every premillennial scholar agrees that specific signs, giving detailed information about events which will transpire during the tribulation period, are found in Scripture. The overwhelming verdict of those who hold to a pretribulation rapture is that this so-called *signless event* is followed immediately by the seven-year tribulation period. Thus, immediately following the rapture of the Church, Israel and the Antichrist will enter into a covenant. *Three-and-a-half years before the second coming of Christ*, says Dr. Walvoord, *the dictator in the Mediterranean will desecrate a future Jewish temple and stop sacrificial worship of God being carried on in this temple* (*Armageddon*, p. 95). The obvious is all too apparent. There could be no rapture until the Jews come back to Palestine and Jerusalem is in their hands so they can rebuild the temple. This rebuilding of the temple could not take place unless Israel was in the land and in control of old Jerusalem unless the rapture occurs at an indefinite period of time before the Day of the Lord commences. The Jews must be in the land before the tribulation begins. The Jews are in the land, although the rapture has not yet taken place. Thus, it becomes plain that the signs having to do with the tribulation are pertinent to the rapture and that these signs make an any-moment rapture from the days of the apostles an invalid thesis. (p. 137)

148

Oliver Greene
(1915-1976)

Dr. Oliver Greene did not fully believe in *imminence*. He said before the Rapture takes place the divinity of Jesus Christ will be stripped away, and the people of the world would be conditioned to worship an image:

> All of this will lead to mass idolatry; and **when the world is educated** to the point where the masses will fall down and worship an image, the **Rapture will occur** and the Church will be caught up. Immediately after the Rapture the Antichrist will make his appearance and offer peace and prosperity to the world – the Utopia the Post-Millennialists have talked about but have never brought about. (*The Epistles of Paul the Apostle to the Thessalonians*, p. 251, emphasis mine)

We know, as Greene noted, the unsaved must be conditioned to worship an image. We have seen maniacal dictators seek worship in the recent past such as Lenin, Stalin, Hitler, Mao and Obama. When the Antichrist rises to power the lost will be fully conditioned to worship a man and his image, or the Antichrist will condition them before the Rapture.

Chuck Smith

Chuck Smith does not believe the full doctrine of *imminence*. He says Christ can return only during the "age when the church was to be taken out":

> As we approach the day in which the Lord takes His church out of this world, it would only be fitting that He make us more aware of the promise to the church of being caught up before the great tribulation. Why would the Lord reveal it to Martin Luther, John Calvin, or any Reformation church leaders? **They weren't living in the age when the church was to be taken out.** (*The Final Act*, p. 192, emphasis mine)

Smith is correct that there was no need for Jesus to give the Reformers insight into eschatology. They were not living in the time of His return.

He is not certain which event is *imminent* – the Rapture or the Russian invasion of Israel:

> As I understand Bible prophecy, one of the next major events to take place in the Biblical order of events will be either Russia's attacking Israel or the Rapture of the Church. **Which is going to come first we don't know.** (*The Soon to be Revealed Antichrist*, p. 4, emphasis mine)

In the very next paragraph he had this to say concerning the *imminence* of the Rapture:

> In reality, the rapture of the Church can take place at any time. (Ibid.)

Smith is not certain which event is *imminent*, yet he contends that the Rapture is *imminent*. If the Russian invasion of Israel takes place first, then the Rapture is not an *imminent* event.

In an answer to a question on Pastor's Perspective radio program, Smith said that certain things had to take place prior to the Rapture such as Israel being back in the land, and weapons of mass destruction being developed.[3]

He defends the doctrine of *imminence* as many do by arguing it is necessary for Christians to believe it to continue serving God. In a response to the doctrine of Preterism he said:

> I think that when you deny and take away the expectancy of the imminent return of Jesus Christ that you are opening the door to a lot of, you might say, slothful Christian living. It's no longer an urgency in our getting the gospel out to the world. It's no longer something that, you know, we need to do. We see things in a totally different light, and so I think it has brought spiritual death wherever the doctrine has gone. ("Pastor's Perspective," 1.09.2006)

Belief in the doctrine of *imminence* is not necessary to keep Christians from "slothful living." It is also not needed to make Christians understand the urgency of sharing the gospel with the lost, and it also does not bring "spiritual death." None of the reformers believed in the 20th century doctrine of *imminence*. Some thought the Rapture would take place in their lifetime because they thought all of the *signs* of Christ's return had been fulfilled. They turned the world upside down just as the apostles did (Acts 17.6).

Christians who are not motivated to live a holy life with a zeal to share the gospel with the lost because of the incredible gift of eternal life, and the indwelling of the Holy Spirit will not be motivated by believing in *imminence*.

Timothy LaHaye

Dr. Timothy LaHaye does not fully believe in the doctrine of *imminence* either. The following is a most insightful statement:

> I personally believe Christ's return will occur after Russia is destroyed, as I explain more fully in the next chapter. I am convinced that the destruction of Russia will appear as a supernatural event that will cause all the world to know that God has acted. During the aftermath of this catastrophe, millions of people will seek the Lord. In fact, the greatest soul harvest in the history of mankind may result from that moment of divine retribution. If so, there will be a need for harvesters; since this event takes place before Israel's conversion and the sealing of the 144,000 during the first half of the Tribulation, who will be better equipped to do the harvesting than the church of Jesus Christ and her worldwide host of missionaries?
>
> I risk the criticism of colleagues when I suggest that Christ may rapture His church *after* the destruction of Russia – particulary (sic) because there

is no conclusive biblical teaching for this view. I may be influenced by my yearning to see the mighty soul harvest, as related in the next chapter. But I caution the reader not to be dogmatic. We know Russia will be destroyed, but we cannot determine exactly when in the scenario it will happen. (*The Coming Peace in the Middle East*, p. 150, emphasis added, T.L.)

LaHaye added to the above statement by saying:

Yes, **I am inclined to believe** that as members of the body of Jesus Christ **we will see the destruction of Russia** and have an opportunity to share in an unprecedented soul harvest. This is one reason why I challenge Christians everywhere to develop the practice of sharing their faith effectively and to appropriate the maximum means of communication in this day. (Ibid., p. 152, emphasis mine)

And what about the Rapture? I *think* it will occur after the destruction of Russia, so Christians will be on the scene to be the soul-winning harvesters when as much as 20-25 percent of the world's population receives Christ. He *could* come to take away His church *before* the invasion. The Rapture could take place at anytime. Even today. (Ibid., p. 188, emphasis T.L.)

The statement by LaHaye that the Rapture will take place after Russia is defeated is significant. It is an extremely important *warning sign* that we should look for to know how near the Rapture is.

Jack Van Impe

Dr. Jack Van Impe teaches the doctrine of *imminence*. He believes it is not a new doctrine claiming that the early Church fathers "believed it" as well as some of the reformers. "The Church was told to live in the light of the imminent coming of the Lord to translate them into His presence... The return of Christ for His Church is a signless and always imminent event" (*Jack Van Impe Study Bible*, pp. 45, 81). Yet he understands some prophecies could not be fulfilled until the 20th century. This is what he wrote in 1983 about Russia invading Israel, as Ezekiel prophesied in chapters 38 and 39:

Let me repeat that Russia could not march until Israel became a nation, and there was no Israel until 1948. Thus, this event could not have taken place in past history. Because Israel now exists as a nation, and because Russia moves against Israel when she is a nation, I want you to follow a thrilling outline with me. (*11:59 and Counting*, p. 100)

Van Impe showed the Rapture was not *imminent* until at least 1948. Since he believes there is no *gap* between the Rapture and the Tribulation as noted in Chapter 6 of this book (p. 116), it means he cannot reasonably believe the doctrine of *imminence*. There are 16 more prophecies that must be fulfilled before the Tribulation starts (Appendix A). It is impossible for them to be fulfilled on the day the Tribulation starts. They must be fulfilled before that day, therefore the Rapture, which takes place on the same 24-hour day the Tribulation starts, cannot take place at *any moment*.

In his video entitled, "AD 2000, the End?" he said he believes in the 6 day 6000 year hypothesis. Any prophecy teacher who believes that hypothesis cannot reasonably believe in the doctrine of imminence until the 6000 years are up. Van Impe believed it would be up in the year 2000 AD. Since that year has come and gone he can now say he believes the Rapture is an *imminent* event.

Dave Hunt

Dave Hunt is a leading Pre-Tribulationist, and an ardent defender of the doctrine of *imminence*. Yet he believes there will be a definite *sign* just prior to the Rapture. In Chapter 19 of his book, *How Close Are We?,* he had this to say about the timing of the Rapture:

The **Rapture comes in the midst of peace** (I Thessalonians 5:3); the Second Coming in the midst of war (Revelation 19:11-21). (p. 204, emphasis mine)

Hunt clearly understands that the Rapture will take place during a time of universal peace, just as Paul said:

When they are saying, Peace and safety, then sudden destruction will come upon them as travail upon a woman with child; and they shall in no wise escape. But you, brethren, are not in darkness, that that day should overtake you as a thief. (1 Thessalonians 5.3-4)

Paul said Christians of the Church Age will see this period of false "*peace and safety,*" and they should not be caught by surprise when it is broken by the Rapture and the start of the Tribulation. It is one of the last major *warning signs* that will alert Christians to the *imminence* of the Rapture.

Hunt and others say *imminence* keeps Christians from backsliding:

And what an encouragement to carnality and worldly living it would have been to know that the Lord couldn't come at any moment and catch one by surprise doing, perhaps, those things that no Christian should. Much would have been lost by giving the date of the Rapture – and nothing would have been gained. (*How Close Are We?,* p. 316)

Only if His imminent return is our constant hope will we live as true followers of Christ... (Ibid., p. 320)

Millions of Christians have lived holy lives without believing in *imminence*. Belief in that doctrine does not edify one to live a holy life.

Joel Rosenberg

Joel Rosenberg, a New York Times best-selling author and founder of the Joshua Fund, is a strong Pre-Tribulationist who believes in *imminence*, but he thinks it is possible the Russian invasion of Israel could take place before the Rapture. He answered the question, "Will the War of Gog and Magog happen before or after the Rapture?" by saying:

> The truth is we simply **do not know the answer for certain**, because Ezekiel does not say. Many of the theologians I have cited in this book believe the war will occur after the Rapture. In the novel Left Behind, Tim LaHaye and Jerry B. Jenkins describe the War of Gog and Magog as having already happened before the Rapture takes place. In The Ezekiel Option, I also chose to portray the war occurring before the Rapture. (Emphasis mine)

He went on to argue:

> It would certainly be consistent with God's heart for humanity that he would cause this cataclysmic moment to occur before the Rapture in order to shake people out of their spiritual apathy and/or rebellion and give them at least one more chance to receive Christ as their Savior before the terrible events of the Tribulation occur.
>
> But let me be clear: I believe that the Rapture could occur at any moment, and I would certainly not be surprised in any way if it occurred before the events of Ezekiel 38 and 39 come to pass.
>
> Christian theologians speak of the "doctrine of imminence." This means that according to the Bible there is no prophetic event that has to happen before Jesus snatches his church from the earth. That is, the Bible teaches us that we should be ready for Jesus to come for us at any moment. I fully believe that. But it should be noted with regard to this doctrine that while no major prophetic event has to happen before the Rapture, that doesn't mean no such event will happen first. Perhaps the clearest evidence of this truth is the rebirth of Israel. This major prophetic event was foretold in Ezekiel 36–37, yet **its fulfillment happened before the Rapture**. Thus, it is **certainly possible that other events—such as the events of Ezekiel 38–39—could happen before the Rapture as well**.[4] (Emphasis mine)

"Couldda" Dispensationalism

Dr. Wouldda Shouldda Couldda believes the Rapture became an *imminent* event that could have taken place *any moment* since Pentecost or the destruction of Jerusalem in 70 AD. This idea is not prevalent, but a few hold to it.

One argument says the command by Jesus to "*look up*" when the things spoken of in the Olivet Discourse begin to come to pass (Luke 21.28), referred to the destruction of the Temple (Luke 21.21-24). When the Temple was destroyed "that fulfilled every and any prophecy that had to be fulfilled before the Rapture." That event "rendered the Rapture of the Church imminent." (Fruchtenbaum, Arnold, *The Footsteps of the Messiah*, 2003, pp. 636-637).

This quasi-Preterist thinking ignores some very important facts. According to this hypothesis the Rapture could have taken place before the book of Revelation was written about 25 years after the destruction of the Temple. It also rejects the fact that Israel had to return to Palestine and become a functioning nation so it could fulfill the prophecy that says she will make a covenant with the Antichrist (Isaiah 28.15-18; Daniel 9.27). The only way to get around this prophecy that had to be fulfilled as we saw in 1948 is to argue there could be a *gap* between the Rapture and the start of the Tribulation. That *gap* could have been over 1900 years according to this hypothesis! We know this hypothesis is not valid because we are still here, the book of Revelation was written, Israel became a nation and many other pre-tribulational prophecies have been fulfilled (Appendix A). We also know it is not biblical because the Bible teaches there is no *gap* between the Rapture and the Tribulation as explained in the previous chapter.

This hypothesis also ignores verses 25 through 27 of Luke 21 which says that just prior to the Rapture there will be signs in the sun, moon and stars, and dismay among nations. The oceans will be roaring and people will be fainting from fear of what is about to happen. It is after this prophecy of cosmic *warning signs* that Jesus commanded all Christians to "*look up, and lift up your heads; because your redemption draweth nigh.*" According to the Bible the Rapture cannot take place until those cosmic *warning signs* come to pass.

Fruchtenbaum also believes the 7 churches in the book of Revelation (Chapters 2-3), are symbolic of 7 periods in the Church Age. The promise of being kept from the "*hour of trial,*" which he interprets as a promise of the Pre-Tribulation Rapture, was made to the church of Philadelphia (Revelation 3.10). He believes the period of the Philadelphia church ran from 1648-1900 (Ibid., pp. 48-50).

His beliefs that the Rapture became an *imminent* event that can take place at *any moment*, and the Philadelphia church was promised to escape the "hour of trial" (Tribulation) are contradictory. If the Rapture has been *imminent* since 70 AD the Philadelphia church could not be symbolic of the Church from 1648-1900. If the Philadelphia church is symbolic of the Church from 1648-1900 the Rapture could not have been *imminent* since 70 AD as he says. Therefore the Rapture could not have become *imminent* until after 1648.

Another mistake that Fruchtenbaum and others make who believe the seven churches are symbolic of seven periods of Church history is that the Philadelphia church period is over, and the Rapture has not taken place. Since, according to Fruchtenbaum, the Philadelphia church period ended in 1900 the promise of being raptured could not have been to that church. Instead the apostate Laodecian church will be spared the "*hour of trial*" (Tribulation) because it began in 1900. We believe the Philadelphia church period began in 1792 when William Carey sailed to India and opened the door of foreign missions. It will continue until the Rapture, thus receiving the promise of being kept from the "*hour of trial*" (Revelation 3.10). This is the answer to the disciples' prayer "*lead us not into temptation*" (Matthew 6.13). The Greek word that is translated "*trial*" and "*temptation*" is *peirasmos*.

Dave Hunt is another who holds to "Couldda" dispensationalism. Here is his argument:

> Would it have been possible for a previous generation to go from knights in armor, for example, to nuclear arms in such a short period of time? That particular leap in technology may not have been necessary. There may be other weapons more ingenious and far more horrible which **could have** been developed and used more simply and quickly. No one can dogmatically rule out such a possibility. Human genius is unpredictable. (Ibid., pp. 260, emphasis mine)

> Once again, while admitting that such a feat would not seem likely under ordinary circumstances, one cannot say it would have been impossible. There may well have been some other more ingenious method of accomplishing more simply the same end which **could have** been developed quickly had the Rapture occurred at any previous time in history.
> It is certainly possible that some former generation, with incredible genius, **could have** developed within seven years or less the weapons and technologies necessary to fulfill all prophecies concerning Daniel's seventieth week. That simple possibility preserves imminency. The Rapture **could have** come at any time and these developments followed immediately and swiftly, perhaps with techniques even more ingenious than our generation has used. (Ibid., p. 261)

> A major factor, of course, is the necessity for Israel to be back in her land, where last days prophecies place her, immediately after the Rapture. This is required by the fact that Antichrist makes a covenant involving Israel at the very beginning of Daniel's seventieth week. Would that not mean, then, that the Rapture could not occur until Israel had once again become a nation? If so, we have lost imminency. (Ibid., p. 263)

Hunt's unlikely hypothesis that past generations "couldda" developed weapons of mass destruction and technology to create and run a world economic system is mute. It could not have been accomplished by "human genius" – only by divine intervention. Since it did not happen, it means it could not have happened. Why does anyone argue about what "couldda" happened?

Conclusion

The arguments for *imminence* are not based on Scripture. Most who teach it say there are *signs* of the approaching Tribulation and the Glorious

Appearing of Jesus Christ. Those *signs* are also *signs* of the Rapture. The Rapture is either an *imminent* event with no *warning signs*, or it is not *imminent* and *signs* precede it.

Other eschatologians believe *imminence* is necessary to motivate Christians to serve Christ. "I believe if you remove the imminent return of Jesus Christ you remove, perhaps, the greatest motivation for service to Christ that a believer has" (MacArthur, John Jr., *The Second Coming of the Lord Jesus Christ*, p. 57)

The doctrine of *imminence* is not necessary to motivate Christians to live holy lives. They should because of their love for Jesus Christ, and the sacrifice He made for us on the cross. They should also do so because they are commanded to (Leviticus 11.44; 19.2; 20.7; Matthew 5.48; 1 Peter 1.14-16). Another reason for holiness is the sobering fact that one may die at *any moment*. No one has a guarantee they will live another day; therefore, Christians should live holy lives each and every day. The knowledge that today may be one's last day should be a greater incentive to live a holy life than the thought that Christ may return at *any moment*.

Some eschatologians also argue that the doctrine is extremely important to keep Christians on their spiritual toes. Dave Hunt and others say *imminence* keeps Christians from backsliding and without that doctrine it could cause God to question our motives:

> And what an encouragement to carnality and worldly living it would have been to know that the Lord couldn't come at any moment and **catch one by surprise doing**, perhaps, **those things that no Christian should**. Much would have been lost by giving the date of the Rapture – and nothing would have been gained. (Hunt, Dave, *How Close Are We?*, p. 316, emphasis, mine)

> **Only** if His imminent return is our constant hope will we live as **true followers of Christ**... (Ibid., p. 320, emphasis mine)

> If we knew the exact time in advance, it would **call our motivation into question and ruin an opportunity to prove that our devotion to Him is pure**. (MacArthur, John Jr., *The Second Coming*, p. 139, emphasis mine)

Millions of Christians have lived holy lives without believing in *imminence*. Belief in that doctrine does not edify one to live a holy life. Jesus does not have to return at *any moment* to "catch one by surprise doing those things that no Christian should" do. He knew everything everyone would do before He created the universe.

Some pastors believe the Holy Spirit deliberately wanted Christians throughout the Church Age to believe Christ could return at *any moment*. We must always keep in mind that the Holy Spirit is omniscient, and He knew that Christ was not scheduled to return for over 1900 years when He inspired Paul, James, Peter and John to write their letters. The Holy Spirit did not deceive the disciples into thinking Christ could return in their lifetime, and in no way did

He seek to have millions of Christians misled into believing Christ could return at *any moment* with no *warning signs* preceding His return!

To say the Holy Spirit deliberately deceived the apostles, and that He has deceived Christians for the last 1900 years into believing Christ could return at *any moment* would be accusing Him of Jesuit casuistry (the end justifies the means).

STUDY QUESTIONS

Chapter 12

1. In one sentence explain what the doctrine of *imminence* teaches.

2. Is the doctrine of *imminence* clearly stated in the Bible or is it based on personal opinion?

3. Do those who teach *imminence* frequently contradict that doctrine by claiming specific *signs* have been fulfilled?

4. Did God put numerous passages in the Bible about the Antichrist to help Christians identify him before the Rapture or to help the unsaved identify him after he becomes dictator of the world?

5. Did the Holy Spirit deliberately mislead the apostles into believing Christ could return at *any moment* even though He knew Christ would not return for over 1900 years?

6. Has the Holy Spirit misled Christians throughout the Church Age into believing Christ can return at *any moment*?

7. What event, that everyone experiences, is a greater incentive to serve the Lord faithfully than the doctrine of *imminence*?

THIRTEEN

IS THE RAPTURE IMMINENT?

The doctrine of *imminence* is based on a few passages which do not teach it directly while there are some passages that teach the opposite.

Passages that seem to allude to Imminence

The defenders of the doctrine of *imminence* argue that key phrases prove the Rapture has been an *imminent* event since Pentecost. The phrase "at hand" (Romans 13.12; Philippians 4.5; James 5.8; 1 Peter 4.7; Revelation 1.3) is the phrase they rely upon.

The Greek adverb *eggus*, that is found in the above verses means "to bring near, to draw nigh, be at hand" (*Liddell & Scott, Greek Lexicon*, p. 189). Greek language expert Dr. Joseph Thayer says that when it is used in reference to time it is "concerning things imminent and soon to come to pass" (*Greek-English Lexicon*, p. 164).

The passages noted above do not concern "time" and they do not teach that the return of Jesus was "*at hand*" in the first century. Instead, they say that the return of Christ is certain. The Holy Spirit knew that Christ was not scheduled to return for over 1900 years when He inspired Paul, James, Peter and John to write their letters. The Holy Spirit did not deceive the disciples into thinking Christ could return in their lifetime, and in no way did He seek to have millions of Christians misled into believing Christ could return at *any moment* with no *warning signs* preceding His return!

Evidence that this is correct is the fact that Jesus told His disciples directly that He would not return while they were alive:

> And He said unto the disciples, "The days will come, when you will desire to see one of the days of the Son of man, and you will not see it." (Luke 17.22)

This statement is clear that the disciples would not be alive when Jesus returns. They understood this. That is why none of them taught that Christ could return at *any moment* and it proves that the above passages have nothing to do with the timing of the Rapture.

Passages that do not teach Imminence

There is no passage that teaches the doctrine of *imminence*, and there are several passages that teach just the opposite. These passages are: Isaiah 13.6, 17.1; 19.1; Ezekiel 30.3; Joel 1.15; 2.1; Obadiah 15 and Haggai 2.6.

Isaiah wrote around 700 BC that the "the *day of Jehovah is at hand*" (13.6). It does not seem correct that 2700 years is "near" or "at hand." The only meaning that makes sense is that it is certain it will come to pass. It does not mean that 2700 years is "near" to God. Every event is "near" to God because He lives outside of the property of time. Remember, the Bible was written by God to mankind.

Isaiah also wrote that Damascus is "about" to be destroyed, yet it has been more than 2700 years, and it is still a thriving city. It is obvious that the word "about" has nothing to do with time. It has to do with certainty. We can be confident that the city of Damascus will be destroyed in the future. The King James translators rendered this verse more accurately:

> *The burden of Damascus. Behold, Damascus is taken away from being a city, and it shall be a ruinous heap.* (Isaiah 17.1)

Isaiah prophesied that Jehovah "*is about to come out from His place to punish the inhabitants of the earth for their iniquity...*" (26.21). It should be translated "*For behold, Jehovah will certainly come out from His place...*"

The King James translators rendered it:

> *For, behold, the LORD cometh out of His place to punish the inhabitants of the earth for their iniquity: the earth also shall disclose her blood and shall no more cover her slain.* (Isaiah 26.21)

Ezekiel also wrote that the "*Day of Jehovah*" is "near":

> *For the day is near, even the day of Jehovah is near; it shall be a day of clouds, a time of doom for the nations.* (Ezekiel 30.3)

This is a prophecy of the Tribulation, not of local judgment, because it is a time of doom for the nations. The nations to be judged are listed – Egypt, Ethiopia, Put, Lud, Arabia and Libya. These are the nations that team up with Gog and Magog for the attack on Israel in the last days (Ezekiel 38.5). Only Ethiopia and Put are mentioned in Chapter 38 of Ezekiel, but it is understood that these other nations will be in league with Gog and Magog. Many times there is more than one passage describing a single event. All of the passages must be pieced together as a jigsaw puzzle to see the entire picture.

The Tribulation was in no way "*near*" when Ezekiel wrote this prophecy. Near has nothing to do with time. It has to do with certainty. We can be certain that Christ will return and judge the nations.

Joel prophesied that *"the day of Jehovah is at hand"* (1.15), and he also wrote that *"the day of Jehovah cometh, for it is nigh at hand"* (2.1). If he meant the Tribulation was near (time-wise), he was mistaken. Yet, if he meant that it was "certain" that Christ would come to judge the world, he was correct.

Obadiah also prophesied of the Second Coming of Jesus Christ:

For the day of Jehovah is near upon all the nations. (v. 15a)

Obadiah was saying what Joel said – the judgment of Jehovah is certain and no one can escape it. He did not mean it was "near" time-wise.

Haggai used the phrase *"a little while"* (2.6) concerning the Second Coming of the Messiah. It is hard to believe that 2500 years is *"a little while."* This phrase was used to remind people that there would be a day of judgment. The context is vengeance. God is reminding Israel that no matter how bad things may be they should not lose hope, but trust in Him. He will judge the wicked and reward the faithful.

These passages could not be saying the Lord Jesus Christ would return to judge the world in a short period of time. How could He come to judge the world before He came to die for the world? No one today would dare to say the Second Coming of Jesus Christ was *imminent* during the Old Testament dispensation based on phrases that seem to say that, because He had yet to come the first time to die for mankind.

We also know Christ could not have returned to judge the world until the fourth kingdom of Daniel's prophesy (Rome) was established (Daniel 2.31-45; 7.2-28). When these prophets wrote, the third kingdom (Greece) had not yet risen.

If the words in the Old Testament, *"near"* and *"about"* and *"a little while,"* have nothing to do with the timing of the Rapture and the Second Coming, neither do similar words that are used in the New Testament. We know this because it has been over 1900 years since the New Testament was written and Christ has not returned. As noted before, they have to do with the "certainty," not the "nearness" of those events.

Another way to look at passages that use words which imply an event will take place in the near future is to understand that the prophet was carried forward by the Holy Spirit in a prophetic vision (1 Peter 1.21), and what he saw in the vision was about to take place.

Jesus Christ did not teach the doctrine of Imminence

Jesus Christ did not teach that He could return at *any moment* after Pentecost. He made it clear to His disciples that they would not see His return; that Peter would die first; that the gospel would be preached to all the world; that He would build His Church; that the disciples would be persecuted and martyred; that Paul would go to Rome; that John would prophesy again after writing the book of Revelation; and that the city of Jerusalem would be trodden down until the times of the Gentiles was fulfilled.

Jesus told His disciples they would not see Him return
(Luke 17.22; Acts 1.7-8)

Jesus plainly told His disciples that they would not see His return:

And he said unto the disciples, "The days will come, when you will desire to see one of the days of the Son of man, and you will not see it." (Luke 17.22)

Jesus made it clear by that statement that none of His disciples would be alive when He returns. He also told His disciples that they should not concern themselves with the timing of the establishment of the Kingdom. Just prior to His ascension, the 11 disciples asked Him if He would establish the Kingdom. He responded by saying:

"It is not for you to know times or seasons, which the Father has set within His own authority. But you will receive power when the Holy Spirit is come upon you. And you will be My witnesses both in Jerusalem and in all Judaea and Samaria and unto the uttermost parts of the earth." (Acts 1.7-8)

Jesus said Peter would be martyred
(John 21.18-19)

Jesus said that Peter would grow old and die a martyr's death:

"Verily, verily, I say unto you, when you were young you dressed yourself and walk wherever you wanted, but when you are old, you shall stretch forth your hands and another shall dress you and carry you where you do not want to go." Now this he spoke, signifying by what manner of death he should glorify God. And when he had spoken this, he said unto him, "Follow me."

John said it signified *"by what manner of death he should glorify God"* (John 21.19). The Rapture could not take place until after Peter had grown old and died, otherwise Jesus would have made a false prophesy. Since all of the New Testament books were written prior to the death of Peter (except the book of Revelation), it is clear that the doctrine of *imminence* is not taught in the New Testament. Later it will be shown that it is also not taught in the book of Revelation.

Jesus said other disciples would be martyred
(John 16.2)

Jesus also prophesied that other disciples and believers would be persecuted and killed:

They will put you out of the synagogues: yes, the hour comes, that whosoever kills you will think that he offers service unto God.

We know that all of the apostles, except John, were martyred for their faith. The last to be martyred was most likely Peter, under the reign of Nero, around 67 AD. Jesus could not have returned until His disciples, except John, had been martyred.

The apostles would make disciples of all nations
(Matthew 28.19-20)

The Lord could not have returned at *any moment* after His ascension, because He commanded the apostles to make disciples of all nations:

"Go therefore and make disciples of all the nations, baptizing them into the name of the Father and of the Son and of the Holy Spirit, teaching them to observe all things whatsoever I commanded you and lo, I am with you always, even unto the end of the world."

It took the eleven disciples, Paul, Barnabas, Timothy, other evangelists and thousands of believers a few decades to just preach the gospel to the entire known (Roman) world. Paul said in his letter to the Colossians that the gospel had been "proclaimed in all creation under heaven" (1.23). That letter was written around 60 AD. If we use that date as the fulfillment of taking the gospel to the entire world, Jesus could not have returned prior to 60 AD.

Jesus said He would build His Church
(Matthew 16.18)

Jesus told His disciples that He would build His Church through them:

"And I also say unto you that you are Peter and upon this rock I will build my church and the gates of Hades will not prevail against it."

History tells us that it took several decades to build the Church. John most likely did not write his gospel, his three letters and the book of Revelation until the time of Domitian, who reigned from 81-96 AD. Those books were written for the Church. Christ obviously could not have returned until all the books of the Bible had been written.

Jesus told Paul he would testify in Rome
(Acts 23.11)

Jesus visited Paul in Jerusalem after he appeared before the Sanhedrin and told him that he would preach the gospel in Rome:

And the night following the Lord stood by him and said, "Be of good cheer: for as you have testified concerning me at Jerusalem, so must you bear witness also at Rome."

Paul recounted this incident when the ship he was sailing to Italy on sank (Acts 27.24). It is evident that the Rapture could not possibly take place before Paul went to Rome.

Jesus said Jerusalem would be captured
(Luke 21.20-24)

Jesus also prophesied in the Olivet Discourse that the city of Jerusalem would be captured by the Gentiles:

"But when you see Jerusalem compassed with armies, then know that her desolation is at hand. Then let them that are in Judaea flee unto the mountains and let them that are in the midst of her depart. And let not them that are in the country enter therein. For these are days of vengeance, that all things which are written may be fulfilled. Woe unto them that are with child and to them that give suck in those days! There shall be great distress upon the land and wrath unto this people. And they shall fall by the edge of the sword and shall be led captive into all the nations. And Jerusalem shall be trodden down of the Gentiles until the times of the Gentiles be fulfilled."

The Gentiles would control Jerusalem until the *"times of the Gentiles"* was fulfilled. It is obvious that Jesus could not rapture the Church until after Jerusalem was captured by the Gentiles. That means the Rapture was not *imminent* until at least 70 AD. The Rapture could not take place until the *"times of the Gentiles"* was completed. It is now understood that the *"times of the Gentiles"* ended in 1967 when Israel took control of Jerusalem. We have the benefit of hindsight and know that the Rapture has not been an *imminent* event that could happen at *any moment* for more than 1900 years.

Jesus said John would prophesy by writing Revelation
(Revelation 10.11)

John was given the revelation of Jesus Christ on the island of Patmos:

And they say unto me, "You must prophesy again concerning many peoples and nations and tongues and kings."

We know that Jesus could not have raptured the Church until John completed the book of Revelation which took place around 95 A.D. Jesus could not return until at least the start of the 2nd century.

It is therefore hard to imagine why eschatologians today teach that Jesus Christ could have returned at *any moment* since Pentecost. History shows that it is not possible. Harold Lindsell explained why no one today should believe in the doctrine of *imminence*:

> We can understand and excuse earlier earnest students of the Word who were wrong about this matter. But we have further light and can see now that those who held to an any-moment rapture were incorrect in their interpretation of Scripture. (*The Gathering Storm,* p. 121)

The parables of the talents
(Matthew 25.14-30; Luke 19.12-27)

Jesus Christ also taught against His soon return through the parables of the talents. The parable about a nobleman, who went to a distant country to receive a kingdom and then returned (Luke 19.12-27), and the Olivet Discourse parable about a man who went on a journey (Matthew 25.14-30), refute the doctrine of *imminence*. These two parables were given at different times, but they speak of the same subject. He said, *"A certain nobleman went to a distant country to receive a kingdom for himself, and then returned"* (Luke 19.12), and *"Now after a long time the master of those slaves came and settled accounts with them"* (Matthew 25.19). The phrases, *"went to a distant country"* and *"after a long time,"* are the key.

All dispensational theologians agree that the parables concern the Church. We now understand the phrases *"went to a distant country"* and *"after a long time"* mean more than 1900 years. Did the early Church understand this? They may not have thought it would be 1900 years before Jesus would return, but they knew it would be a *"long time."* They heard Jesus read Isaiah 61, which said that there would be a long period of time between the First and Second Comings of the Messiah.

More parables of Jesus
(Matthew 13.3-8; 24-30; 31-33; 44-46; 47-50)

Four of the seven parables of Matthew Chapter 13 prove the Rapture was not an *imminent* event. In the first four parables, Jesus explained that a long period of time would elapse between His resurrection and His return.

The first parable is about Jesus and the apostles sowing the gospel (v. 3-8). The second parable (v. 24-30) concerns the fact that tares (the unsaved) would grow up alongside the wheat (saved). The wheat and the tares are allowed to mature until the harvest (Second Coming). The third parable is of the mustard seed (v. 31-33). It was the smallest seed in the Middle East, yet it grew into a large tree. The tree is symbolic of Christendom. Yet every bird nested in the tree. Birds are always symbolic of the unsaved. We see in this third parable that there would be a period of time for the tree (the Church) to grow to maturity, and once it was fully grown, the unsaved would become part of it. The fourth parable is about the apostasy (leaven) in the Church (v. 33). Leaven always represents false teaching (Matthew 16.6). The parable describes false teaching that leavens the whole lump (the Church) after it is mature, just as in the parable of the mustard seed. It has been over 1900 years, and the Church is still growing in its apostasy. The first four parables show that there would be a considerable amount of time between the founding of the Church (day of Pentecost) and the Second Coming of Christ.

Jesus commanded us to be "*alert*" and to "*watch*" for His return (Matthew 24.33, 42; Mark 13.37; Luke 21.34, 36). The only way we can look for His return is to "*watch*" for prophecies to be fulfilled that will take place before the Rapture and the start of the Tribulation.

Paul did not teach the doctrine of Imminence

Acts 20.28-30

Paul knew Jesus could not return at *any moment* during his final visit to the church of Ephesus around 60 AD. He warned the elders:

Take heed unto yourselves, and to all the flock, in which the Holy Spirit hath made you bishops, to feed the church of the Lord which he purchased with his own blood. I know that after my departing grievous wolves shall enter in among you, not sparing the flock; and from among your own selves shall men arise, speaking perverse things, to draw away the disciples after them.

One might argue that this could take only a few years, but we know that it usually takes many years for false teachers to work their way into an established church and lead it astray. One thing is certain – Paul knew Jesus could not return at *any moment* when he made that prophecy.

Romans 13.11-12

Paul did not teach in his letter to the Romans, that Jesus could return at *any moment*:

And this, knowing the season, that already it is time for you to awake out of sleep: for now is salvation nearer to us than when we first believed. The night is far spent, and the day is at hand: let us therefore cast off the works of darkness, and let us put on the armor of light.

The word "nearer" simply means that the return of Christ is nearer than it has been. This is a commonsense statement. It is not a doctrinal statement that the Rapture has been *imminent* since Pentecost. The phrase "*the day is at hand*" (v. 12), should be translated "the day has drawn near." All Paul was saying is that the "*night*" (time of doing evil) is almost over and the "*day*" (time of doing good) *"has drawn near,"* so we should live holy lives. This passage is an admonishment to live a holy life; it is not a doctrinal statement.

The literal meaning of the Greek adverb *engus* is "bring near, to draw nigh, be at hand" (*Liddell & Scott, Greek-English Lexicon,* p. 189), as noted previously. If the correct understanding is that the Second Coming was being brought *"near"* or *"at hand,"* and that it was *imminent* in the time that Paul wrote his letter to the Romans (57 AD), there is a problem.

It has been over 1900 years since the letter was written, and the Rapture has not taken place. No one can believe that 1900 years is *"near"* or *"at hand."* It may be to God, but not to us. The Bible was written for us, not for God. All time references must be accepted as being from our perspective.

The meaning of the phrase *"at hand"* is a statement of certainty (the event will take place), as we noted previously, or it is a reference to the statement by Jesus concerning His return. Jesus said in the Olivet Discourse, *"Even so ye also, when ye see all these things, know ye that he is nigh, even at the doors"* (Matthew 24.33). Every statement in the New Testament about the timing of the return of Jesus is a reference to this statement by Jesus. This is called "the law of first mention." Jesus said that when the things He spoke of in the Olivet Discourse start to take place (the two World Wars and the birth of the nation of Israel, Matthew 24.6-8, 32), then the time of His return will be *"at hand."*

When Paul said, *"the day is at hand,"* he was making a reference to the statement by Jesus in the Olivet Discourse. In other words, he was saying that when his readers see the events described in that discourse start to take place, they would know the return of Jesus is *"at hand."*

This law of first mention applies to the other uses of the phrase *"at hand"* and the word *"near,"* that are found in Philippians 4.5; James 5.8; 1 Peter 4.7 and Revelation 1.3.

1 Corinthians 15.51-52

Some believe that a passage in Paul's first letter to the church in Corinth teaches *imminence*:

Behold, I tell you a mystery: We all shall not sleep, but we will all be changed, in a moment, in the twinkling of an eye, at the last trump: for the trumpet will sound, and the dead shall be raised incorruptible, and we will be changed.

This passage does not teach *imminence*. The transforming of mortal bodies to immortal ones takes place in the *"twinkling of an eye."* That happens after all the *warning signs* of the Rapture have been fulfilled, including the 2 that take place on the day of the Rapture (Joel 2.30-31; Luke 21.25-27). It is also important to notice the order of events. The last trumpet sounds first, the dead are raised incorruptible and then Christians who are alive and remain will be changed. It is the changing of our mortal bodies to immortal ones that takes place in the *"twinkling of an eye,"* not the entire Rapture event as explained in Chapter 2.

Philippians 3.20

Paul said Christians should wait for the return of Christ, but he did not imply His return was an *imminent* event:

For our citizenship is in heaven; whence also we wait for a Savior, the Lord Jesus Christ.

This passage has nothing to do with *imminence*. It tells us to *"wait"* for the Lord's return. Jesus said He would go *"to a distant country to receive a kingdom"* (Luke 19.12), and be gone a *"long time"* (Matthew 25.19). Christians are to patiently *"wait"* for the return of Christ just as James said (5.7-8). As noted several times before, Christians do that by watching for the *signs* of His coming to be fulfilled.

Philippians 4.5

Paul told the believers at Philippi that the Lord was *"at hand"*:

Let your forbearance be known unto all men. The Lord is at hand.

If he meant the return of Christ was *"at hand"* when he wrote the letter (62 AD), he was wrong. As noted several times before, 1900 years is not *"near"* or *"at hand."* The proper understanding is that the return of Christ is "certain," or it is a reference to the statement by Jesus in the Olivet Discourse. When the events described by Jesus begin to take place, then His return will be *"at hand."*

Colossians 3.4

In his letter to the Colossians, Paul said Jesus would return; he did not say His return was *imminent*:

When Christ, who is our life, shall be manifested, then will you also with him be manifested in glory.

This passage does not support the doctrine of *imminence* either. It simply says Christ will return.

1 Thessalonians 1.10

This is another passage that commands us to *"wait"* for the return of Christ, but it does not support *imminence*:

> *For they themselves report concerning us what manner of entering in we had unto you; and how you turned unto God from idols, to serve a living and true God, and to wait for his Son from heaven, whom He raised from the dead, even Jesus, who delivers us from the wrath to come.*

This is one of many passages that command Christians to *"wait."* Waiting for the return of Christ does not mean He can return at *any moment.* Christians are also told many times to be *"looking"* and to *"watch"* for His return. The way one *"waits"* is to *"watch"* for the *warning signs* of His return.

1 Thessalonians 5.1-6

Paul warned the Thessalonians in his first letter to be spiritually awake at all times so the *"Day of the Lord"* (Rapture/Tribulation) would not overtake them like a thief. He said they did not need anything to be written to them about the *"times and seasons,"* because he had already taught it to them:

> *But concerning the times and the seasons, brethren, ye have no need that aught be written unto you. For yourselves know perfectly that the day of the Lord so cometh as a thief in the night. When they are saying, Peace and safety, then sudden destruction cometh upon them, as travail upon a woman with child; and they shall in no wise escape. But ye, brethren, are not in darkness, that that day should overtake you as a thief: for ye are all sons of light, and sons of the day: we are not of the night, nor of darkness; so then let us not sleep, as do the rest, but let us watch and be sober.*

We know from this passage that Jesus will not return to rapture believers until after there is a false peace. According to the book of Revelation, the Antichrist comes to power through peace (6.1-2), and then war breaks out (6.3-4). The Antichrist will bring about a short period of *"peace and safety,"* and then make the *"covenant of death"* with Israel (Isaiah 28.15). The Rapture will take place on the day that this covenant of death is made.

This passage clearly teaches that all Christians should be spiritually awake and *"watch"* for the return of Christ. They do this by watching for the *warning signs* of the Rapture. As the *signs* are fulfilled one will know how close the Rapture is. Once all of the *warning signs* have been fulfilled, then one will know the Rapture is at hand, and that it finally is an *imminent* event.

2 Thessalonians 2.1-3

In his second letter to the church at Thessalonica, Paul explained what must take place prior to the start of the *"Day of the Lord"*:

> *Now we beseech you, brethren, touching the coming of our Lord Jesus Christ, and our gathering together unto him; to the end that ye be not quickly shaken from your mind, nor yet be troubled, either by spirit, or by word, or by epistle as from us, as that the day of the Lord is just at hand; Let no man beguile you in any wise: for it will not be, except the falling away come first, and the man of sin be revealed, the son of perdition...*

Someone had forged a letter claiming that the *"Day of the Lord,"* which starts with the Tribulation, was *"just at hand."* Paul cleared up the confusion by explaining that two things had to take place before the Tribulation could start – the *"falling away"* and the revealing of the *"man of sin."*

The "it" here is the start of the Tribulation. It cannot take place until the *"falling away"* of the Church from the faith, and the *"man of sin"* is revealed. Many eschatologians believe that we are in this time of the *"falling away,"* but the Antichrist has yet to be revealed. Until he is revealed, the Tribulation cannot start.

1 Timothy 6.14

Paul told Timothy to live a holy life until the return of Jesus, but that does not mean that he was saying Christ could return at *any moment*:

> *That thou keep the commandment, without spot, without reproach, until the appearing of our Lord Jesus Christ:*

Paul simply told Timothy and all Christians throughout the Church Age to live holy lives. Even if this passage were taken by itself, it does not support the doctrine of *imminence*. Nothing is said about when Christ will return. It does not say He will return at *any moment*. It merely says that He will return. We know from numerous passages throughout the Bible that specific *warning signs* must take place before the Tribulation starts.

2 Timothy 4.3-4

Paul warned Timothy about a time of apostasy in the future:

> *For the time will come when they will not endure the sound doctrine; but, having itching ears, will heap to themselves teachers after their own lusts; and will turn away their ears from the truth, and turn aside unto fables.*

That letter was written around 65 AD. Paul knew that Jesus could not return at *any moment* when he wrote it. He knew it would be many years before Christ could return.

2 Timothy 4.6-7

Paul did not look for the *imminent* return of Jesus, instead he awaited his death:

For I am already being offered, and the time of my departure is come. I have fought the good fight. I have finished the course. I have kept the faith...

Titus 2.11-13

A statement by Paul to Titus is also misunderstood by some eschatologians:

For the grace of God has appeared, bringing salvation to all men, instructing us, to the intent that, denying ungodliness and worldly lusts, we should live soberly and righteously and godly in this present world; looking for the blessed hope and appearing of the glory of the great God and our Savior Jesus Christ.

This passage clearly refutes the doctrine of *imminence*. Instead of it saying Christ can return at *any moment*, believers are commanded to be "looking" for His return. The only way to be "*looking*" for His return is to "*watch*" for specific *warning signs* that will be fulfilled prior to His return as Scripture says. Then, as they are fulfilled one will know the Rapture is that much closer. All of the passages that command us to be "*looking*" for and to "*watch*" for the return of Christ refute the doctrine of *imminence*.

Hebrews 10.25, 37

The following verses in Hebrews do not support the doctrine of *imminence*:

Not forsaking our own assembling together, as the custom of some is, but exhorting one another; and so much the more, as you see the day drawing near. (v. 25)

For yet a very little while, He that comes will come, and will not tarry (v. 37).

The phrase "*as you see the day drawing near*" (Hebrews 10.25) implies there is something for us to "*watch*." The only things Christians can possibly "*watch*," to know how near the Rapture is, are *warning signs*. Without *warning signs* to look for, one cannot possibly know if the Rapture is near.

The phrases, "*in a very little while*," and "*will not delay*" (Hebrews 10.37), are quoted from Habakkuk 2.3:

> *For the vision is yet for the appointed time, and it hastens toward the end, and will not lie: though it tarry, wait for it; because it will surely come, it will not delay.*

The passage in Habakkuk does not say Christ can return at *any moment*. It says that He will not return soon, but will tarry. Yet, even though the Bible teaches there would be a long span between the First and Second Comings of Jesus Christ, Christians are commanded to eagerly "*wait*" for His return.

Why are Christians commanded to eagerly "*wait*" for the return of Christ? No believer in the Church Age can know the exact day of His return years in advance (Matthew 24.36), but they can know the approximate time by waiting and watching. The way Christians eagerly "*wait*" and "*watch*" for His return is by "*looking*" for the *warning signs*.

Similar phrases, such as "*near*" and "*at hand*," were used by the Old Testament prophets concerning the Second Coming, as we noted earlier – (Isaiah 13.6; 26.21; 29.17; Ezekiel 30.3; Joel 1.15; 2.1; Obadiah 15; Haggai 2.6; Zechariah 8.1-8). It is obvious that the Second Coming of Christ was not a "*near*" event that was "*at hand*" because His First Coming was more than 500 years away. The context of these passages is not about the timing of the Second Coming – that it was "*near*" or "*at hand*." The context is about the certainty of that event, as noted previously.

If you replace the words "*near*" or "*at hand*" with the words "a certainty" the statements make sense. Here is an example using Isaiah 13.6:

> *Wail, for the day of Jehovah is at hand; as destruction from the Almighty will it come.*

> *Wail, for the day of Jehovah is a certainty; as destruction from the Almighty will it come.*

The prophet was not saying that the "*day of Jehovah*" (Tribulation) was "*near*" in his day. Instead, he was saying the "*day of the Jehovah*" would certainly take place.

James did not teach the doctrine of Imminence

James did not teach the doctrine of *imminence*. Instead, he exhorted his readers to not give up, "*due to the persecution they suffered*" and to patiently "*wait*" for the return of Christ.

James 5.7-8

James used the analogy of a farmer to explain that it would be some time before Christ would return. He emphasized the need to be "*patient*" (thrice) and to "*wait*" for His return:

> Be **patient** therefore, brethren, until the coming of the Lord. Behold, the husbandman **waits** for the precious fruit of the earth, being **patient** over it, until it receives the early and latter rain. Be **patient** and establish your hearts for the coming of the Lord is at hand. (Emphasis mine)

Most teachers of *imminence* miss the object of the passage – "patience." James is admonishing believers three times to be "*patient*." Why? Because the Rapture was a long way off. The phrase "*the coming of the Lord is at hand*" does not mean Jesus could return at *any moment*; it means His return is certain. Jesus could not return around the time James wrote this letter (45 AD) because the temple had not been destroyed. Remember, Jesus prophesied that the temple would be destroyed (Matthew 24.2).

James did not teach the doctrine of *imminence*. He taught that it was an event that certainly would take place, but he knew it would take place a long time in the future. That is why he told his readers to be "*patient*." He knew, as did the Christians of the 1st century, that specific prophecies had to be fulfilled before Christ could return. He knew Peter had to die a martyr's death (John 21.18-19) and that the Temple would be destroyed (Matthew 24.1-2).

Noted collector of ancient Greek manuscripts Dr. Craig Lampe stated that the Greek word *eggus* which is translated "*near*" or "*at hand*" in James 5.8 means "certainty of the event without relationship to time."

Peter did not teach the doctrine of Imminence

Peter also did not teach the doctrine of *imminence*, even though some argue that he did.

1 Peter 4.7-8

The passage below appears to support the doctrine of *imminence*, but a closer look reveals that it does not:

> But the end of all things is at hand: therefore be of sound mind, and be sober unto prayer: above all things being fervent in your love among yourselves; for love covers a multitude of sins.

If Peter meant that the "*end of all things*" was "*at hand*" in 64 AD, when he wrote his first letter, he was wrong! No one can believe that 1945 years is "*at hand*." It may be for God, since 1000 years is as one day (2 Peter 3.8), but it is not for us. The only way this passage and other passages that use similar phrases make sense is if these are not time references.

Instead of being statements of time, they are statements of certainty. If we substitute "certain" for "*at hand*" the passage becomes crystal clear – "*But the end of all things is certain.*" The only ones who believe these phrases "*At hand*" and "*near*" are time references are the Preterists.

2 Peter 2.1-3

Peter prophesied around 64-68 AD that false teachers would sneak into the Church and introduce destructive heresies, denying Jesus is Lord:

But there arose false prophets also among the people, as among you also there shall be false teachers, who shall privily bring in destructive heresies, denying even the Master that bought them, bringing upon themselves swift destruction. And many shall follow their lascivious doings; by reason of whom the way of the truth shall be evil spoken of. And in covetousness shall they with feigned words make merchandise of you: whose sentence now from of old lingereth not, and their destruction slumbereth not.

Peter knew it would take some time for this prophecy to be fulfilled and that it would happen after he died. Remember, he wrote this letter a couple of years before he was martyred. A few decades later when John wrote the book of Revelation it was confirmed they had sneaked in (Revelation 2.14-15, 20).

2 Peter 3.1-5

Peter prophesied that in the "*last days*" men would ridicule the promise of the return of Christ:

This is now, beloved, the second epistle that I write unto you; and in both of them I stir up your sincere mind by putting you in remembrance; that ye should remember the words which were spoken before by the holy prophets, and the commandments of the Lord and Saviour through your apostles: knowing this first, that in the last days mockers shall come with mockery, walking after their own lusts, and saying, Where is the promise of his coming? for, from the day that the fathers fell asleep, all things continue as they were from the beginning of the creation. For this they willfully forget, that there were heavens from of old, and an earth compacted out of water and amidst water, by the word of God.

Peter knew he would grow old and die before Jesus would return. He also knew, when he wrote his second letter, that there would be an indeterminate time before his prophecy about the mockers and false teachers would be fulfilled. That period of time would have to be several decades at least, because the mockers will say that *"since the fathers fell asleep"* everything has remained the same just as it was from the beginning of creation. If the *"fathers"* is a reference to the apostles, there would have to be a lengthy delay between their deaths and the time of the mockers.

Peter may have known that the delay would be decades or hundreds of years long. The use of the statement, *"that one day is with the Lord as a thousand years and a thousand years as one day"* (2 Peter 3.8), could mean that he understood Jesus would not return for a very long time. We can be confident that the above statement was a reference to the delay of the return of Christ as being an extremely long period of time.

The statement about the mockers is a prophecy that some would ridicule the teaching of the return of Jesus Christ, because He has not returned. They are ignorant of the two parables of Jesus in which He said that He would be gone a *"long time"* (Matthew 25.19), because he was going to a *"distant country"* (Luke 19.12).

Peter knew he would be martyred
(2 Peter 1.13-14)

Peter knew that he must die before the Lord could return, because Jesus prophesied he would die (John 21.18-19). He looked forward to that day:

And I think it right, as long as I am in this tabernacle, to stir you up by putting you in remembrance; knowing that the putting off of my tabernacle cometh swiftly, even as our Lord Jesus Christ signified unto me.

Peter awaited martyrdom, as Paul did, not the Rapture. He knew that he had to die before the Rapture could take place.

John did not teach the doctrine of Imminence

Some eschatologians are certain that John taught the doctrine of *imminence* in his first letter, and also in the book of Revelation, but he did not.

1 John 3.2-3

Beloved, now are we children of God, and it is not yet made manifest what we shall be. We know that, if he shall be manifested, we shall be like him; for we shall see him even as he is. And every one that hath this hope set on him purifieth himself, even as he is pure.

The *imminent* return of Christ is not stated here. The purifying effect of His return is not our belief that He can return at *any moment*, it is our assurance that when He returns we will be with Him and be like Him.

Revelation 1.1

This verse is a favorite among Preterists. They claim that it proves Jesus Christ returned in 70 AD:

The Revelation of Jesus Christ, which God gave Him to show unto His servants, even the things which must shortly come to pass: and He sent and signified it by His angel unto His servant John.

The phrase *"the things which must shortly take place"* has nothing to do with chronological time. The Greek words, *en tachei* can mean "with all speed" (Liddell & Scott, *Greek-English Lexicon*, p. 693), but in Romans 16.20 it deals with the certainty of the event:

And the God of peace will bruise Satan under your feet (en tachei) shortly. The grace of our Lord Jesus Christ be with you.

Satan was not bruised "shortly" or in a "brief space of time," after the letter was written. Instead the Greek word *en tachei* shows the certainty of Satan's coming judgment in the future.

The meaning of a word depends on the context. The context of Revelation 1.1 means Jesus will "certainly" return in manner just as He said He would, like a thief in the night (Luke 12.39). We know He certainly will return, and we can know the approximate time of His return by watching the *warning signs* so we will not be caught by surprise, as the unsaved will be (1 Thessalonians 5.3-4).

The clear meaning of this verse is seen once the word "certainly" is substituted for "shortly":

*The Revelation of Jesus Christ, which God gave Him to show unto His servants, even the things which must **certainly** come to pass: and He sent and signified it by His angel unto His servant John.*

This is a paraphrased version that makes it clear what Jesus was saying:

*The Revelation of Jesus Christ, which God gave Him to show unto His servants, even the things which must **certainly** come to pass: and He sent and signified it by His angel unto His servant John.*

Revelation 1.3

This is another favorite verse of the Preterists, but as you can see it does not support their doctrine that Christ had to return soon after the book of Revelation was written, as they claim around 68 AD:

Blessed is he that reads, and they that hear the words of the prophecy, and keep the things that are written therein: for the time is at hand.

The phrase, *"for the time is at hand,"* also has nothing to do with chronological time. The Greek word for "time" is not *"chronos"* (the time of day) but *"kairos"* (opportune time). *"Chronos* marks quantity, *kairos,* quality" (*Vine's Expository Dictionary,* p. 333). A better reading of this verse is:

> *Blessed is he that reads and they that hear the words of the prophecy, and keep the things that are written therein: for it is an opportune time.*

Jesus Christ is telling us that it is always an "opportune time" to study the book of Revelation. By careful study of prophecy we can see the *warning signs* as they are fulfilled, and we can determine how close we are to the Rapture. Jesus is telling Christians to look for the **What** (*warning signs*) so they can know the **When** (time of His return).

The Greek word *"kairos"* is derived from Caerus, the Greek god of opportunity, luck and favorable moments. This youngest child of Zeus had one lock of hair. When he ran by, a person had to grab his lock of hair to get good luck. The use of the word *kairos* in this verse means the time of opportunity to understand what is written is certain. As noted in the passage of James 5.8, the Greek word *eggus* means the event is "certain."

Conclusion

The doctrine of *imminence* is not taught in the Bible. Instead, there are several passages that say just the opposite (Isaiah 13.6, 17.1; 19.1; Ezekiel 30.3; Joel 1.15; 2.1; Obadiah 15; Haggai 2.6). Jesus did not teach it and neither did Paul, James, Peter or John.

The Bible says specific prophecies (*warning signs*) must be fulfilled before the start of the Tribulation. Many of those prophecies have been fulfilled, but several more must be fulfilled. If there is no *gap* between the Rapture and the Tribulation as explained in Chapter 10, then all of the *signs* that must be fulfilled before the Tribulation starts will be fulfilled before the Rapture.

It may be some time before all of these prophecies are fulfilled. A world government, economy and church will not spring up overnight. It most likely will take a few years at least to establish a "New World Order." Christians should keep a close eye on the news, and *"watch"* for the creation of this new world order. They must also be prepared for the increased spiritual warfare (Ephesians 6.10-18) that they will fight as the Tribulation draws closer.

We must always keep in mind that the Holy Spirit is omniscient, and He knew that Christ was not scheduled to return for over 1900 years when He inspired Paul, James, Peter and John to write their letters. The Holy Spirit did not deceive the disciples into thinking Christ could return in their lifetime, and in no way did He seek to have millions of Christians throughout the Church Age misled into believing Christ could return at *any moment* with no *warning signs* preceding His return!

STUDY QUESTIONS

Chapter 13

1. Should a doctrine be based on clear or unclear passages?

2. Did Jesus, Paul, James, Peter or John teach the doctrine of *imminence*?

3. Does the Bible clearly state that specific *warning signs* will be fulfilled before the Tribulation starts?

4. Did Jesus Christ want Christians throughout the Church Age to believe He could return at *any moment*?

5. Since Jesus knew after His resurrection that He would not return for over 1900 years is it possible He would have said something that would make His disciples believe He could return at *any moment*?

6. Would the Holy Spirit, who clearly knew Jesus would not return to Earth for over 1900 years, inspire Peter, Paul, James and John to write something that would make Christians believe that Jesus could return at *any moment*?

7. Can the end ever justify the means?

8. Would a person who teaches that Jesus and the Holy Spirit deliberately sought to make Christians believe Jesus could return at *any moment* be in danger of committing blasphemy?

9. If a person thinks the Greek word *eggus*, which is translated "*at hand*" or "*near*," means Jesus Christ can return at any moment does that make him a pseudo-Preterist?

FOURTEEN

THE OLIVET DISCOURSE

Shortly before Jesus went to the cross, He gave His inner circle of disciples a special briefing, called the Olivet Discourse. In it, He said the Temple would be destroyed, as well as the nation of Israel. He also explained what would take place prior to and during the Tribulation. This special briefing is recorded in Matthew 24-25, Mark 13 and Luke 21. The following quotations are taken from all three books, weaved together to make one narrative.

Jesus used the illustration of a pregnant woman to describe what the Church Age would be like. It would be a long period of time, and at the end there would be two birth pains, and then a birth. We saw almost 1900 years pass from the start of the Church Age (33 AD) until the first birth pain, World War I (1914). The second birth pain came in 1939 with the Second World War, and then the birth of the nation of Israel in 1948. The Lord will return before Israel becomes an old man by age 80 in 2028, and 7 years earlier to rapture the Church (Psalm 90.10).

The Prophecy of the Temple
(Matthew 24.1-3; Mark 13.1-4; Luke 21.5-7)

Jesus began His briefing on the "last days" saying the Temple would be destroyed:

And Jesus went out from the temple, and was going on his way; and his disciples came to him to show him the buildings of the temple. But he answered and said unto them, See ye not all these things? verily I say unto you, There shall not be left here one stone upon another, that shall not be thrown down. And as he sat on the mount of Olives, the disciples came unto him privately, saying, Tell us, when shall these things be? and what shall be the sign of thy coming, and of the end of the world? (Matthew 24.1-3)

This news stunned the disciples. They asked three specific questions:

1. When will the Temple be destroyed?
2. What will the *sign* be of its destruction?
3. What will the *sign* be of the return of Jesus and the end of the age?

The disciples asked the **When** and the **What**. The **What** is the *warning signs* of the Rapture, and the **When** is the Rapture.

Persecution of believers before the Temple's destruction (Luke 21.12-20)

Later in His prophetic discourse, Jesus explained what will occur prior to the destruction of the Temple. This was only recorded by Luke:

> But before all these things, they shall lay their hands on you, and shall persecute you, delivering you up to the synagogues and prisons, bringing you before kings and governors for my name's sake. It shall turn out unto you for a testimony. Settle it therefore in your hearts, not to meditate beforehand how to answer: for I will give you a mouth and wisdom, which all your adversaries shall not be able to withstand or to gainsay. But ye shall be delivered up even by parents, and brethren, and kinsfolk, and friends; and some of you shall they cause to be put to death. And ye shall be hated of all men for my name's sake. And not a hair of your head shall perish. In your patience ye shall win your souls. But when ye see Jerusalem compassed with armies, then know that her desolation is at hand.

The phrase, "*but before all these things,*" is the key to knowing that this refers to the 1st century, and not the time prior to the Rapture. From 33 to 70 AD, Christians were persecuted by both Jews and non-Jews. Thousands were thrown in prison, and some were killed. Nero was said to have slaughtered thousands for mere entertainment. Peter and Paul are the two most famous Christians to die during the reign of Nero.

Destruction of the Temple (Luke 21.20-24)

Jesus then explained how the Temple would be destroyed. Again, this was only recorded by Luke:

> But when ye see Jerusalem compassed with armies, then know that her desolation is at hand. Then let them that are in Judaea flee unto the mountains; and let them that are in the midst of her depart out; and let not them that are in the country enter therein. For these are days of vengeance, that all things which are written may be fulfilled. (Luke 21.20-22)

General Vespasian surrounded the city of Jerusalem in 66-67 A.D. The Roman legions dug a trench around the entire city. Everyone who was caught attempting to escape was crucified. Yet, before he attacked the city, he received word that Emperor Nero had died. He returned to Rome to take control of the empire in 69 AD, and left his eldest son, General Titus, in Judea. The siege was lifted for a year, and after the reprieve General Titus led the final assault on the city.

The Christians who knew what Jesus had told His disciples concerning the siege of Jerusalem left the city during the reprieve. They saw the **What** (*sign* of the surrounding of Jerusalem), and knew the **When** (destruction of the Temple) was *imminent*. Those who did not depart the city had no opportunity to leave later.

Jesus gave Christians of the 1st century the specific *warning sign* to know when the Temple would be destroyed – the surrounding of the city of Jerusalem. He then gave this grave warning:

> *Woe unto them that are with child and to them that give suck in those days! for there shall be great distress upon the land, and wrath unto this people. And they shall fall by the edge of the sword, and shall be led captive into all the nations: and Jerusalem shall be trodden down of the Gentiles, until the times of the Gentiles be fulfilled.* (Luke 21.23-24)

Those who did not heed the warning by Jesus to depart from Jerusalem when they saw the city surrounded by armies suffered through the worst period in her history. Over one million people died by starvation, disease and the sword. Josephus, a Jewish historian of the 1st century, said about 98,000 Jews were taken captive, as Jesus prophesied.

We see the importance of paying attention to the **What** to know the **When**. The Christians, who knew the sign of Jerusalem being surrounded, knew the destruction of the Temple was at hand. Josephus tells us that the "holy people" (Christians) fled Jerusalem during this time and were spared. Christians today can know the **What** (*signs* of the Rapture), and be fully ready for the **When** (Rapture).

Beginning of birth pains
(Matthew 24.4-8; Mark 13.5-8; Luke 21.8-11)

Jesus explained what will happen before the Tribulation starts:

> *And Jesus answered and said unto them, Take heed that no man lead you astray. For many shall come in my name, saying, I am the Christ; and shall lead many astray. And ye shall hear of wars and rumors of wars; see that ye be not troubled: for these things must needs come to pass; but the end is not yet. For nation shall rise against nation, and kingdom against kingdom; and there shall be famines and earthquakes in divers places. But all these things are the beginning of travail.* (Matthew 24.4-8)

182

These verses cover the time preceding the Tribulation. Full-Preterists and Partial-Preterists believe this was fulfilled in 70 AD. During this time, which covers the 19th, 20th and 21st centuries, many false messiahs will try to mislead the elect and the unsaved. There have been false messiahs (antichrists), false teachers and false prophets since the start of the Church Age (Acts 20.29-30; 2 Peter 2.1; 1 John 2.18; 4.1), yet an increasing number of these deceivers have plagued mankind during the last two centuries, and now in the 21st century. Some of the more infamous false prophets were William Miller, Joseph Smith, Jr., Charles Taze Russell, Joseph Franklin Rutherford, Ellen G. White, Herbert W. Armstrong, Sun Myung Moon, Jim Jones and Elizabeth Clare Prophet.

The phrase, *"nation against nation,"* is a Hebrew idiom. It is found in two places in the Old Testament (2 Chronicles 15.1-8; Isaiah 19.1-5). Its four-fold meaning describes:

1. A war
2. that begins in a small way
3. and grows
4. to include all the lands before the eyes of the prophet.

It is a perfect picture of the two world wars. The first started with conflict between the Austro-Hungarian and Serbian empires after Gavrilo Princip shot and killed Archduke Franz Ferdinand of Austria. It quickly activated a series of alliances that set off a chain reaction of war declarations. Within a month, much of Europe was in a state of open warfare. Out of that Great War came the Balfour Declaration, which prepared the land of Israel for the Jews.

World War II escalated in a similar fashion. Germany invaded Poland, and the subsequent declarations of war launched the Second Great War. Eventually, most of the nations of the world were dragged into it. The destruction of the Jewish people by Adolf Hitler and his butchers prepared the Jews for the land of Israel.

A mother carries her unborn child for a period of nine months; when she is gripped by the initial birth pains she knows she is nearing the time to deliver her child. Likewise, Jesus said we will know when we come near the end of this Christian dispensation when we see the beginning of the birth pains – the two world wars. A mother, gripped with the first birth pain, cannot say the exact day or hour her child will be born, yet she knows that she has come near to the end of her time of waiting.

The remaining warning signs, *"plagues," "famines," "great earthquakes in various places"* and *"terrors and great signs from heaven"* started with World War I. They will continue and grow in number and severity as we approach the Rapture and the start of the Tribulation.

Dave Hunt explained this in his book, *How Close Are We?* saying, "Jesus is apparently revealing that these signs will begin to occur substantially ahead of the Second Coming. They will increase in frequency and intensity like birthpangs. Moreover, it would seem that these **signs begin prior to the Rapture**" (p. 116, emphasis mine).

Once these *warning signs* have come to pass, Christians will know the Rapture is very near. There are many other *signs* that are given elsewhere in the Bible that will enable Christians to know how close the Rapture is.

Persecution of the elect during the Tribulation
(Matthew 24.9-14; Mark 13.9-13)

According to the "Law of Double Reference" Jesus changes the subject from the events of World War II and jumps over the years in which we are now living, and begins to talk about the Tribulation in verses 9 through 28. He explains how the elect (believers in Him) will be persecuted during the first half of the Tribulation:

> *But take ye heed to yourselves: for they shall deliver you up to councils; and in synagogues shall ye be beaten; and before governors and kings shall ye stand for my sake, for a testimony unto them. And the gospel must first be preached unto all the nations. And when they lead you to judgment, and deliver you up, be not anxious beforehand what ye shall speak: but whatsoever shall be given you in that hour, that speak ye; for it is not ye that speak, but the Holy Spirit. They shall deliver you up unto tribulation, and shall kill you: and ye shall be hated of all the nations for my name's sake, but he that endureth to the end, the same shall be saved. And then shall many stumble, and shall deliver up one another, and shall hate one another. And brother shall deliver up brother to death, and the father his child; and children shall rise up against parents, and cause them to be put to death. And many false prophets shall arise, and shall lead many astray. And because iniquity shall be multiplied, the love of the many shall wax cold. And this gospel of the kingdom shall be preached in the whole world for a testimony unto all the nations; and then shall the end come.*

During the Tribulation, the 144,000 of the 12 tribes of Israel (Revelation 7.1-9) will preach the Gospel throughout the entire world. Billions will be saved because of their preaching (Revelation 7.13-14). Many of them will also share the gospel and lead millions more to Jesus. No one knows how many people will be saved during the Tribulation, but it could be several billion, possibly half the world's population (Isaiah 26.9).

Those who trust in Jesus Christ during the Tribulation will be hated and persecuted in large numbers during the Tribulation. They will be put in prison, and most will be killed. Untold millions of people, who are saved after the Rapture and the start of the Tribulation and are not of the 144,000, will be put to death by the executioners working for Antichrist (Revelation 6.9-11). Some will have the opportunity to speak before governors and kings (presidents, prime ministers, etc.). They are to rely on the Holy Spirit to speak through them rather than devise their own defense.

Family members will turn on each other because of the massive persecution of believers throughout the world. The unsaved will turn in true believers to the authorities. The few believers, who survive this massive persecution, will enter the Millennial Kingdom in mortal bodies and repopulate the world (Isaiah 65.17-25).

The second half of the Tribulation
(Matthew 24.15-28; Mark 13.14-23)

The Lord explains what will happen at the mid-point of the Tribulation and beyond:

When therefore ye see the abomination of desolation, which was spoken of through Daniel the prophet, standing where he ought not, in the holy place (let him that readeth understand), then let them that are in Judaea flee unto the mountains: let him that is on the housetop not go down to take out things that are in his house: and let him that is in the field not return back to take his cloak. But woe unto them that are with child and to them that give suck in those days! And pray ye that your flight be not in the winter, neither on a Sabbath. For those days shall be tribulation, such as there hath not been the like from the beginning of the creation which God created until now, and never shall be And except the Lord had shortened the days, no flesh would have been saved; but for the elect's sake, whom he chose, he shortened the days. Then if any man shall say unto you, Lo, here is the Christ, or, Lo, there; believe it not. For there shall arise false Christs, and false prophets, and shall show great signs and wonders; so as to lead astray, if possible, even the elect. Behold, I have told you all things beforehand. If therefore they shall say unto you, Behold, he is in the wilderness; go not forth: Behold, he is in the inner chambers; believe it not. For as the lightning cometh forth from the east, and is seen even unto the west; so shall be the coming of the Son of man. Wheresoever the carcass is, there will the eagles be gathered together.

The abomination of desolation marks the mid-point of the Tribulation. This event signals the beginning of the greatest time of tribulation in the history of the world. This tribulation from the devil, his horde of fallen angels, the Antichrist and his minions will be very severe, worse than all previous persecutions by the forces of darkness and wickedness (Ephesians 6.12). The tremendous persecution by the forces of evil will be minimal compared to the final wrath of God, which will be greater than at any other time in history. The second half of the tribulation will be so great, that if God were to let it go on more than 3 ½ years, everyone would be killed, and there would be no one to populate the Millennial Kingdom. As it is, very few people survive (Isaiah 13.12).

The abomination of desolation was prophesied in Daniel 9.27. The Beast (little horn) confirms a covenant with many nations, including Israel, at the start of the Tribulation. The signing of this covenant is the beginning of the Tribulation. It lasts seven years, and in the middle of the covenant the Beast (Antichrist) breaks the covenant and puts an end to the sacrifices that are made in the rebuilt Temple in Israel. Putting a stop to the sacrifices is not the abomination of desolation. It is the act, by the Antichrist and the False Prophet, of erecting a statue of the Antichrist in the Holy of Holies and declaring himself to be "God" (2 Thessalonians 2.4). The False Prophet will then force everyone on Earth to worship the Antichrist and his image (Revelation 13.15).

In the middle of the Tribulation the Antichrist will make Jerusalem his second headquarters (the first will be in Babylon). He will then launch a massive pogrom of persecution against the Jews and Christians. The world church, which will be headquartered in Rome prior to this time, will move out. It will establish its new headquarters in the rebuilt city of Babylon (Zechariah 5.7-11).

Believers and religious Jews will flee from Jerusalem and hide in the mountains when the Antichrist moves in. He will begin to persecute Jews immediately after he proclaims himself to be God. Jews in Israel will not have time to pack their bags. When the Antichrist erects the abomination of desolation, they might make it out with just the clothes on their backs if they leave before the Antichrist finishes his show. Pregnant women and mothers with infant children will be very fortunate if they escape. If the persecution begins in the winter, fewer still will be able to escape with their lives (Matthew 24.15-22). Many eschatologians speculate that they will flee to the wilderness of Petra (Revelation 12.14). It will be reminiscent of when they departed Egypt and ate the unleavened bread.

During the second half of the Tribulation, there will be false messiahs and prophets who will perform spectacular signs and wonders. They will almost, but not quite, mislead the elect. Believers will not be fooled, because they know that Jesus Christ is to return quickly with the speed of lightning, and wipe out the armies of the world that have surrounded the city of Jerusalem to fight Him (Revelation 19.17-21).

The Glorious Appearing of Jesus Christ
(Matthew 24.29-31; Mark 13.24-27)

Jesus concluded by explaining what would happen when He returns:

But immediately after the tribulation of those days the sun shall be darkened, and the moon shall not give her light, and the stars shall fall from heaven, and the powers of the heavens shall be shaken: and then shall appear the sign of the Son of man in heaven: and then shall all the tribes of the earth mourn, and they shall see the Son of man coming on the clouds of heaven with power and great glory. And he shall send forth his angels with a great sound of a trumpet, and they shall gather together his elect from the four winds, from the uttermost part of the earth to the uttermost part of heaven.

The Olivet Discourse

24: 1,2 **Prophecy** Concerning the temple: there shall not be left one stone upon another.

Questions:

24: 3(b) What shall be the sign: { of thy coming?
and of the end of the world?

(a) When shall these things (fall of Jerusalem, destruction of temple) be?

◀

Answers:

24: 5   Many shall come saying, "I am the Christ".

24: 6   And ye shall hear of wars and rumors of wars,

(b)   But the end is not yet.

24: 7   For nation shall rise against nation and kingdom against kingdom, prophecy of World War I 1917-1918 - first birth pain.

24: 8   All these things are the beginning of travail, Literally - birth pains, World War II -1941-1945 - second birth pain.

24: 34   This generation, Literally - this "born one", the birth of the nation of Israel May 14, 1948 which is the sign of Christ's coming and the end of the world [age].

Just before Christ returns at the end of the Tribulation, the Earth will be going through massive convulsions. The waves of the oceans will be much larger than normal, bombarding the costal regions with massive breakers. This unusual activity will cause people to fear the worst. This could be caused by a polar shift (Isaiah 24.1, 20), a partial melting of the polar ice caps, a shift in the moon's orbit or a combination of those things.

The sun and the moon will also be darkened, either by natural or supernatural causes. The heavens will be shaken and stars will fall from the sky. The shaking of the heavens (stars in space) is the work of God, for He is the only one who can shake them (Isaiah 13.13; Joel 3.16; Haggai 2.6, 21; Hebrews 12.26); the devil can only shake the nations (Isaiah 14.16).

The stars falling out of the sky is the language of appearance. We call a meteor a "falling star." The ancients referred to asteroids, meteors and comets as "stars." Asteroids, meteors and comets will strike the Earth just prior to the Second Coming of Christ. Since the heavens will be physically shaken, it is logical that asteroids and comets could be moved out of their orbits and strike the Earth.

Immediately before Christ returns, His *sign* will appear in the sky. Everyone will see it and understand that the time of His Glorious Appearing is at hand.

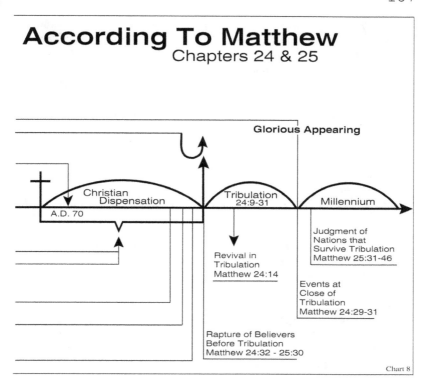

According To Matthew
Chapters 24 & 25

Glorious Appearing

Christian Dispensation

A.D. 70

Tribulation
24:9-31

Millennium

Revival in
Tribulation
Matthew 24:14

Judgment of
Nations that
Survive Tribulation
Matthew 25:31-46

Events at
Close of
Tribulation
Matthew 24:29-31

Rapture of Believers
Before Tribulation
Matthew 24:32 - 25:30

Chart 8

When Jesus returns to Earth, everyone will see Him returning in the same manner that He departed (Acts 1.11). He will also be accompanied by His holy angels (2 Thessalonians 1.7), and by believers of the Church Age. They will be riding flying horses just as Christ will (Revelation 19.7-8, 14), His will be a cherub in the form of a horse (Psalm 18.10). Some of the holy angels will come in their chariots of fire (Isaiah 66.15).

Christ will execute the wicked who are hiding in the ancient land of Edom (Isaiah 63.1-6; Habakkuk 3.3), and then travel to Jerusalem to destroy the armies of the Antichrist, who have surrounded the city to do battle with Him (Revelation 17.14). He will slay them with fire that comes from His mouth (Isaiah 66.15-16; Revelation 19.21), and strike the wicked with *"rays coming forth from his hand"* (Habakkuk 3.4). He also strikes them with pestilence (Habakkuk 3.5).

The command to be ready for the Rapture
(Matthew 24.32-51; Mark 13.28-37; Luke 21.29-36)

According to the Law of Recurrence, Jesus returns to the subject of verses 7 and 8 of Matthew 24, and tells the parable of the Fig Tree. He also explains what will happen in the "last days" and why Christians should watch for *warning signs*:

Now from the fig tree learn her parable: when her branch is now become tender, and putteth forth its leaves, ye know that the summer is nigh; even so ye also, when ye see all these things, know ye that he is nigh, even at the doors. Verily I say unto you, This generation shall not pass away, till all these things be accomplished. Heaven and earth shall pass away, but my words shall not pass away. But of that day and hour knoweth no one, not even the angels of heaven, neither the Son, but the Father only. And as were the days of Noah, so shall be the coming of the Son of man. For as in those days which were before the flood they were eating and drinking, marrying and giving in marriage, until the day that Noah entered into the ark, and they knew not until the flood came, and took them all away; so shall be the coming of the Son of man. Then shall two men be in the field; one is taken, and one is left: two women shall be grinding at the mill; one is taken, and one is left. Watch therefore: for ye know not on what day your Lord cometh. But know this, that if the master of the house had known in what watch the thief was coming, he would have watched, and would not have suffered his house to be broken through. Therefore be ye also ready; for in an hour that ye think not the Son of man cometh.

Who then is the faithful and wise servant, whom his lord hath set over his household, to give them their food in due season? Blessed is that servant, whom his lord when he cometh shall find so doing. Verily I say unto you, that he will set him over all that he hath. But if that evil servant shall say in his heart, My lord tarrieth; and shall begin to beat his fellow-servants, and shall eat and drink with the drunken; the lord of that servant shall come in a day when he expecteth not, and in an hour when he knoweth not, and shall cut him asunder, and appoint his portion with the hypocrites: there shall be the weeping and the gnashing of teeth. (Matthew 24.32-51)

The Lord described the Tribulation and His return at the end of it. He then returned to the events that will take place before the start of the Tribulation in this passage. We find here the "law of recurrence" principle. This hermeneutical law can be likened to painting a portrait. The artist blocks out different parts of one's features, and the next day he fills in the details. Jesus takes up where He left off by the "law of double reference" in verse 8 of Matthew 24. He continues to explain what will happen after the beginning of birth pains which were the first two world wars.

The parable of the fig tree is a prophecy of the rebirth of the nation of Israel. The Greek phrase *"panta tauta,"* that is translated *"all these things,"* refers to the beginning of birth pains (Matthew 24.8). Jesus was saying, in effect, that when you see the birth pains – World War I and II, that are accompanied by famines, pestilence and earthquakes – you will know that His return is drawing near.

The Greek word *genea* is translated "generation." The words *gene, genetic,* and *gynecology* are derived from it. It literally means *"born one"* (Thayer's *Greek-English Lexicon,* p. 112). Jesus said that this "born one" (nation of

Israel) will be in existence when He returns. The same word is used in John 3.16 and is translated "begotten."

Luke recorded the parable of the fig tree, *"And he spake to them a parable: Behold the fig tree, and all the trees"* (Luke 21.29). He added *"all the trees"* which is a reference to the United Nations. That political organization is the foundation for the creation of the "end-times" world government that is still many years away. In 1948, the fig tree (Israel) put forth its leaves – it became a nation. Israel could not have been recognized as a nation without the United Nations to do it.

Remember, Jesus said there would be birth pains – World Wars I and II. Birth pains always indicate there will be a birth. What is this birth about which Jesus was talking? There can be no question that He was referring to the birth of the nation of Israel, which took place on May 14, 1948. This was also prophesied in Isaiah 66.7, where the prophet used this same term, *travail*:

> *"Before she travailed, she brought forth; before her pain came, she delivered a man child. Who has heard such a thing? Who has seen such things? Shall the earth be made to bring forth in one day? Or shall a nation be born at once? For as soon as Zion travailed she brought forth her children. Shall I bring to the birth, and not cause to bring forth?"* says Jehovah. *"Shall I cause to bring forth, and shut the womb?"* says your God. (Isaiah 66.7-9, KJV)

> *When Israel was a child, then I loved him, and called my son out of Egypt.* (Hosea 11.1)

The birth of a man-child, preceded by a time of travail, is what the above passages prophesied. The nation of Israel is Jehovah's son. Those birth pains were World Wars I and II. Finally the birth of this man-child took place on May 14, 1948. Jesus said "this born one" would not pass away until all these things are fulfilled.

The *signs* Jesus gave were the beginning of birth pains, followed by the *super-sign* – the birth of the nation of Israel, and its growth from a baby to a mature man. Note the analogy of the growth of a Jewish child into manhood with the development of the nation of Israel. The nation of Israel was born in 1948. Then war broke out and the Arabs vowed to behead Israel in 10 days. All they were able to do was give Israel a mild circumcision in 8 days. A Jewish boy's Bar Mitzvah (his coming of age), occurs at age 13; at Israel's "Bar Mitzvah" (1961), Adolf Eichmann was captured (1961) and hung for his role in the Holocaust. That marked the year Israel was recognized by the United Nations as a developed nation. A Jewish boy was not supposed to go to war until after his 19th birthday (Numbers 1.3). Israel became a man of war by taking back the city of Jerusalem during the Six-Day War of 1967. A Jewish male could only become a priest (a man of peace) in his 30th year. On September 17, 1978, Egyptian President Anwar El Sadat, and the Prime

Minister of Israel, Menachem Begin, signed the Camp David Accord. That led directly to the Israel-Egypt Peace Treaty, signed on March 26, 1979.

The phrase, *"but of that day and hour knows no one"* (Matthew 24.36), is a reference to the Pre-Tribulation Rapture, not the Second Coming. We know this because anyone alive when the Antichrist commits the abomination of desolation can simply count the days (1260) until the Second Coming (Daniel 12.11).

When will the Rapture take place? As noted early, it cannot be pinned down several years beforehand to the exact day and hour. The Second Coming should take place by 2028 at the latest, and the Rapture 7 years earlier. Jesus said that the generation that sees the birth of Israel will be alive when He returns: *"this generation* (born one - Israel) *shall not pass away."* If the re-establishment of the nation of Israel is the starting date of that generation, 80 years brings us to 2028 (Psalm 90.10).

Jesus did not know the day of His Second Coming prior to His death and resurrection because He voluntarily gave up knowledge of certain things when He came to Earth. He did not give up His divinity, but voluntarily *"emptied himself, taking the form of a servant, being made in the likeness of men"* (Philippians 2:7).

It is possible that we may be able to pin down the day of the Rapture when we come to the last year of the Church Age through the study of the 7 major feasts celebrated by the Hebrew people (Leviticus 23). They are: Passover (14th of Nisan-March/April), Unleavened Bread (15th of Nisan); First Fruits (1st day after the Sabbath after Passover); Weeks or Pentecost (50 days after First Fruits); Trumpets (1st of Tishri-September/October); Atonement (10th of Tishri); and Tabernacles or Booths (15th of Tishri).

Four of these 7 feasts were fulfilled by Jesus during His First Coming. He died on Passover (John 13:1; 19:17-18), being the final Passover Lamb (John 1:29). He was buried on the Feast of Unleavened Bread (John 19:42), and rose from the tomb on the Feast of First Fruits (Matthew 28:1-7; Mark 16:1-7; Luke 24:1-8), being the First Fruit (1 Corinthians 15:20-23). On the feast of Pentecost, the Holy Spirit came and took up permanent residence inside the bodies of 120 believers (Acts 1.15; 2:1-4). Four of the 7 feasts were fulfilled on the very day of the feasts, leaving 3 to be fulfilled.

The remaining 3 feasts await fulfillment, and some believe they could be fulfilled on the day of each feast. The Rapture may be the fulfillment of the Feast of Trumpets (1 Corinthians 15:52; 1 Thessalonians 4:16-17). The Second Coming of Jesus could then fulfill the Feast of Atonement, and the establishing of the Millennial Kingdom on Earth could be the fulfillment of the Feast of Booths.

Of the 3 major events to come, the Rapture will take place first. Therefore, it should take place on the day of the next feast – the Feast of Trumpets. We cannot know in advance which year the Rapture will take place, but if this position which some take is correct, the Rapture would take place on the Feast of Trumpets at the blowing of the last of the many trumpets of that two-day feast.

Dr. Jack Van Impe believes that it is possible the remaining prophecies will be fulfilled on the days of the three remaining feasts – Feast of Trumpets, Feast of

Atonement and Feast of Booths. He explained his belief that the history of man may be completed by the year 2000 in his 1990 video, "A.D. 2000 – the End?"

We also know that God *"will do nothing, except he reveal his secret unto his servants the prophets"* (Amos 3:7). Is it possible that God has revealed when the Rapture will take place through the feasts? If the 3 major events yet to be fulfilled – Rapture, and Coming and Millennial Kingdom are fulfilled on the last 3 feasts they will be fulfilled in different years.

Some eschatologians agree that the warning by Jesus concerning His return (Matthew 24.32-51) is a reference to the Second Coming, and not the Pre-Tribulation Rapture. Arnold Fruchtenbaum explained why it refers to the Pre-Tribulation Rapture:

> Within premillennial and pretribulational circles, the majority view today is that this passage is speaking of the Second Coming rather than the Rapture. Two main reasons are given. *First*: contextually, Jesus has been speaking about the Second Coming and since this passage follows that discussion, then, logically, it would mean that He is speaking of the same thing. *Second*: the "taking away" of Matthew 24:40-41 is taken to be the same as verse 39, which is a "taking away" in judgment. Hence, the "taking away" is in judgment at the Second Coming, and not the blessing of the Rapture.
>
> In answer to the first point, Matthew 24:36 begins with the word *But*, which in Greek is *peri de* construction in Greek is a contrastive introduction of a new subject and, hence, is often translated as *But concerning* (I Cor. 7:1; 8:1; 12:1; I Thes. 5:1; etc.). The usage of this construction points to the introduction of a new subject. So yes, He has been discussing the Second Coming until this point. However, the *peri de* means that He is now introducing a new subject, and that is the Rapture. This would not be the first time the chronological sequence of the Olivet Discourse was broken to speak of an earlier event. It also happened in Luke 21:12. In answer to the *second* point, in Greek, the "taking away" in verses 40-41 is a different Greek word than the one used in verse 39, and so it need not be interpreted as the same kind of "taking away." (*The Footsteps of the Messiah*, 2003 edition, pp. 640-641)

Jesus said in Matthew 24.38 that the Rapture would take place in a time like days of Noah. Mankind will be *"eating and drinking, marrying and being given in marriage"* just as they did in the time of Noah. This must describe a period of time prior to the Tribulation. During the Tribulation, one-fourth of the world's population will be killed in the first few months (Revelation 6.1-8). Things get much worse. So many people will die during the Tribulation that man will be scarcer than the gold of Ophir (Isaiah 13.12). It is unlikely that people at the end of the Tribulation period will be living life as they did in the time of Noah before the flood. The context depicts a normal type of living before the start of the Tribulation. During the Tribulation food will be extremely scarce and expensive

(Revelation 6.6), and marriage will be a rare event. Seven women will beg one man to be their husband (Isaiah 4.1).

Arnold Frutchenbaum is right that there are two different Greek words used in Matthew 24.39-41 that are translated "taken." In verse 39 it says, "*they knew not until the flood came, and took them all away.*" The Greek word is *airo* which means "to take up or away." It is a reference to being taken away in judgment. In verses 40-41 the Greek word is *paralambano* which is made up of two words – *para*, which means "alongside of" or "with," and *lambano* which means "to take." It is the same word that is used in John 14.3 where it is translated "*receive you unto myself,*" referring to the return of Christ for His Church at the Rapture. All Pre-millennial Bible teachers understand that. It could not have a different meaning when He was speaking to the same group of disciples not more than 72 hours earlier on the Mount of Olives. Some scholars say the passage refers to the wicked being taken into judgment at the end of the Tribulation and believers left behind to go into the glorious Millennial Kingdom. However, *aphiemi*, the Greek word for "*left*" means "to send away" or "leave behind." It is used in 1 Corinthians 7.12-13 of a husband leaving his wife. Paul says a believing husband should not "*leave*" an unbelieving wife if she consents to live with him.

Certainly the statement, "*two men in the field, one will be taken and one will be left. Two women will be grinding in the mill, one will be taken and one will be left,*" is a description of the Pre-Tribulation Rapture as it is in John 14.3.

Some argue that *paralambano*, as is used John 19.17, means that since Jesus was taken away in judgment to be crucified the word has a negative connotation. The passage simply means the soldiers took Jesus with them. Then the words describing where they took Him are added. The word is also used in Matthew 4.5, 8 where the devil took Jesus to a high place and told Him to jump, and to a high mountain where he showed Him the kingdoms of the world. The word does not have any connotation of good or evil. It means to take along side of. It is the word that is used in John 14.3 and translated "*receive you unto myself.*"

Jesus, in a previous account, said that when He returns it will be like the days of Noah. The time of the Rapture would be in a day similar to that of the time of Noah and Lot:

> *And as it came to pass in the days of Noah, even so shall it be also in the days of the Son of man. They ate, they drank, they married, they were given in marriage, until the day that Noah entered into the ark, and the flood came, and destroyed them all. Likewise even as it came to pass in the days of Lot; they ate, they drank, they bought, they sold, they planted, they builded; but in the day that Lot went out from Sodom it rained fire and brimstone from heaven, and destroyed them all: after the same manner shall it be in the day that the Son of man is revealed. In that day, he that shall be on the housetop, and his goods in the house, let him not go down to take them away: and let him that is in the field likewise not return back. Remember Lot's wife. Whosoever shall seek to gain his life shall lose it: but whosoever shall lose his life shall preserve it. I say unto you, In that night there shall be two men on one bed; the one shall be taken, and the*

other shall be left. There shall be two women grinding together; the one shall be taken, and the other shall be left. There shall be two men in the field; the one shall be taken, and the other shall be left. And they answering say unto him, Where, Lord? And he said unto them, Where the body is, thither will the eagles also be gathered together. (Luke 17.26-37)

This passage contains more information about the Rapture. We see that on the very 24-hour day that Noah entered the ark (Genesis 7.13-17), and on the day that Lot departed the city of Sodom (Genesis 19.15-16, 23-25), the wrath of God fell upon the wicked. The Tribulation will start within 24 hours of the Rapture. (There will be no *gap*, as some eschatologians argue.)

Just before the Lord returns Christians are to take heed to the words of Jesus who said, *"But when these things begin to come to pass, look up, and lift up your heads; because your redemption draweth nigh"* (Luke 21.28). When He returns, there is nothing for us to do but look up and wait to be caught up. Christians should also remember the warning Jesus gave concerning Lot's wife, *"Remember Lot's wife. Whosoever shall seek to gain his life shall lose it: but whosoever shall lose his life shall preserve it"* (Luke 17.33).

Believers who know what to do and who are "watching" for the *warning signs,* will know when that day has arrived. They will also know what to do – just lift up their heads and wait for the "catching up." Christians who do this will receive the special crown for *"looking"* for the return of Christ, and be caught up alive:

Henceforth there is laid up for me the crown of righteousness, which the Lord, the righteous judge, shall give to me at that day; and not to me only, but also to all them that have loved his appearing. (2 Timothy 4.8)

All believers, who know what to "look" for on the day of the Rapture as noted above, and have been "eagerly awaiting" His return, will receive that special crown. They will also receive the *"day-star"*:

And we have the word of prophecy made more sure; whereunto ye do well that ye take heed, as unto a lamp shining in a dark place, until the day dawn, and the day-star arise in your hearts. (2 Peter 1.19)

The *"day dawn"* refers to the *signs* of Christ's coming. The *"day-star"* is the assurance that God will give to diligent students of Bible prophecy that the Rapture is about to occur just before it takes place. When those final *warning signs* appear, (Luke 21.25-28) all believers, who love the appearing of Jesus, will look up and await His arrival because they will have been given the *"day-star"* – the assurance that the events that will take place just before the Rapture are indeed the final *warning signs*, and thus be enabled to *"look up"* and be caught up alive.

Noah knew when to enter the ark because God told him when (Genesis 7.4). Lot knew when to depart Sodom because the angels told him and dragged him and his family out (Genesis 19.12-16). On the day of the Rapture

Christians who are looking for Christ's return will know it is the day of their departure because the *"day star"* will arise in hearts giving them the assurance of the **When**.

The warning by Jesus for Christians to remember Lot's wife, and to look up and wait for His return when the *warning signs* He spoke of start to take place is a proof that the Rapture cannot take place at *any moment*. If there are no *warning signs* to look for just prior to His return, the warning to remember Lot's wife makes no sense.

Jesus concluded this passage by saying that pairs of people will be separated at His return. Christians will be caught up to meet Him in the air, and the others will be left behind to go through the Tribulation.

The *warning signs* will grow in intensity before and after the day of the Rapture/Tribulation. Before that day and on that day there will be *signs* in the sun, moon and stars (Joel 2.30-31), and distress and fear among the nations (Luke 21.25-27). There are also *"lightnings and voices and thunders"* that proceed from the throne of Jehovah (Revelation 4.5). During the Tribulation the intensity of judgment grows with the breaking of the 7th Seal – *"thunders, and voices, and lightnings, and an earthquake"* (Revelation 8.5). When the 7th angel blows his trumpet, there will be *"lightnings, and voices, and thunders, and an earthquake, and great hail"* (Revelation 11.19). The final judgment comes when the 7th angel pours out his bowl, there is *"lightnings, and voices, and thunders; and there was a great earthquake"* (Revelation 16.18). It flattens every mountain and sinks every island on Earth (Revelation 16.20). Hailstones also fall from the sky about the *"weight of a talent"* (100 pounds).

Before the Tribulation the *warning signs* become more spectacular. The last seven *warning signs* will be obvious to everyone and they grow in importance. The final two *warning signs* will be so obvious and spectacular that many people around the world will literally pass out due to fear (Luke 21.26).

When we come to the days just before the Rapture/Tribulation so many *warning signs* will have been fulfilled that all students of Bible prophecy will clearly understand that the Rapture/Tribulation is a very short time away, and that all of the prophecies that must be fulfilled before the Tribulation starts will be fulfilled before the Rapture.

Parable of the ten virgins
(Matthew 25.1-13)

Before concluding His prophetic briefing, Jesus gives two parables, the first being that of the ten virgins:

Then shall the kingdom of heaven be likened unto ten virgins, who took their lamps, and went forth to meet the bridegroom. And five of them were foolish, and five were wise. For the foolish, when they took their lamps, took no oil with them: but the wise took oil in their vessels with their lamps. Now while the bridegroom tarried, they all slumbered and slept. But at midnight there is a cry, Behold, the bridegroom! Come ye forth to meet him. Then all those virgins arose, and trimmed their lamps. And the foolish said unto the wise, Give us of your oil; for our lamps are going out. But the wise answered, saying, Peradventure there will not be enough for us and you: go ye rather to them that sell, and buy for yourselves. And while they went away to buy, the bridegroom came; and they that were ready went in with him to the marriage feast: and the door was shut. Afterward came also the other virgins, saying, Lord, Lord, open to us. But he answered and said, Verily I say unto you, I know you not. Watch therefore, for ye know not the day nor the hour.

This parable shows that Jesus would be gone a long time before returning to rapture His bride. Notice that it says the bridegroom *"tarried."* He was gone so long that all of the virgins fell asleep. If the virgins are symbolic of the Church, it means that Jesus will be gone so long that the majority of Christians will give up looking for His return (2 Peter 3.3-4). This is true today, even though hundreds of books have been written about the Rapture and the Second Coming. Most pastors rarely teach on eschatology because they do not understand it. Very few Christians study the subject because they consider it to be too complex to understand. The vast majority do not even know what the word "eschatology" means. The five foolish virgins represent unsaved people who go to church and think they are saved.

Parable of the talents
(Matthew 25.14-30)

The last parable Jesus gave emphasized the fact that He would return after a long period of time:

For it is as when a man, going into another country, called his own servants, and delivered unto them his goods. And unto one he gave five talents, to another two, to another one; to each according to his several ability; and he went on his journey. Straightway he that received the five talents went and traded with them, and made another five talents. In like manner he also that received the two gained another two. But he that received the one went away and digged in the earth, and hid his lord's money. Now after a long time the lord of those servants cometh, and maketh a reckoning with them. And he that received the five talents came and brought another five talents, saying, Lord, thou deliveredst unto me five talents: lo, I have gained another five talents. His lord said unto him, Well done, good and faithful servant: thou hast been faithful over a few things, I will set thee over many things; enter thou into the joy of thy lord. And he also that received the two talents came and said, Lord, thou deliveredst unto me two talents: lo, I have gained another two talents. His lord said unto him, Well done, good and faithful servant: thou hast been faithful over a few things, I will set thee over many things; enter thou into the joy of thy lord. And he also that had received the one talent came and said, Lord, I knew thee that thou art a hard man, reaping where thou didst not sow, and gathering where thou didst not scatter; and I was afraid, and went away and hid thy talent in the earth: lo, thou hast thine own. But his lord answered and said unto him, Thou wicked and slothful servant, thou knewest that I reap where I sowed not, and gather where I did not scatter; thou oughtest therefore to have put my money to the bankers, and at my coming I should have received back mine own with interest. Take ye away therefore the talent from him, and give it unto him that hath the ten talents. For unto every one that hath shall be given, and he shall have abundance: but from him that hath not, even that which he hath shall be taken away. And cast ye out the unprofitable servant into the outer darkness: there shall be the weeping and the gnashing of teeth.

This parable shows that Jesus would go into a far country (Heaven), and be gone for a long period of time before returning. He told the same parable earlier in His ministry (Luke 19.12-27). Both parables emphasize the truth that Jesus would be gone for a very long time. These parables are strong proof that Jesus could not return at *any moment* since Pentecost. He had to be gone a very long time, and we know that period of time will be about 2000 years.

The two servants, who doubled their talents, represent true believers of the Church Age who are faithful in serving Jesus. The servant, who hid his one talent, represents unsaved people who go to church and think they are saved. (Some Christians do not serve the Lord. They are saved, but they will receive few rewards as Paul explained in 1 Corinthians 3.11-15.)

Judgment of the nations
(Matthew 25.31-46)

Jesus concluded by saying He would judge the wicked and reward the righteous when He returns:

But when the Son of man shall come in his glory, and all the angels with him, then shall he sit on the throne of his glory: and before him shall be gathered all the nations: and he shall separate them one from another, as the shepherd separateth the sheep from the goats; and he shall set the sheep on his right hand, but the goats on the left. Then shall the King say unto them on his right hand, Come, ye blessed of my Father, inherit the kingdom prepared for you from the foundation of the world: for I was hungry, and ye gave me to eat; I was thirsty, and ye gave me drink; I was a stranger, and ye took me in; naked, and ye clothed me; I was sick, and ye visited me; I was in prison, and ye came unto me. Then shall the righteous answer him, saying, Lord, when saw we thee hungry, and fed thee? or athirst, and gave thee drink? And when saw we thee a stranger, and took thee in? or naked, and clothed thee? And when saw we thee sick, or in prison, and came unto thee? And the King shall answer and say unto them, Verily I say unto you, Inasmuch as ye did it unto one of these my brethren, even these least, ye did it unto me. Then shall he say also unto them on the left hand, Depart from me, ye cursed, into the eternal fire which is prepared for the devil and his angels: for I was hungry, and ye did not give me to eat; I was thirsty, and ye gave me no drink; I was a stranger, and ye took me not in; naked, and ye clothed me not; sick, and in prison, and ye visited me not. Then shall they also answer, saying, Lord, when saw we thee hungry, or athirst, or a stranger, or naked, or sick, or in prison, and did not minister unto thee? Then shall he answer them, saying, Verily I say unto you, Inasmuch as ye did it not unto one of these least, ye did it not unto me. And these shall go away into eternal punishment: but the righteous into eternal life.

Jesus Christ first returns to the ancient land of Edom (Isaiah 63.1-6; Habakkuk 3.3). He marches up through the forces of the Antichrist to Jerusalem to destroy the armies of the Antichrist that have surrounded it (Revelation 19.17-21). Everyone who survives the Tribulation is then gathered before the Lord Jesus Christ to be judged. The righteous enter into the Millennial Kingdom (Matthew 25.31-34). They are the ones who did not take the mark of the Beast, and were kind and helpful to the Jews. They will be saved at the Glorious Appearing of Christ when they are given the gospel in its fullness. That is what is meant by the statement of the Lord, *"But he that endureth to the end, the same shall be saved"* (Matthew 24.13). They will enter the Millennial Kingdom in their mortal bodies, and repopulate the Earth.

Jesus will explain to the wicked why they are condemned. During the Tribulation they did not help those who were hungry, thirsty, sick or in prison. They did not help those in need, because they were not saved (Matthew 25.41-46).

Chapter review

Special instructions to believers prior to the Rapture

By way of review we will recap the major points of this chapter. Jesus gave special instructions to the believers who will be living in the last days:

And there shall be signs in sun and moon and stars; and upon the earth distress of nations, in perplexity for the roaring of the sea and the billows. (Luke 21.25)

And I will show wonders in the heavens and in the earth: blood, and fire, and pillars of smoke. The sun shall be turned into darkness, and the moon into blood, before the great and terrible day of Jehovah cometh. (Joel 2.30-31)

These *signs* will begin before the Rapture, increase in intensity during the Tribulation, coming to an end at the return of the Lord in glory. Jesus said, *"But when these things begin to come to pass, look up, and lift up your heads; because your redemption draweth nigh"* (Luke 21.28). We take that literally. Jesus said that those who are looking up when they see these *signs* will receive a special reward, that is, to be caught up alive.

The second special instruction is, *"Remember Lot's wife"* (Luke 17.32). Jesus has told us that when these signs immediately preceding the Rapture are manifested, we are to look up. What happened to Mrs. Lot? God told Lot, his wife and his children not to look back when Sodom is destroyed. Mrs. Lot could not resist and was turned into a pillar of salt (Genesis 19.26). The Lord then gave the warning, *"Whosoever shall seek to gain his life shall lose it: but whosoever shall lose his life shall preserve it."* That is the lukewarm Christian who, when he sees these events immediately preceding the Rapture of the Church and is more interested in his own life and his own affairs than he is in the coming of the Lord. He will still be caught up in the Rapture, but he will lose his reward.

> *I say unto you, In that night there shall be two men on one bed; the one shall be taken, and the other shall be left* (apheime, deserted). *There shall be two women grinding together; the one shall be taken, and the other shall be left* (Luke 17.34-35). (The word *"taken"* is *paralambano* which means *"taken with"* and *"along side of."*)

The last instruction is:

> *But take heed to yourselves, lest haply your hearts be overcharged with surfeiting, and drunkenness, and cares of this life, and that day come on you suddenly as a snare.* (Luke 21.34-35)

Most of us are not touched by either of these two words *"surfeiting"* and *"drunkenness,"* but we are by this next statement:

> *For so shall it come upon all them that dwell on the face of all the earth. But watch ye at every season, making supplication, that ye may prevail to escape all these things that shall come to pass, and to stand before the Son of man.* (Luke 21.34-36)

The word *"stand"* indicates "standing innocent, unashamed." Jesus has given special instructions to believers living immediately preceding the Rapture. That is, we are to look up, stop where we are, turn our heads toward heaven, and watch for our coming Redeemer. If we do not, how embarrassed we will be, having failed God's last test. There are many people who are saying, "Oh, I'm anxious for the Lord's return; and if He comes today I'm ready." God is going to give one final test to show us if we are truly ready. So be ready to look up. If we look up in obedience we will not be harmed, but will be caught up alive and receive the *"crown of righteousness"* (2 Timothy 4.8).

The Day-Star

The *"day-star"* is a promise from God given through Peter. He urges all Christians to study prophecy:

And we have the word of prophecy made more sure; whereunto ye do well that ye take heed, as unto a lamp shining in a dark place, until the day dawn, and the day-star arise in your hearts. (2 Peter 1.19)

The *"day dawn"* refers to the signs of Christ's coming. The *"day-star"* is the assurance that God will give to diligent students of prophecy that the Rapture is about to occur just before it takes place. We have seen there will be signs in the sun, moon, stars and upon the earth immediately prior to the Rapture. Jesus told us when we see these *signs* begin to come to pass we are to look up (Luke 21.28). How will we know to look up? That is the *"day-star."* Sincere students of prophecy who truly love his appearing will be given the assurance that this is the time to look up for their redemption (the Rapture) draweth nigh.

Christians are not to go back to their homes if they are outside when Christ returns:

In that day, he that shall be on the housetop, and his goods in the house, let him not go down to take them away: and let him that is in the field likewise not return back. (Luke 17.31)

The truths in this book will lead to this gift of the *"day-star"* in your life, so that you can be obedient to God's last test and be caught up alive, receive your crown and *"stand"* before the Lord.

How embarrassing it will be for those Christians who do not obey this last test:

And now, my little children, abide in him; that, if he shall be manifested, we may have boldness, and not be ashamed before him at his coming. (1 John 2.29)

Have you ever thought how wonderful it would be living back in the days just prior to the birth of Christ? Days when great prophecies were fulfilled, when Christ's birth was coming near and you would have been one of those shepherds who heard the angel's announcement; or maybe, one of the Wise Men from the East who saw the star, and came and saw the baby Jesus; or to be present at the empty tomb? Wouldn't it have been wonderful to see some great prophetic events like that being fulfilled? You may not realize it, but in the lifetime of every person reading this, some of the most significant Bible prophecies in the entire Word of God have been fulfilled.

Days of Noah and Lot

Jesus made it clear that His Second Coming would be a long way off, and his disciples had no reason to look for His return in the near future:

And he said unto the disciples, The days will come, when ye shall desire to see one of the days of the Son of man, and ye shall not see it. And they shall say to you, Lo, there! Lo, here! go not away, nor follow after them: for as the lightning, when it lighteneth out of the one part under the heaven, shineth unto the other part under heaven; so shall the Son of man be in his day. (Luke 17.22-24)

Luke 17.23 refers to the Glorious Appearing of Christ at the end of the Tribulation; but in verse 25, we read that He must suffer many things and be rejected by this generation. Jesus then spoke about the events of the Rapture of the Church:

And as it came to pass in the days of Noah, even so shall it be also in the days of the Son of man. (Luke 17.26)

While the days of Noah were very wicked, Jesus did not particularly deal with the wickedness of Noah's time, but rather with the normalcy of the way people lived in Noah's day:

And as it came to pass in the days of Noah, even so shall it be also in the days of the Son of man. They ate, they drank, they married, they were given in marriage, until the day that Noah entered into the ark, and the flood came, and destroyed them all. (Luke 17.26-27)

Jesus showed that the sin of Noah's day was that people lived as though they would never die despite predictions of coming destruction within 120 years (Genesis 6.3). *"Likewise even as it came to pass in the days of Lot; they ate, they drank, they bought, they sold, they planted, they builded..."* (Luke 17.28). The verbs here, by the way, are in the imperfect mode and should be translated, "they kept on" eating and drinking.

But in the day that Lot went out from Sodom it rained fire and brimstone from heaven, and destroyed them all: after the same manner shall it be in the day that the Son of man is revealed. (Luke 17.29-30)

Many Bible scholars put Luke 17.26 and the following verses at the end of the Tribulation. This cannot be because Jesus was showing by the days of Noah and the days of Lot, normal living – buying and selling in a normal way, eating and drinking in a normal way. At the end of the Tribulation, the people will not be buying and selling in a normal way, nor marrying and giving in marriage. The mark of the Beast will have been established, and people will not be able to buy or sell unless they have that mark. Marriage will have been virtually abolished (Isaiah 4.1). These phrases, "*days of Noah*" and "*days of Lot*" refer to the days immediately prior to the Rapture of the Church. "*In that day* (that is in the day of the Rapture), *he that shall be on the housetop, and his goods in the house, let him not go down to take them away: and let him that is in the field likewise not return back* (Luke 17.31).

And he spake to them a parable: Behold the fig tree, and all the trees: when they now shoot forth, ye see it and know of your own selves that the summer is now nigh. Even so ye also, when ye see these things coming to pass, know ye that the kingdom of God is nigh. Verily I say unto you, This generation shall not pass away, till all things be accomplished. (Luke 21.29-32)

The Greek word *genea* that is translated "generation" means "born one." Jesus referred to the birth of Israel. May 14, 1948, and likened it to the birth of a Jewish boy. Israel (that Jewish boy) will not grow up and become an old man in the eightieth year of his life before all the things He mentioned in the Olivet Discourse come to pass.

Heaven and earth shall pass away: but my words shall not pass away. (Matthew 24.35)

Conclusion

Do not wait until the Tribulation starts to trust in **Jesus Christ** to save you. If you go into the Tribulation, there is no guarantee you will survive it for very long. Within the first year or so, one-fourth of the world's population will die from war, famine, pestilence and wild animals (Revelation 6.8). By the middle of the Tribulation, one-third of the remaining population of the world will be dead (Revelation 9.15), leaving half of the world's population alive. Things only get worse. So many people die during the Tribulation that man becomes rarer than gold (Isaiah 13.12). (If you have not trusted **Jesus Christ** to save you turn to Appendix B.)

STUDY QUESTIONS

Chapter 14

1. What is the "**What**" and what is the "**When**"?

    A.

    B.

2. What were the first birth pains and what was the birth that followed those birth pains?

    A.

    B.

    C.

3. Will Christians, who know Bible prophecy, be surprised by the Rapture?

4. Will students of Bible prophecy receive a special crown for eagerly "looking" for the return of Jesus?

PART V

THE COMING NEW WORLD ORDER

This section is included to prove beyond a shadow of a doubt that the prophecies (*warning signs*) that have yet to be completely fulfilled are in the process of being fulfilled before our very eyes. There is a lot of information in this book concerning the "New World Order" that is racing toward us. We have placed most of the details of this conspiracy in the Appendices F and G.

Below are quotes by two of the most senior members of the "New World Order Gang" that are working feverishly to usher in the Old World Nightmare:

We have had **250 years** or so of **family involvement** in the finance business. We provide advice on **both sides** of the balance sheet, and we do it **globally**. (David Rothschild)

Some even believe we (the Rockefeller family) are part of a **secret cabal** working **against the best interests of the United States**, characterizing my family and me as **"internationalists"** and of **conspiring** with others around the world to build a more integrated **global** political and economic structure – **one world**, if you will. If that's the charge, **I stand guilty**, and **I am proud of it**. (David Rockefeller)

FIFTEEN

WORLD CHURCH

A World Church will be established before the Tribulation. There has been much work to unite the world's religions. The first attempt at a global dialogue of faiths (Parliament of the World's Religions) was held in 1893. Roman Catholics, Protestants, Hindus, Buddhists, Muslims, Theosophists and others prayed together and dialogued for 17 days. The event was celebrated by another conference on its centennial in 1993. This led to a new series of conferences under the official title, "Parliament of the World's Religions." It held meetings in 1999, 2004, 2007 and 2009.

Ecumenical organizations

The World Council of Churches (WCC) was formed in 1948 to unite the Protestant denominations. The Roman Catholic Church is not a member of the WCC, but has worked closely with it and sends representatives to all of its conferences. The Vatican's Pontifical Council for Promoting Christian Unity nominates 12 members to the WCC's Faith and Order Commission as full members. The International Missionary Council merged with the WCC in 1961, and the World Council of Christian Education merged in 1971.

The Three Faiths Forum was founded in 1997 to encourage friendship, goodwill and understanding among people of the three monotheistic faiths Christianity, Judaism and Islam.

The Conference of European Churches (CEC) was founded in 1959 to assist Protestant, Orthodox and Catholic churches to cooperate. In 1999 the CEC and European Ecumenical Commission on Church and Society merged.

The Federal Council of Churches (1908) and International Council of Religious Education (1905) merged in 1950 to form the National Council of Churches.

Christian Churches Together is a Christian ecumenical group formed in 2006 to "broaden and expand fellowship, unity and witness among the diverse expressions of Christian faith today."

The Tony Blair Faith Foundation, created in 2007 by former British Prime Minister Tony Blair, aims to promote respect and understanding about the world's major religions and show how faith is a powerful force for good in the modern world. Rick Warren is a member of this ecumenical foundation.

More inter-faith organizations will continue to be created. Prior to the Rapture/Tribulation a world religion will be formed. Christians should not be involved in this work. They should oppose it, and share the gospel of eternal life through Jesus Christ with the lost. There is only one way to be saved:

Jesus saith unto him, I am the way, and the truth, and the life: no one cometh unto the Father, but by me. (John 14.6)
And in none other is there salvation: for neither is there any other name under heaven, that is given among men, wherein we must be saved. (Acts 4.12)

Templeton Prize

The Templeton Prize for Progress Toward Research or Discoveries about Spiritual Realities, established in 1972, is awarded to the person who tried "various ways for discoveries and breakthroughs to expand human perceptions of divinity and to help in the acceleration of divine creativity." The panel of judges consists of Hindus, Christians, Jews, Buddhists, Muslims and atheists. Some of its winners have been: Mother Teresa (1973), Billy Graham (1982), James I. McCord of the Princeton Theological Seminary (1986), Charles Colson, founder of the Prison Fellowship (1993) and Bill Bright, founder of Campus Crusade for Christ (1996).

Ecumenical advocates

Numerous people in the religious community are working to bring members of different religions together. Some of the more notable individuals who were and are active in this effort are: Jack Van Impe, Billy Graham, Bill Bright, Jerry Falwell, Rick Warren, Robert Schuller, Pat Robertson, Richard Land, James I. Packer, Larry Lewis, Richard Mouw, Mark Noll, Jesse Miranda, Os Guinness, William Swing, Richard John Neuhaus, John White, Pope John Paul II, Pope Benedict XVI, Hans Kung, Charles Colson and Robert Muller. (Warren called for cooperation between Muslims and Christians – Washington Times, 7.05.2009, Julia Duin.)

Hans Kung, a notable Catholic priest, Swiss philosopher and professor of ecumenical theology at University of Tubingen in Germany, desires a world church. In his book, *Global Responsibility: In Search of a New World Ethic* (1991), he made it clear that the world needs an "ecumenical world order":

If ethics is to function for the wellbeing of all, it must be undivided ethic. Post modern men and women need common values, goals, ideals, visions. But the great question in dispute is: does not all this presuppose a religious faith?... What we need is an ecumenical world order. (Citing Gary Kah, *The New World Religion*, p. 212)

The United Religions Initiative was founded by William E. Swing, formerly Bishop of the Episcopal Diocese of California. Its purpose is to bring people of diverse faith into cooperation for peace through the United Nations. The movement to found it began in 1996, culminating in the signing of the United Religions Initiative Charter in 2000. Its charter states:

The purpose of the United Religions Initiative is to promote enduring, daily interfaith cooperation, to end religiously motivated violence and to create cultures of peace, justice and healing for the Earth and all living beings.

Robert Muller, former assistant Secretary General of the United Nations for 40 years, has become known as "Philosopher of the UN." He sees a "new world" coming:

May the kind divine providence help us start a new history and prepare the advent of a new age, a new world, a new philosophy and new human relationships, as we approach the bi-millennium. (*New Genesis: Shaping a Global Spirituality*, p. 168, citing Kah, *The New World Religion*, p. 231)

Roman Catholic Church

In 1994, Roman Catholic and Protestant evangelical scholars signed an ecumenical document in the United States called "Evangelicals and Catholics Together" (ECT). The co-signers of the document were Charles Colson and Richard Neuhaus, representing each side of the discussions. It was part of a larger ecumenical rapprochement in the United States that had begun in the 1980s with Catholic-Evangelical collaboration in para-church organizations such as Jerry Falwell's Moral Majority.

Some of the more notable evangelical signatories include the late Bill Bright of Campus Crusade, Os Guinness of the Trinity Forum, Richard Mouw of Fuller Theological Seminary, Mark Noll of Wheaton College, James I. Packer and Pat Robertson of Regent University, Larry Lewis of the Home Mission Board of the Southern Baptist Convention, Richard Land of the Christian Life Commission, Jesse Miranda of the Assemblies of God and John White of Geneva College.

The Joint Declaration on the Doctrine of Justification (between Lutherans and Catholics) of 1999, says many of the same things as the ECT. It emphasizes Sola gratia (grace alone) over Sola fide (faith alone).

John Paul II (1920-2005), Roman Catholic Pope (1978-2005), made a few comments concerning a possible "World Church" in 2004:

VATICAN CITY (AP) – Pope John Paul II rang in the New Year on Thursday with a renewed call for peace in the Middle East and Africa and the creation of a new world order based on respect for the dignity of man and equality among nations.

But he stressed that to bring about peace, there needs to be a new respect for international law and the creation of a "new international order" based on the goals of the United Nations.

He called for "an order that is able to give adequate solutions to today's problems based on the dignity of the human being, on an integral development of society, on solidarity among nations rich and poor, on the sharing of resources and the extraordinary results of scientific and technical progress."[1]

Pope John Paul II also said, about his goal of creating a "World Church":

It is necessary for humanity to achieve **unity** through plurality, to learn to come together in the **one Church**, even while presenting a plurality of ways of thinking and acting, of cultures and civilizations. (Gary Kah, *A New World Religion*, p. 237, emphasis mine)

The "one Church" is the Roman Catholic Church, which has been working behind the scenes with all the major religions to form a world religion. Its hierarchy has been talking with high-level members of Protestantism, Buddhism, Hinduism and Islam. Progress has been made, yet there is much more that needs to be accomplished before a world religion is established. As noted previously, Christians should not participate in that effort.

Conclusion

The Bible clearly teaches that before the Antichrist rises to power there will be a World Church. The *"great harlot"* (World Church) rides the beast (Antichrist) from the beginning of the Tribulation. That one-world false religion must be in place before the start of the Tribulation. It controls the Antichrist from the start, but loses control of him at the mid-point.

Every religion, denomination, cult and church will be part of this world religion. The churches and people who do not join it will have to operate in an "underground" manner as the early Christian churches did. Persecution of true Christians and Christian churches will become prevalent throughout the world and more intense as we draw closer to the start of the Tribulation. Prepare for persecution.

STUDY QUESTIONS

Chapter 15

1. Is there a concerted effort by most religions of the world to unite?

2. Are many leading Protestant pastors calling for the religions of the world to work together?

3. Is the ecumenical movement a fulfillment of Bible prophecy?

4. Will most Protestant churches eventually join the World Church before the start of the Tribulation?

SIXTEEN

WORLD ECONOMY

The "powers that be," thousands of politicians, bureaucrats and civilians, have worked openly and behind the scenes to establish a world economic system for their "New World Order."

Public organizations and treaties

In the past several decades, the conspirators have created numerous institutions to form a world economic system. The most notable are the: Federal Reserve Banks of the United States (1913), Commonwealth of Nations (1926), Bank for International Settlements (1930), International Monetary Fund (1944), World Bank (1945), Organization for Economic Co-operation and Development (1948), Council of Arab Economic Unity (1957), European Free Trade Association (1960), Group of 77 (1964), Council of the Americas (1965), Americas Society (1965), Association of Southeast Asian Nations (1967), Group of 24 (1971), Worldwide Interbank Financial Telecommunication (1973), Group of 8 (1975), the Group of 30 (1978), Organization of Eastern Caribbean States (1981), Gulf Cooperation Council (1981), South Asian Association for Regional Cooperation (1985), World Trade Organization (1994), and the Group of 20 (1999).

These organizations have helped politicians and bureaucrats create treaties and agreements that are the foundation of a world economic system: the General Act for Pacific Settlement of International Disputes (1929), the Oslo Agreements (1930), the Bretton Woods Agreement (1944), the General Agreement on Tariffs and Trade (1947), the Asia-Pacific Economic Cooperation (1989), the European Free Trade Agreement (1992), the North American Free Trade Agreement (NAFTA) (1994), the Dominican Republic-Central America Free Trade Agreement (2004), the South Asian Association for Regional Cooperation (2004) and the Constitutive Treaty (Union of the South American Nations) (2008).

The organizations and agreements above are the foundation of the coming new world economic system. It is likely that within a decade or so the conspirators will merge the various free trade agreements into a world free trade agreement. They will probably introduce the amero currency to replace the American dollar, the Canadian loonie and the Mexican peso. Other supranational currencies will be created to replace all national currencies and eventually a world currency will replace all forms of currency. Once that is accomplished the world currency will be replaced by an implantable computer chip. Before the Tribulation starts, many will have a chip implanted in their bodies with which to make economic transactions.

Union Currencies

The European Union officially adopted the *euro* on December 16, 1995. It was introduced to world financial markets as an accounting currency on January 1, 1999, replacing the former European Currency Unit (ECU). Euro coins and banknotes entered circulation on January 1, 2002. It is currently in use in 16 of the 27 member states and on December 1, 2009 the Treaty of Lisbon entered into force, and with it the euro became the official currency of the European Union.

The monetary union pact of the Cooperation Council for the Arab States of the Gulf (Gulf Cooperation Council), which called for the launch of a single currency, went into effect in December 2009. "The Gulf monetary union pact has come into effect. Accordingly, GCC central bank governors will work out a timetable for the establishment of the Gulf central bank to ultimately launch the single currency," said Kuwait's Finance Minister Mustafa al-Shamali Shamali as reported by the official KUNA news agency.[1]

Under the pact, a Gulf monetary council will be established in 2010 to create a central bank which will take the required measures to issue a single currency.

The European Union has its own currency, and the North American Union will soon has its own, the "amero." Other unions around the world will follow suit, and then all currencies will be replaced by a world currency.

Calls for a world economic system

Council on Foreign Relations

The Council on Foreign Relations has been calling for a world economic system for over two decades. Council member Richard Cooper called for "the creation of a common currency for all the industrial democracies, with a common monetary policy." The "determination of monetary policy" must be turned over "to a supra-national body." (Foreign Affairs magazine, Fall 1984)

Financial gurus

The financial gurus of the Group of Twenty, IMF, World Bank, World Trade Organization, United Nations and U.S. Treasury Secretary Timothy Geithner, French President Nicolas Sarkozy, British Prime Minister Gordon Brown, Russian President Dmitry Medeved have all called for a world economic system.

Group of Twenty

The London Telegraph reported on the Group of Twenty (G20) saying in the headline, "The G20 moves the world a step closer to a global currency." The sub-title read, "The world is a step closer to a global currency, backed by a global central bank, running monetary policy for all humanity." The article explained the significance of what the G-20 accomplished:

> In effect, the G20 leaders have activated the IMF's power to create money and begin global "quantitative easing." In doing so, they are putting a **de facto world currency into play**. It is **outside the control** of any sovereign body. **Conspiracy theorists will love it.**[2] (Emphasis mine)

Gordon Brown

Gordon Brown, Prime Minister of England (2007-present) and former Chancellor of the Exchequer (1997-2007), called for global cooperation to implement a "new Bretton Woods" international agreement to prevent a repeat of the global financial meltdown. This is a snippet of what he had to say:

> Rebuilding **global** financial stability is a **global** challenge that needs **global** solutions.[3] (Emphasis mine)

Confessions about bankers

The bankers around the world have controlled governments for hundreds of years, and today they have a stranglehold on virtually every nation. Dozens of men have spoken out concerning the machinations of the bankers exposing their criminal actions. Some of these brave men are – Carroll Quigley, Louis T. McFadden, Woodrow Wilson, Henry Ford, Charles Lindberg, Sr., Andrew Jackson, James Madison and Thomas Jefferson.

Robert Reich

Robert Reich, Secretary of Labor (1993-1997), stated bluntly that bankers make domestic and foreign policy, not Congress:

> The **dirty little secret** is that both houses of **congress** are **irrelevant**. America's **domestic policy** is now **being run by** Alan Greenspan and the **Federal Reserve**. America's **foreign policy** is now being **run by the International Monetary Fund**.[4] (Emphasis mine)

Louis T. McFadden

Louis T. McFadden (1876-1936), Congressman from Pennsylvania (1915-1935), and Chairman of the House Banking Committee, condemned the Federal Reserve Act of 1913, which gave international bankers absolute control over the banking industry in America. He also condemned the Federal Reserve banks and the bankers in a speech before Congress during the Great Depression on June 10, 1932:

Mr. Chairman, we have in this country one of the most **corrupt institutions** the world has ever known. I refer to the Federal Reserve.

From the Atlantic to the Pacific our country has been ravaged and laid waste by the **evil practices** of the **Federal Reserve Board** and the **Federal Reserve banks** and the **interests which control them** ... This is an **era of economic misery**, and for the conditions that caused that misery, the **Federal Reserve Board** and the **Federal Reserve banks are fully liable**.[5] (Emphasis mine)

Smedley Butler
(1881-1940)

Major General Smedly Butler was the most highly decorated Marine in American history at the time of his death. He was the only soldier to be awarded the Brevet Medal and a Medal of Honor for two different actions. He spoke out against military adventurism, and stopped a military coup in America. Butler told a congressional committee in 1934 that a group of wealthy industrialists had approached him to lead a military coup to overthrow Franklin D. Roosevelt's government, allegations that came to be known as the "Business Plot." A long congressional investigation concluded that there was some truth in the allegations, though those involved denied it, and no arrests were ever made.[6]

Concerning the profits that were made from World War I, Butler wrote this in his stunning expose of the money making racket called war:

And let us not forget the **bankers** who **financed** this **great war**. If anyone had the **cream of the profits** it was the bankers. Being partnerships rather than incorporated organizations, they do not have to report to stockholders. And their profits were as secret as they were immense. How the bankers made their millions and their billions I do not know, because those little secrets never become public – even before a Senate investigatory body. (*War is a Racket*, p. 25, emphasis mine)

North American Union

The Council on Foreign Relations studied the concept of a North American Union and issued a 175 page report in May 2005 called, "Task Force Report No. 53." The chairs of the report were John P. Manley, Pedro Aspe and William F. Weld; and the vice chairs are Thomas P. D'Aquino, Andres Rozental and Robert A. Pastor. The conclusion of their study is:

> To that end, the Task Force proposes the creation by 2010 of a North American community to enhance security, prosperity, and opportunity. We propose a community based on the principle affirmed in the March 2005 Joint Statement of the three leaders that "our security and prosperity are mutually dependent and complementary." Its boundaries will be defined by a common external tariff and an outer security perimeter within which the movement of people, products, and capital will be legal, orderly, and safe. Its goal will be to guarantee a free, secure, just, and prosperous North America.[7]

It is unlikely the North American community will be fully formed by 2010, but it will be established in the near future. Other unions (African, Asian, Middle Eastern, Pacific, South American) will be formed before the Tribulation. Once these unions are formed they will then be merged into a World Union. As we noted a world government will be fully established as prophesied by Daniel (7.23). That world government will also have its world economic system in place.

The foundation for the North American Union was laid on March 24, 2005, when representatives from America, Canada and Mexico signed the Security and Prosperity Partnership of North America (SPP).

Conclusion

A world economic system will be created before the Tribulation that will give the conspirators complete control over the people. The economic unions, agreements and organizations are the building bricks of this conspiracy. The Antichrist will inherit that control, and midway through the Tribulation he will force everyone on Earth to take his "mark" to be able to buy or sell.

As noted previously Scripture says there will be a world government established before the Tribulation begins (Daniel 7.23). That world government will have a world economic system in place. The world government will break into 10 divisions, and after that the Antichrist will rise to power (Daniel 7.24). The Tribulation begins after the Antichrist rises to power and signs a covenant with Israel (Isaiah 28.15-18; Daniel 9.27).

According to the biblical sequence of events there will be a world government with a world economic system, it will break into 10 divisions, the Antichrist will rise to power and then he will sign a covenant with Israel marking the start of the Tribulation.

STUDY QUESTIONS

Chapter 16

1. Are numerous billionaires (bankers, financial advisers, industrialists, etc.) conspiring with politicians and bureaucrats to create a world economic system?

2. Will the North American Union be fully established before the Tribulation starts?

3. Will the Asian Union and the African Union also be established before the Tribulation starts?

4. Will all the unions of the world eventually be united into a World Economic Union before the start of the Tribulation?

5. Will a world currency replace all union and national currencies before the start of the Tribulation?

SEVENTEEN

WORLD GOVERNMENT

A world government is not far-fetched. There has been a movement to create a world government for more than a century. The conspirators have created myriad political unions and alliances, private organizations, institutions, foundations, think-tanks and "shadow" organizations to bring into fruition their dream of a world government.

Political unions

The first political union, the Western European Union, was formed in 1948. It was quickly followed by the Council of Europe (1949) and the European Coal and Steel Community in 1951, an industrial coalition of 6 nations (Germany, France, Italy, Netherlands, Belgium and Luxembourg). In 1957, the European Atomic Energy Community and the European Economic Community were created. These three communities, called the European Community, were joined by the United Kingdom, Ireland and Denmark (1973), Greece (1981) and Spain and Portugal (1986). It has grown to 27 nations, with plans to expand. It is currently called the European Union.

There is an intensive effort to create a North American Union, a Central American Union and a South American Union. Once these unions are established, they will merge into a Western Union. Other unions will be created and fully developed prior to the Rapture/Tribulation, and then merged into a World Union to create a world government and economy.

Some other unions are the: Arab League (1945), Organization of American States (1948), Association of Southeast Asian Nations (1967), Pacific Islands Forum (1971), Cooperation Council for the Arab States of the Gulf (1981), South Asian Association for Regional Cooperation (1985), Commonwealth of Independent States (1991), Association of Caribbean States (1994), African Union (2002), Union of South American Nations (2008) and the Union for the Mediterranean (2008).

Public and private organizations

Some of the public organizations that have been and are working for a "New World Order" are the: League of Nations (1920-1946), International Criminal Police Organization (INTERPOL) (1923), United Nations (1945), International Court of Justice (1945), North Atlantic Treaty Organization (1949) and the International Criminal Court (2002).

Conspirators

There are hundreds of foundations, institutes, associations and think-tanks that are involved in the conspiracy to create a "New World Order." The most prominent of these "shadow" organizations are: Knights of Malta (1080), Knights Templar (1118), Freemasons (1314 or 1717), Illuminati Order (1776), Skull and Bones Society (1832), Bohemian Club (1872), Royal Institute for International Affairs (1920), Council on Foreign Relations (1921), Bilderberg Group (1954), Club of Rome (1968), the Trilateral Commission (1973).

Thousands of people in key positions in politics, law enforcement, finance, business, religion, education and the military have been members/attendees of "shadow" organizations. Most have worked to create a "New World Order" while others are ignorant of the end game. The more notable members or attendees of the "shadow" organizations are: **Foreign potentates** – King Juan Carlos I of Spain (B), Queen Elizabeth II (PS), Queen Beatrix of the Netherlands (B), Prince Philip of England (BC, M); **U.S. Presidents** – George Bush (BC, SB), George H.W. Bush (B, BC, CFR, SB, TC), Bill Clinton (B, CFR, M, TC), Ronald Reagan (BC, M), James Carter (CFR, TC), Gerald Ford, Jr. (B, BC, CFR, M), Richard Nixon (BC, CFR), Lyndon Johnson (M), Dwight D. Eisenhower (BC, CFR), Harry Truman (M), Franklin Roosevelt (M); **Vice-Presidents** – Richard Cheney (BC, CFR, PNAC, TC), Al Gore, Jr. (B, BC, TC), Nelson Rockefeller (BC); **Secretaries of State** - Hillary Clinton (B, CFR), Alexander Haig (BC, CFR, KM), Henry Kissinger (B, BC, CFR, TC), Colin Powell (B, BC, CFR, KM); **Governors:** Jeb Bush (BC, CFR, PNAC), Rick Perry (B), Arnold Schwarzenegger (BC); **Senators:** Prescott Bush (CFR, SB), John Kerry (CFR, SB), John McCain, Jr. (B, CFR, M), John Rockefeller IV (B, CFR, TC); **Bankers:** Ben Bernanke (B), Alan Greenspan (BC, CFR, TC), Timothy Geithner (B), Henry Paulson, Jr. (B), Jakob Meyer Rothschild (M); **Billionaires:** David Rockefeller, Sr. (B, BC, CFR, PS, TC), David Rockefeller, Jr. (BC, CFR, M), Edmond de Rothschild (B), Evelyn de Rothshild (B), Guy de Rothschild (B), Lionel Rothschild (B), George Soros (B); **Media:** Tom Brokaw (CFR), William Buckley (B, BC, CFR, SB), Walter Cronkite (BC), Peter Jennings (B), Dan Rather (CFR), Diane Sawyer (CFR); **Preachers:** Joseph Smith, Sr. & Jr. (M), Rick Warren (CFR), Brigham Young (M); **Others:** Zbigniew Brzezinski (BC, CFR, TC), Benjamin Franklin (M), Albert Pike (M), Karl Rove (BC), Adam Weishaupt (I, M). **Key:** Bilderberg (B), Bohemian Club (BC), Club of Rome (CR), Council on Foreign Relations (CFR), Masons (M), Illuminati (I), Knights of Malta (KM), Pilgrims Society (PS), Project for a New American Century (PNAC), Skull and Bones (SB), Trilateral Commission (TC). (An expanded list can be found in Appendix G.)

Confessions of the conspirators

Bill Clinton

We can't be so fixated on our **desire to preserve the rights of the ordinary Americans.**[1] (42nd President of the United States, 1993-2001, emphasis mine)

Hillary Clinton

We get a **lot of advice** from the Council, so this will mean I won't have as far to go **to be told what we should be doing** and **how we should think** about the future. (Secretary of State, Foreign Policy Address at the Council on Foreign Relations, 7.15.2009, emphasis mine)

David Rothschild

David René James de Rothschild was born in New York City in 1942 because his father fled Nazi Germany. He is a prominent European banker and a member of the famous Rothschild banking family of France. He is the son of Guy de Rothschild who passed away in 2007 at the age of 98. David had this to say about his family:

We have had **250 years** or so of **family involvement** in the finance business. We provide advice on **both sides** of the balance sheet, and we do it **globally.**[2] (Emphasis mine)

This is what was said of Rothschild in the same article:

Baron Rothschild shares most people's view that there is a **New World Order**. In his opinion, banks will deleverage and there will be a new form of **global governance.**[2] (Emphasis mine)

The Rothschild family is heavily involved in creating a "New World Order" just as the Rockefeller family is. Their banking motto is: Concordia, Integritas, Industria (Unity, Integrity, Industry). The founder of the Rothschild banking family, Mayer Amschel Bauer (1744-1812), is alleged to have said, "Give me control of a nation's money and I care not who makes her laws." Forbes ranked him the 7th most influential businessman of all time, yet J.P. Morgan #2 and John D. Rockefeller #3 worked for the Rothschild family.

At its height in the mid-19th century the total family worth in today's terms is estimated at least in the many hundreds of billions of dollars, if not in the trillions (Ferguson, Niall, *The House of Rothschild: Money's prophets, 1798-1848*, Volume 1, pp. 481-85). Some conspiriologists believe the net assets of the Rothschild family are well over 500 trillion dollars, and the net assets of the Rockefeller family are about half that.

David Rockefeller

David Rockefeller is the only surviving grandson of John D. Rockefeller, who founded the largest oil empire in the world and the Council on Foreign Relations (CFR). David's father, John D. Rockefeller II, donated the land for the United Nations building. David, former president of the CFR and founder of the Trilateral Commission, the Council of the Americas and the Americas Society, and financial supporter of the Institute for International Economics, is considered by many historians to be an influential "New World Order" player. He freely admits his desire to see a world order established:

Some even believe we (the Rockefeller family) are part of a **secret cabal** working **against the best interests of the United States**, characterizing my family and me as **"internationalists"** and of **conspiring** with others around the world to build a more integrated **global** political and economic structure – **one world**, if you will. If that's the charge, **I stand guilty**, and **I am proud of it**. (*Memoirs*, p. 405, emphasis mine)

This present window of opportunity, during which a truly peaceful and interdependent world order might be built, will not be open for too long. All we need is the right **major crisis** and the nation will accept the **New World Order**. (UN Business Conference, September 1994, emphasis mine)

He allegedly stated at the June 1991 Bilderberg meeting:

We are grateful to The Washington Post, The New York Times, Time Magazine and other great publications whose directors have attended our meetings and respected their promise of discretion for almost forty years. It would have been impossible for us to develop our plan for the world if we had been subjected to the bright lights of publicity during those years. But the world is now more sophisticated and prepared to march towards a **world government**. The **super-national sovereignty** of an intellectual **elite** and **world bankers** is surely preferable to the national auto-determination practiced in past centuries.[3] (Emphasis mine)

After a trip to China in 1973, David Rockefeller praised Mao Tse-tung, the man who butchered over 60 million Chinese:

One is impressed immediately by the sense of national harmony.... Whatever the price of the Chinese Revolution it has obviously succeeded in fostering high morale and community purpose. General social and economic progress is no less impressive.... The enormous social advances of China have benefited greatly from the singleness of ideology and purpose.... The **social experiment** in China under Chairman Mao's leadership is one of the **most important and successful in history**.[4] (Emphasis mine)

Maurice Strong

Maurice Strong, former Under Secretary-General of the United Nations, Chairman of the Earth Council Institute, advisor to the Secretary-General of the United Nations and advisor to the President of the World Bank, has made some interesting comments:

> The time has come when we need to act both globally and locally, and that requires the cooperation of all of us, from individuals to grassroots groups to business, governments and supranational organizations.[5]

> The concept of national sovereignty has been an immutable, indeed sacred, principle of international relations. It is a principle which will yield only slowly and reluctantly to the new imperatives of **global environmental cooperation**. It is simply not feasible for sovereignty to be exercised unilaterally by individual nation states, however powerful. The **global community** must be assured of environmental security.[6] (1992 Earth Summit, emphasis mine)

Statements by the media and historians

Several newspapers and journalists have written and commented about the plan to establish a "New World Order."

Eric Arthur Blair
(1903-1950)

Eric Blair (a.k.a. George Orwell) was a British journalist and novelist. His most famous books – *1984* and *Animal Farm* – were warnings to the people of the world that powerful men were working to create a nightmarish world dictatorship. That warning is summarized in this classic statement from *1984*:

> If you want a picture of this future, imagine a boot stamping on a human face–**forever**. (p. 220, emphasis mine)

Walter Cronkite
(1916-2009)

Walter Cronkite, the CBS anchorman from 1962 to 1981, was considered to be the greatest television anchorman, and the most trusted man in America during his reign at CBS.

> I believe, as Norman Cousins did, that the **first priority of human kind** in this difficult era is to **establish an effective system of world law** that will **assure peace and justice among the peoples of all the world**...

First, **we Americans** are going to have to **yield up some of our sovereignty**.

We need a system of **enforceable world law**, a democratic federal **world government**. **Well join me, I'm glad to sit here at the right hand of Satan.**[7] (Emphasis mine)

H. G. Wells

H. G. Wells (1866-1946), historian and science fiction writer (*War of the Worlds, The Time Machine, The Invisible Man, The Island of Doctor Moreau, The Shape of Things to Come, The First Men in the Moon, When the Sleeper Wakes, etc.*), believed a "New World Order" was inevitable:

Countless people will hate the **New World Order** – and will **die protesting against it**. (*The New World Order*, 1940, emphasis mine)

Statements by past politicians

Some politicians have spoken out and written about the conspiracy to establish a "New World Order." One of them paid the ultimate price for telling the truth.

Barry Goldwater

Barry Goldwater (1909-1998), senator from Arizona (1969-1987) and presidential candidate (1964), spoke out about a conspiracy to gain control of the governments of the world. He said the Council on Foreign Relations (CFR) "is the American branch of a society" that was organized in England (Royal Institute of International Affairs), and it "believes national boundaries should be obliterated and one world rule established" (*With No Apologies*, p. 126).

Concerning the CFR, he said it "is intended to be the vehicle for multinational consolidation of the commercial and banking interests by seizing control of the political government of the United States" (Ibid., p. 293).

In 1979, Senator Goldwater wrote an intriguing paper, "Goldwater Sees Elitist Sentiments Threatening Liberties," in which he said:

I believe that the Council on Foreign Relations and its ancillary **elitist groups** are indifferent to communism. They have **no ideological anchors**. In their pursuit of a **New World Order** they are prepared to deal without prejudice with a communist state, a socialist state, a democratic state, a monarchy, an oligarchy – it's all the same to them.

Their goal is to impose a benign stability on the quarreling family of nations through merger and consolidation. They see the **elimination of national boundaries**, the suppression of racial and ethnic loyalties, as the most expeditious avenue to world peace. They believe economic competition is the root cause of international tension.[8] (Emphasis mine)

Conclusion

The "New World Order" conspirators openly boast of their goal to create a "New World Order." They have been working tirelessly for hundreds of years, and they are confident that they will be able to establish their satanic dictatorship over the peoples of the world within a decade or so.

The idea that thousands of people have been working to create a "New World Order" for centuries is biblical. The Bible states that just before Jesus Christ returns a world government, economy and religion will be in place. This world order must have people working publicly and secretly to form it.

Satan is the prince of this world (John 12.31; 14.30; 16.11; 2 Corinthians 4.4), who deceives the entire world (Revelation 20.3). The devil and the fallen angels are the "powers that be" – "*the principalities*," "*the powers*," "*the world-rulers of this darkness*," "*the spiritual hosts of wickedness in the heavenly places*" (Ephesians 6.12) – behind this vast, right/left-wing conspiracy. Every nation has powerful fallen angels who rule over it (Daniel 10.20) and many politicians, bureaucrats, businessmen, preachers, educators, etc. are under their influence (2 Corinthians 11.13-15).

We must never lose sight of the fact that Jehovah is in control of the entire universe, including Earth. He puts rulers in positions of power and removes them (Daniel 4.17, 25, 32; 5.21). He also causes them to fulfill His will:

For God did put in their hearts to do his mind, and to come to one mind, and to give their kingdom unto the beast, until the words of God should be accomplished. (Revelation 17.17)

STUDY QUESTIONS

Chapter 17

1. Are there myriad proofs that thousands of men and women are working together to create a "New World Order"?

2. Who is guiding the "New World Order" conspirators?

3. Do the conspirators work with communists, fascists, socialists, liberals and conservatives alike?

4. Have some of the conspirators admitted they want a world government?

5. Are Christians commanded to oppose the efforts to create a "New World Order" in a legal and non-violent manner?

6. Will millions of Christians be persecuted and martyred by the "New World Order" gangsters before the Rapture?

7. Have millions of Christians been persecuted and martyred by dozens of tyrannical governments around the world during the last 1900 years?

8. How can Christians prepare for the persecution they will suffer before the Rapture and the start of the Tribulation?

EIGHTEEN

BIG BROTHER

Big Brother is a term that was coined by Eric Blair (a.k.a. George Orwell) in his book *1984*. It referred to the government. Most people understand that Big Brother refers to government, but it goes beyond that. Today we know that virtually all the governments in the world are controlled by powerful families that have been controlling the major powers of the world for hundreds of years. The leading families that have ruled and are ruling the world are – Bush, DuPont, Forbes, Kennedy, Rockefeller, Rothschild, Sassoon, Schiff, Tudor, Vanderbilt, Warburg and the House of Witten-Saxe-Coburg-Gotha-Windsor. (An expanded list can be found in Appendix G.)

The powerful families of the past and present who rule the world have also used myriad organizations and corporations to guide and direct politicians and bureaucrats to further their goals. These families, and their corporations and organizations have been pressuring the governments of the Western nations for several decades to impose tyrannical laws and technology on their citizens. Politicians and bureaucrats are taking most rights and freedoms away from the people in the name of security. Soldiers are performing police duties in most countries, including America. The nightmare scenario depicted by Eric Blair in his masterpiece novel *1984* is unfolding before our very eyes.

Big Brother is working steadily toward his goal of imposing an overt dictatorship upon every nation through a World Government. Before his goal can be achieved he must coerce every government to establish a dictatorship over its people. The politicians and bureaucrats of most nations are passing laws and regulations that will eventually strip a citizen of all rights, freedoms and privacy.

Along with these tyrannical laws and regulations, technology is being developed to insure Big Brother will know everything each citizen does, says, hears and even thinks. Fantastic surveillance technology has already been developed, and it is being used to track where people go, what they do, what they see and hear, and what they say. Big Brother's surveillance web is growing larger every day, and few are able to keep from being caught in it.

Surveillance

Big Brother is using a variety of surveillance technologies to keep watch of you. He watches you from space, from the air and from the ground. Some of the surveillance tools that Big Brother is currently using are: satellites, blimps, helicopters, planes, unmanned aerial vehicles (UAVs), mini-UAVs, Closed-

226

circuit television systems (CCTV) – road cameras, sidewalk cameras, school cameras, office cameras, retail store cameras, cable boxes and cop cams. [1-12]

Global Positioning System (GPS) tracking of vehicles is also becoming a standard technology for trucking, taxi, limousine, courier and delivery companies. Some automobile manufacturers are installing GPS technology in their passenger vehicles. It will only be a matter of time before every vehicle, motorcycle, boat, ship and airplane will have a GPS transponder in it.

Tracking people with GPS is becoming commonplace. Parents can buy shoes and backpacks equipped with it.[13] The latest GPS technology is tracking people via their cell phones. Google is offering a service that enables those who pay for the service to track others using the service.[14]

Eavesdropping

Big Brother is not only watching everything you do and everyplace you go he is also listening to everything you listen to and everything you say. He is listening to you through the OnStar[15] service, with roving cellphone eavesdropping,[16] and through your landline telephone.[17]

Carnivore & NarusInsight

Carnivore was a system implemented by the Federal Bureau of Investigation during the Clinton administration designed to monitor email and electronic communications. In 2001 it was replaced with improved commercial software such as NarusInsight.[18-19]

Big Brother watches everything everyone does on the Internet. He reads all emails and tracks every website you visit. Watch where you go!

ECHELON

ECHELON is a signals intelligence (SIGINT) network operated for the United States, United Kingdom, Canada, Australia and New Zealand. The AUSCANNZUKUS security agreement was reportedly created to monitor the military and diplomatic communications of the Soviet Union and its Eastern Bloc allies during the Cold War in the early 1960s. Yet since the end of the Cold War it is also being used to search for hints of terrorist plots, the plans of drug dealers, and political and diplomatic intelligence.[20-22]

"In 1975, a congressional investigation revealed that the NSA had been intercepting, without warrants, international communications for more than 20 years at the behest of the CIA and other agencies. The spy campaign, code-named 'Shamrock,' led to the Foreign Intelligence Surveillance Act (FISA), which was designed to protect Americans from illegal eavesdropping."[23-24]

Spying on the people

COINTELPRO

COINTELPRO (an acronym for Counter Intelligence Program) was a series of covert, and often illegal, projects conducted by the Federal Bureau of Investigation (FBI) aimed at investigating and disrupting dissident political organizations within America. The FBI has used covert operations from its inception, however formal COINTELPRO operations took place between 1956 and 1971. The FBI's stated motivation at the time was "protecting national security, preventing violence, and maintaining the existing social and political order." [25-26]

InfraGard

InfraGard is a FBI Public-private partnership that began in the Cleveland, Ohio, Field Office in 1996. The program expanded, and in 1998 the FBI assigned national program responsibility for InfraGard to the former National Infrastructure Protection Center (NIPC) directed by R. Adm. James B. Plehal and to the FBI's Cyber Division in 2003.

InfraGard Alliances support FBI priorities in the areas of counterterrorism, foreign counterintelligence, and cybercrime. According to Matthew Rothschild, InfraGard had 23,000 members in 86 chapters around America in 2008. As of December of 2009 it has 32,000 members from all walks of life. He even alleges that the members have the authority during martial law to shoot and kill anyone they deem to be an enemy of the state. [27]

Citizen snitches

As part of the country's war against terrorism, the Bush administration sought to recruit a million letter carriers, utility workers and others whose jobs allow them access to private homes into a contingent of organized government informants. The Terrorism Information and Prevention System (Operation TIPS), a national reporting pilot program, was scheduled to start in August of 2002 in 10 cities, with 1 million informants or nearly 4 percent of Americans initially participating in the program. [28-35]

The program was never implemented, but some local programs of the similar nature have sprung up around the country.

Information gathering

Several thousand law enforcement agencies are creating the foundation of a domestic intelligence system through computer networks that analyze vast amounts of police information to fight crime and uncover terror plots. The Information Awareness Office, formed in 2002 by DARPA, created the "Total

Information Awareness Program" (TIA). The name was changed to "Terrorist Information Awareness Program" and the IAO was defunded by Congress. Yet its most controversial program "TIA" lives on.[36-37]

The Multistate Anti-Terrorism Information Exchange Program, also known by the acronym "MATRIX" was created to analyze government and commercial databases to find associations between suspects or new suspects.[38]

Mark of the Beast technology

We have seen the development of the mark of the Beast technology for the last 58 years. A patent for the universal product code technology was issued in 1952, and it was first used in 1974. The next generation of the mark of the Beast technology was the RFID (radio frequency ID) which was patented in 1973 and first used in the 1990s.

RFID technology

RFID technology has many uses. It can be used to identify products, livestock, fish, birds, pets and people. In the near future it may replace all forms of identification, credit cards, checks and cash.

In July of 2004, Mexico's attorney general had a RFID microchip inserted under the skin of his arm to give him access to a new crime database and also enable him to be traced if he is ever abducted. Attorney General Rafael Macedo said a number of his staff (over 160) had also been fitted with chips which will give them exclusive and secure access to a national computerized database for crime investigators.[39]

The VIP Baja Beach Club in Barcelona, Spain, is chipping its customers. Customers who have a chip implanted do not have to show identification to enter, and all their purchases are made by scanning the chips.[40]

America's Department of Homeland Security is seeking next-generation real ID, and privacy advocates are concerned. The RFID chip in drivers' licenses would allow agents to compile attendance lists at freedom rallies by reading the chips inside wallets and purses by walking through the crowd.[41]

On the "60 Minutes" broadcast of February 10, 2002, Andy Rooney said, "We need some system for permanently identifying safe people. Most of us are never going to blow anything up and there's got to be something better than one of these photo IDs. I wouldn't mind having something planted permanently in my arm that would identify me."

GPS tracking chips

Implantable computer chips with Global Positioning Satellite (GPS) tracking technology will become commonplace and accepted by most people in the near future. They are being marketed today by the Xega Company has created an "injectable chip" the size and shape of a rice kernel.[42]

All 31,000 Metropolitan police officers in London have been "microchipped" so their movements can be monitored. The new technology, the Automated Personal Location System (APLS), replaced the unreliable Airwave radio system.[43]

Electronic ID bracelets

Lamperd Less Lethal, Inc., a firearm training system company, is peddling its Electronic ID Bracelet to the government and airlines. The security bracelet would be worn by all airline passengers replacing the boarding pass. It would contain personal information about the traveler and enable airline employees to monitor the whereabouts of each passenger. In case of an incident the stewards could shock the wearer on command, completely immobilizing him for several minutes.[44]

It is very possible that before the Tribulation starts governments around the world may force all citizens to wear shock bracelets. It would make it easy for law enforcement officers to subdue criminals or citizens who resist arrest.

Dentention centers

The United States government has considered building large dentention centers around the country. This program first came to public view in 1984 with the leaking of the Rex 84 exercise.[45]

About 20 years later the Bush Administration decided to build detention centers to hold "refugees" and "enemies of the state." Those internment centers were built by Kellog Brown and Root (KBR), a subsidiary of Haliburton.[46] The National Guard will be used to man those camps along with other military and police forces. It posted this job listing on its website.[47-48]

Some conspiriologists believe these detention centers could become concentration camps where political dissenters will be taken. We know that during the Tribulation millions of people around the world will be held in concentration camps, and those who refuse to worship the Antichrist, and take his mark will be executed (Revelation 13.15-17).

Guillotine

Some prophecy scholars think execution by guillotine will become the standard method of execution before the Tribulation starts. It has been the preferred method of execution in France since the French Revolution. The coming world government will also be godless so it is possible beheading will become commonplace throughout the world prior to the Tribulation.

As explained in Chapter 5 the Antichrist will force everyone to take his "*mark*" to be able to buy or sell. Those who refuse the "*mark*" will be beheaded (Revelation 20.4). Since 1996 there has been a provision for execution by guillotine in America.[49] It is possible that other countries may adopt this form of execution before the Tribulation. It is even possible that in some Western nations execution by guillotine may be carried out before the Rapture and the Tribulation against Christians who are considered a threat to the state (Mark 13.12).

Conclusion

There are numerous technologies in use that will be used by the Antichrist to keep track of everyone on Earth during his reign of terror. One of these technologies is the implantable computer chip that is currently used to identify pets and livestock. It has also found its way into people. The goal of the "New World Order Gang" is to implant a computer chip in everyone on Earth to replace all forms of identification, credit and cash. These "chips" will become commonplace before the start of the Tribulation giving governments incredible influence over the lives of the people. Future "chip" technology may be the "mark" of the Beast or a new technology may be developed. Whatever technology the Beast uses he will force everyone on Earth to take his "mark" to be able to buy and sell (Revelation 13.16-17).

Big Brother (a.k.a. "New World Order Gang") wants to rule over everyone on Earth. These genocidal megalomaniacs want to have absolute control over you. They want to be able to tell you where you can live, work and where you can travel. They also want to dictate who you marry and how many children you can have. They want to limit your use of the world's natural resources, which they claim is theirs. They even want to listen to and watch everything you say and do in public, and in the privacy of your own domicile. They are peeping perverts. There is much more that they want to do to you and your family but it cannot be put in print.

Eric Blair's book *1984* is a good description of the kind of world Big Brother wants to create. Yet the world that he will eventually impose on the peoples of the world will be even more tyrannical, and far more evil than the one that Blair predicted. The advancement of technology will give Big Brother far greater power and control of the people than has been depicted in television shows that envision a bleak existence in the future such as *Max Headroom* and *The Prisoner*. The village that the "*Prisoner*" was trapped in is the kind of society that Big Brother wants to create in every nation on Earth.

Books and movies that depict a tyrannical Big Brother style society are – *Brave New World, Brave New World Revisited, Comma, Commonwealth Saga, Demolition Man, Escape from LA, Fahrenheit 451, The Iron Heel, It Can't Happen Here, Logan's Run, Men Like Gods, The Running Man, A Scanner Darkly, The Secret of the League, The Sleeper Awakes, Ultraviolet, V for Vendetta, Vineland* and *We*. Big Brother's ultimate goal is to record every second of everyone's life from birth to death as depicted in the movie, *The Truman Show*.

STUDY QUESTIONS

Chapter 18

1. Has Big Brother been watching you for many years?

2. Is Big Brother watching you from space and from the air?

3. Is Big Brother watching everywhere you go on the Internet?

4. Does Big Brother know everything you watch if you have cable or satellite television service?

5. Does Big Brother keep track of where you go with spy cameras scattered all over the streets?

6. Does Big Brother want to put a GPS transponder in every vehicle so he can keep track of where everyone goes?

7. Does Big Brother plan to chip people with GPS technology so he can know where everyone goes?

8. Does Big Brother plan to watch what people do in the privacy of their own homes with cameras built into cable boxes?

9. Is Big Brother listening to everything you say on the telephone?

10. Has Big Brother been collecting all kinds of data about everyone he can for decades?

11. Does Big Brother plan to put Christians, political dissidents and patriots in detention centers?

12. Is it possible, that before the Rapture and the Tribulation, Big Brother will execute Christians who are considered enemies of the state?
13. Is it possible that Christians who are considered to be enemies of the state will be executed by guillotine?

14. Should Christians oppose Big Brother in a legal and non-violent manner?

15. Does the "New World Order" Gang have the technology to impose a dictatorship over every country and person on the planet?

16. Are the conspirators slowly but surely laying their web of technology to keep track of the whereabouts of everyone on Earth, and what everybody on Earth buys and sells?

17. Will a future world currency be replaced by a computer chip?

18. Will most people and some Christians accept a computer chip implanted in their body before the Tribulation to replace all forms of currencies, checks, credit cards and identification?

19. Will the mark of the Beast technology be in use before the Rapture and the start of the Tribulation?

20. Will mark of the Beast technology be so ubiquitous before the Rapture and start of the Tribulation that most non-believers and many believers will use it without knowing what it is?

21. Are you using mark of the Beast technology today?

CONCLUSION

Having seen the "What?" we can ask:

When is the "When?"

When...

we see the destruction of Russia, Islam and Egypt. (Ezekiel 38.8, 11, 14; Ezekiel 38.1-39.16; 30.1-5)

When...

we see the first stage of the conversion of Israel and also Gentiles. (Ezekiel 39.7)

When…

we see the ancient city of Babylon begin to be rebuilt. (Zechariah 5.5-11)

When...

we see a world church and the rise of the False Prophet. (Rev. 17.1-5, 18; 13.11-17)

When…

**we see a world economic system in place.
(Revelation 13.15-17)**

When…

we see a world government.
(Daniel 7.23)

When…

we see the world government break into 10 divisions. (Daniel 7.24)

When…

**we see the rebuilding of the Temple.
(Revelation 11.1-2; 2 Thessalonians 2.4)**

When…

**we see an amazing man rise out of obscurity
and begin to solve the world's problems.
(Daniel 7.20, 24; 8.9; Revelation 13.1-10)**

When…

we see the rumblings of the *"overflowing scourge."* (Joel 2.1-11; Isaiah 28.15)

When…

we see the people of the world say,
"Peace and safety!" **(1 Thessalonians 5.3)**

When…

**we see the prophet Elijah appear in
Jerusalem. (Malachi 4.5)**

When…

we see indications of the impending covenant between Israel and the Antichrist. (Isaiah 28.15; Daniel 9.27)

When

we see *"signs in the sun and moon and stars; and upon the earth distress of nations, in perplexity for the roaring of the sea and the billows; men fainting for fear, and for expectation of the things which are coming on the world: for the powers of the heavens shall be shaken."* **(Luke 21.25-26)**

And when...

those signs begin to take place, the day star will arise in your heart, giving you the assurance that the Lord will appear, and

Then *you* will *know* WHEN!

For this we say unto you by the word of the Lord, that we that are alive, that are left unto the coming of the Lord, shall in no wise precede them that are fallen asleep. For the Lord himself shall descend from heaven, with a shout, with the voice of the archangel, and with the trump of God: and the dead in Christ shall rise first; then we that are alive, that are left, shall together with them be caught up in the clouds, to meet the Lord in the air: and so shall we ever be with the Lord. Wherefore comfort one another with these words. (1 Thessalonians 4.15-18)

Behold, I tell you a mystery: We all shall not sleep, but we shall all be changed, in a moment, in the twinkling of an eye, at the last trump: for the trumpet shall sound, and the dead shall be raised incorruptible, and we shall be changed. For this corruptible must put on incorruption, and this mortal must put on immortality. (1 Corinthians 15.51-53)

AFTERWORD

If there is no gap between the Rapture and the Tribulation as explained in Chapter 10, then the Pre-Tribulation Rapture cannot take place at *any moment*. More than a dozen major prophecies must be fulfilled before the start of the Tribulation and thusly before the Rapture. All students of Bible prophecy should learn what those prophecies (*warning signs*) are, and then carefully "*watch*" for them to be fulfilled.

No one can calculate the exact year, month or day of the Rapture ahead of time. Yet as we "*watch*" the fulfillment of the prophecies that must be fulfilled before the Rapture/Tribulation we will be able to determine how close we are to that "*blessed hope*" (Titus 2.13).

It is important to know what the major Bible prophecies are that must be fulfilled prior to the Rapture/Tribulation. By knowing what those prophecies are we will be able to explain to the lost that the Bible is the Word of God, and that the prophecies concerning the "*last days*" are being fulfilled. Fulfillment of Bible prophecy is one of the most powerful proofs that the Bible is the Word of God.

Knowing Bible prophecy is also important to edify, encourage and stimulate fellow Christians "*unto love and good works*" (Hebrews 10.24). We should do this all the more as "*we see the day drawing nigh*" (Hebrews 10.25). The "*day*" that is "*drawing nigh*" is the day of the Rapture.

Study Appendix A carefully, and then "*watch*" for the fulfillment of those *warning signs*. As you see them be fulfilled share the importance of those prophecies with fellow believers. Also share them with those who are not saved, and pray that they will come to a saving knowledge of Jesus Christ.

All Christians are ambassadors of Jesus Christ:

We are ambassadors therefore on behalf of Christ, as though God were entreating by us: we beseech you on behalf of Christ, be ye reconciled to God. (2 Corinthians 5.20)

And we are commanded to know how to share the gospel:

And having shod your feet with the preparation of the gospel of peace. (Ephesians 6.15)

But sanctify in your hearts Christ as Lord: being ready always to give answer to every man that asketh you a reason concerning the hope that is in you, yet with meekness and fear. (1 Peter 3.15)

A good way to learn how to share the gospel is to memorize the basic salvation verses given in Appendix B. Then find a brother at the church you attend who knows how to share the gospel, and go out with him to share it. Some churches have classes to teach members how to share the gospel and some have evangelistic programs. Every Christian should take advantage of those classes and programs.

As noted in the Preface, all Christians are commanded to resist evil and expose the evil deeds of the wicked, including the coming New World Order:

*Be sober, be watchful: your adversary the devil, as a roaring lion, walketh about, seeking whom he may devour, whom **withstand steadfast** in your faith, knowing that the same sufferings are accomplished in your brethren who are in the world.* (1 Peter 5.8-9)

*And have no fellowship with the unfruitful works of darkness, but rather even **reprove them**; for the things which are done by them in secret it is a shame even to speak of. But all things when they are **reproved** are made manifest by the light: for everything that is made manifest is light.* (Ephesians 5.11-13)

*Put on the whole armor of God, that ye may be able to **stand against the wiles of the devil**.* (Ephesians 6.11)

He that saith unto the wicked, Thou art righteous;
Peoples shall curse him, nations shall abhor him:
*But to them that **rebuke** him shall be delight,*
And a good blessing shall come upon them. (Proverbs 24.24-25)

They that forsake the law praise the wicked;
*But such as **keep the law contend** with them.* (Proverbs 28.4)

*For consider him that hath endured such gainsaying of sinners against himself, that ye wax not weary, fainting in your souls. Ye have not yet resisted unto blood, **striving against sin**.* (Hebrews 12.3-4)

As a troubled fountain, and a corrupted spring,
*So is a righteous man that **giveth way before the wicked**.* (Proverbs 25.26)
(Emphasis mine)

All Christians are commanded to **withstand steadfast against** (resist) the **devil, reprove the wicked** and **their evil deeds, stand against the wiles** (schemes) **of the devil, keep the Law** (of YHWH) **to contend with them, strive against sin** and **not give way before the wicked**. If you are not actively doing these things on a continual basis you are not fully serving the Lord.

Now that you know what you should do, do it and tell others. Share this book and the information in it with as many people as you can. Buy extra copies, and give them to those you love.

R. William Keller
December 2009

GLOSSARY

Angels are created beings who serve God (Daniel 7.10; Hebrews 12.22; Jude 14; Revelation 5.11) and Christians (Hebrews 1.14). One third of them joined Satan in his rebellion (Revelation 12.4). They are called "fallen angels."

Antichrist – He will be the ruler of a Middle Eastern nation who will rise to power prior to the Rapture (Daniel 7.20, 24; 8.9; Revelation 6.1-2), and be identified as the Antichrist before the Rapture (2 Thessalonians 2.1-3). After the Rapture, he will assume control of the world, but will be under the power of the World Church (Rev. 17.3). At the mid-point of the seven-year Tribulation, he will take total control of the world government by the power of Satan (Rev. 13.4), and rule with absolute authority for 42 months (Rev. 13.5). He will blaspheme God (Daniel 7.25; Rev. 13.5-6), and persecute and kill those who are saved after the Rapture (Daniel 7.21, 25; Rev. 13.7).

Any Moment is a term that means Jesus Christ can return to Rapture the Church at any time. There are no *warning signs* or events that must take place first. The idea is not biblical.

Apostasy – It is the *"falling away"* of the Church, from the faith and biblical doctrines, to a false faith and to false doctrines (2 Thessalonians 2.3; 2 Timothy 4.3-4). It started at the end of the 19th century, and will continue until the Rapture.

Apostles – They were the eleven disciples (Judas Iscariot not included), Matthias (Luke 1.26) and Paul, that Jesus chose to preach the gospel, make disciples of all nations (Matthew 28.19-20; Acts 1.8) and build His Church (Ephesians 4.11-13).

Beast – He is the Antichrist. This future world ruler is also called the *"man of sin"* and the *"son of destruction"* (2 Thessalonians 2.3), among other names.

Bible – It is the infallible, holy word of God. It contains all the information that every believer needs to live his life for the Lord Jesus Christ (2 Timothy 3.16). It contains hundreds of prophecies that have been fulfilled in a literal manner, and many more which will be fulfilled prior to the Rapture. They are *warning signs* that all Christians must "look" for to know how near the Rapture is.

Christ – He is the Messiah. Christ is the English word for the Hebrew word Messiah. The Messiah is the one prophesied to first die for mankind, and secondly to rule mankind. Jesus of Nazareth fulfilled all of the prophecies of the First Coming of the Messiah. He is called Christ throughout the New Testament.

Christians are true believers in Jesus Christ. Not everyone who calls himself a Christian is truly *"born anew"* (John 3.3). Jesus said that on judgment day some people, who thought they were saved and serving Him, will be turned away into Hell (Matthew 7.21-23).

Church – It is the body of the Lord Jesus Christ, which consists of all true believers in Christ (1 Corinthians 12.27; Ephesians 4.12).

Day of Christ – It is the same as the Day of the Lord. It is a period of time that begins with the Rapture/Tribulation and ends at the Glorious Appearing.

Day Star – It is the assurance that God will give to diligent students of Bible prophecy that the Rapture is about to occur just before it takes place (2 Peter 1.19).

Devil – He is also known as Satan (see **Satan**).

Disciples (the Twelve) – They were the 12 men that Jesus chose to train (Luke 6.14-16) so they could build His Church after His ascension (Ephesians 4.11-13). They became the apostles, except for Judas Iscariot, who betrayed Jesus and committed suicide. Paul was chosen by Jesus (Acts 9.1-16) to replace him as the twelfth apostle. In our opinion, Matthias (Acts 1.26) was a temporary substitution until Paul was called.

End Times – It is an indeterminate period of time that began with the *"falling away"* (apostasy) of the Church from the faith. It will end with the Second Coming of Jesus Christ. We are living in the "end times."

Eschatologian is a person who studies eschatology and writes books or essays on it.

Eschatology is the study of the "last things" in Bible prophecy (the "end times").

Fallen Angels are the angels that joined the devil in his rebellion. A third of the angels followed the devil (Revelation 12.4), and became the *"principalities,"* the *"powers,"* the *"world-rulers of this darkness,"* and the *"spiritual hosts of wickedness in the heavenly places"* (Ephesians 6.12) that rule the world with the devil.

False Prophet – He will be the religious leader who heads the World Church, enforcing the dictates of Antichrist (Revelation 13.11-18).

Futurist – A person who believes that the prophecies of the Rapture, Tribulation and Second Coming of Christ would be fulfilled after the Bible was completed (around 100 AD). They began to be fulfilled in the 19th century with the apostasy of the Church, and then with the world wars, birth of the nation of Israel, etc.

Gap – It is a period of indeterminate time between the Rapture and the start of the Tribulation. The idea is not biblical.

Gospel – It is the "good news" that Jesus Christ, the Son of God, died to save mankind.

Great White Throne Judgment – It is the final judgment of the unsaved at the conclusion of the Millennial Kingdom (Revelation 20.11-15). They will give an account of every sin they committed in deed (Proverbs 24.12; Ecclesiastes 11.9; Rev. 20.12-13), in word (Matthew 12.36-37), in thought (Psalm 94.11; Proverbs 24.9; Matthew 15.19) and in motive (Proverbs 24.12; Romans 2.16). The unsaved are given a specific level of punishment for their sins, and then cast into the Lake of Fire where they will spend all eternity.

Hell is the place, in the heart of the Earth (Matthew 12.40), where people go who die in their sins (Luke 19.16-31). They are punished with fire, brimstone, burning coals (Psalm 11.6; 140.10) and unquenchable thirst (Luke 16.24), while they wait to be judged at the Great White Throne Judgment (Revelation 20.13-14). The Greek word for Hell is Hades. Some English translations translate the Greek word *Gehenna* as "hell." *Gehenna* is a reference to the Lake of Fire (Matthew 18.9).

Holy Spirit – He is the Third Person of the Trinity. He literally indwells the body of every believer in Jesus Christ. He is a person, not a force.

Imminence is a doctrine that teaches Jesus Christ could have returned to rapture the Church at *any moment* since Pentecost; therefore, there are no *warning signs* or events that must take place before the Rapture.

Jehovah is the proper name of God. It is the English transliteration of the Hebrew name Yahweh. It is used in the American Standard Version that is quoted in this book.

Jesus Christ is God the Son, the Second Person of the Trinity, who died to redeem mankind (Romans 3.24; 5.8). He rose from the tomb after three days (1 Corinthians 15.4), and ascended to Heaven (Acts 1.9; Mark 16.19) where He rules the universe with God the Father and God the Holy Spirit. He will return in the future to rapture the Church (1 Thessalonians 4.16-17); then seven years later, He will return to judge the wicked and establish His Millennial Kingdom (Matthew 25.31-46).

Lake of Fire – It is the final abode of Satan and the fallen angels (Matthew 25.41; Revelation 20.10). It is also the final abode of everyone who dies in their sins without trusting in Jesus Christ for salvation (Rev. 20.11-15). Everyone who is cast into that place of punishment (Proverbs 10.16; Matthew 25.46) has no hope of parole, pardon or escape.

Last Days – See **End Times.**

Mark of the Beast – It is a mark, of some kind, that the Antichrist will force everyone on Earth to take, to be able to buy, or sell, or receive government benefits.

Messiah – See **Christ.**

Millennial Kingdom – Also known as the Millennium, it is a period of time that begins with the Second Coming of Jesus Christ, and ends after 1000 years (Revelation 20.1-10). The major passages describing that age are – Isaiah 4.1-6; 11.6-10; 25.6-7; 60.1-9; 61.3-11; 62.1-9; 65.17-25; 66.22-24; Jeremiah 23.3-8; 30.18-22; 33.6-18; Ezekiel 40-48; Joel 3.18-21; Micah 4.1-8; Zephaniah 3.9-13; Zechariah 14.9-11, 16-21).

Millennialism is a teaching that there will be a literal kingdom on Earth in which Jesus Christ will reign for 1000 years.

Amillennialism teaches there is no literal Millennial Kingdom. Jesus Christ will return, some time in the future, with no *warning signs* to alert us of His return. It is a false teaching that was taught by heretics in the second and third centuries AD – Clement of Alexandria, Caius, Origen and Dionysius. All but Caius were heretics. It was later popularized by Augustine early in the 5th century. Augustine was a faithful Roman Catholic priest who held to all of the false doctrines of the church, including the damnable doctrine of Purgatory.

Postmillennialism teaches that Christians will create a Golden Age, and once their Utopian Paradise is established, Jesus Christ will return.

Premillennialism teaches Jesus Christ will physically return to Earth before the Millennial Kingdom is established. The Lord is the one who establishes it when He returns.

New Testament – It is the second section of the Bible that was written between 45 to 95 AD, by the apostles Matthew, John, Paul and Peter, and also by Luke, Mark and James.

Old Testament – The first section of the Christian Bible was written by many men between 2000 BC and about 430 BC.

Olivet Discourse – It is the private briefing on future events that Jesus gave His disciples shortly before His arrest. It is recorded in Matthew 24-25, Mark 13 and Luke 21.

Pentecost is the day that the Church began (Acts 2.1). On that day, 120 believers in Jesus Christ gathered to pray (Acts 1.12-15), and the Holy Spirit came and took up residence inside of them (Acts 2.1-4). The disciples then went out and preached the Gospel (Acts 2.5-13). Peter gave the concluding sermon on this day (Acts 2.14-40), and about 3000 people were saved (Acts 2.41).

Preterism, Full is the belief that all prophecy in the Bible hitherto unfulfilled was fulfilled in 70 AD. It teaches that Jesus Christ physically returned at that time (in the air), and that He will never return to Earth again. The Great White Throne Judgment took place at that time. There is no Millennial Kingdom, and no more divine intervention on Earth. Mankind will continue to live on a sin-polluted planet until the sun explodes and destroys it.

Preterism, Partial teaches that all Bible prophecies were fulfilled in 70 AD, except for the physical return of Jesus Christ. He will return in the future to judge the righteous and the wicked. There will be no Millennial Kingdom.

Rapture – It is the resurrection and "catching away" of dead believers in Jesus Christ, and the transformation of living believers' mortal bodies to immortal ones, and the "catching away" of them to meet the Lord in the air (1 Corinthians 15.51-53; 1 Thessalonians 4.16-17). It takes place on the day that the Tribulation starts.

Pre-Tribulation Rapture – Jesus Christ will rapture the Church prior to the start of the Tribulation.

Mid-Tribulation Rapture – Jesus Christ will rapture the Church at the mid-point of the Tribulation.

Pre-Wrath Rapture – Jesus Christ will rapture the Church near the end of the Tribulation, just before the pouring out of the wrath of God through the seven bowl plagues (Revelation 16.1).

Post-Tribulation Rapture – Jesus Christ will rapture the Church at the end of the Tribulation, just as He returns.

Resurrection – There are two general resurrections. The first resurrection is divided into four parts. The resurrection of Jesus and a select number of Old Testament saints (Matthew 27.52-53) was the first part. The second part is the resurrection of all believers of the Church Age (1 Thessalonians 4.15-17). The third part is the resurrection of the two witnesses (Revelation 11.11-12). The final part of the first resurrection is that of believers who are martyred during the Tribulation and the Old Testament saints (Rev. 20.4).

The second resurrection, of the unsaved, takes place at the end of the Millennial Kingdom (Rev. 20.5). The unsaved are resurrected, judged, found guilty and cast into the Lake of Fire where they will spend all eternity with no hope of parole, pardon or escape (Rev. 20.11-15).

Satan, the highest-ranking angel, led a rebellion of angels, and was expelled from Heaven, taking one-third of them with him (Revelation 12.4). He is the ruler (John 12.31; 14.30; 16.11; 1 John 5.19) and the god of this world (2 Corinthians 4.4). He is the leader of all the forces of darkness (Ephesians 6.12), and he is the "prince of the power of the air" (Ephesians 2.2).

Second Coming – It is the physical return of Jesus Christ to Earth to judge the wicked and reward the righteous (Matthew 25.31-46; Revelation 19.11-21). He will then establish the Millennial Kingdom. It is also referred to as the Second Advent and the Glorious Appearing.

Signs – See **Warning Signs.**

Tribulation – It is a seven-year period of time during which God pours out His wrath on the world. It is the 70th week of Daniel (9.24-27). It is described in chapters 6-19 of Revelation, the Olivet Discourse and many other passages in the Bible.

Trinity – This is another word for the Godhead, which consists of God the Father, God the Son and God the Holy Spirit. Each is fully God and equal to each other in all ways. Each is omnipotent (all powerful), omniscient (all-knowing), and omnipresent (present everywhere). Together, They created and rule the universe.

Warning Signs are past events that have fulfilled Bible prophesy. They are also prophecies of future events that will be fulfilled before the start of the Tribulation, alerting Christians to the nearness of the Rapture.

World Church – Prior to the start of the Tribulation, a world religion will be established. All of the religions of the world will be part of this false church. When the Tribulation starts, it will have total control over all the churches on Earth. The churches that refuse to be part of the false church will be shut down. It will also control the Antichrist for the first 42 months of the Tribulation (Revelation 17.1-7).

World Economy – A world economic system will be established before the Tribulation starts. During the Tribulation, the Antichrist will use this economic system to force everyone on earth to worship him and take his mark (Revelation 13.15-17).

World Government – Before the Tribulation starts, a super-government will be established that will have control over all the governments of the world (Daniel 7.23). Sometime after this world government is established it will divide into a coalition of ten kingdoms which will then rule all the nations of the world (Daniel 7.23; Revelation 17.12).

APPENDIX A

RAPTURE WARNING SIGNS

The Scriptures clearly teach us that numerous *warning signs* will be fulfilled before the Rapture/Tribulation starts. Several *warning signs* have already been fulfilled, and others are being fulfilled at this time. Below are the past, present and future *warning signs* of the Rapture/Tribulation:

Warning signs that have been fulfilled

1-The Balfour Declaration, 1917 (Zephaniah 2.1a)
2-The Return of the Jews to the Holy Land (Ezekiel 37.1-14; Zeph. 2.1-2)
3-The two World Wars – birth pains (Matthew 24.6-8)
4-Founding of the United Nations, 1945 (Luke 21.29-32)
5-Israel becomes a nation, 1948 (Matthew 24.34)
6-Capture of Jerusalem, 1967, end of *"times of the Gentiles"* (Luke 21.24)
7-Gaza abandoned by Israel in 2005 (Zephaniah 2.4).

Warning signs that are being fulfilled

1-The *"falling away"* (2 Thessalonians 2.3; 2 Timothy 4.3-4)
2-Increase in travel and knowledge (Daniel 12.4)
3-Rise of anti-Semitism (Psalm 83)
4-Mark of the Beast technology (Revelation 13.15-18).
5-Israel dwelling securely (*betach*) (Ezekiel 38.8, 11, 14).

Warning signs yet to be fulfilled

1-Destruction of Russia, Islam and Egypt (Ezekiel 38.1-39.16; 30.1-5)
2-First stage of the conversion of Israel and also Gentiles (Ezekiel 39.7)
3-Rebuilding the ancient city of Babylon (Zechariah 5.5-11)
4-World church & the rise of the False Prophet (Rev. 17.1-5, 18; 13.11-17)
5-World economy (Revelation 13.15-18)
6-World government (Daniel 7.23)
7-World government breaks into 10 divisions (Daniel 7.24)
8-Rebuilding of the Temple (Revelation 11.1-2; 2 Thessalonians 2.4)
9-Rise of Antichrist (Is. 28.15; Dan. 9.27; 7.20, 24; Rev. 6.1-2; 13.1-10)
10-The *"overflowing scourge"* (Joel 2.1-11; Isaiah 28.18-19)
11-A time of *"peace and safety"* (1 Thessalonians 5.3)
12-Appearing of Elijah (Malachi 4.5)
13-Indications of a covenant between Israel and the Antichrist (Is. 28.15).

Warning signs to be fulfilled on the day the Tribulation starts

1-Signs in space and on Earth (Joel 2.30-31)
2-Distress and fear among the nations (Luke 21.25-27).

Watch for the *warning signs* that have yet to be fulfilled. As you see them fulfilled, you will be able to determine how much closer we are to the Rapture and the start of the Tribulation. Now that you know the **What**, you can know the **When**.

APPENDIX B

WHAT YOU MUST DO TO BE SAVED

Do not wait until the Tribulation starts to trust in **Jesus Christ** to save you. If you go into the Tribulation, there is no guarantee you will survive it for very long. Within the first year or so, one-fourth of the world's population will die from war, famine, pestilence and wild animals (Revelation 6.8). By the middle of the Tribulation, one-third of the remaining population of the world will be dead (Revelation 9.15), leaving half of the world's population alive. Things only get worse. So many people die during the Tribulation that man becomes rarer than gold (Isaiah 13.12).

If you have not trusted **Jesus Christ** to save you, do it now! Read the following Scriptures:

For all have sinned, and fall short of the glory of God. (Romans 3.23)

For the wages of sin is death, but the free gift of God is eternal life in **Christ Jesus** *our Lord.* (Romans 6.23)

But God commendeth his own love toward us, in that, while we were yet sinners, **Christ** *died for us.* (Romans 5.8)

For by grace have ye been saved through faith; and that not of yourselves, it is the gift of God; not of works, that no man should glory. (Ephesians 2.8-9)

In whom we have our redemption through His blood, the forgiveness of our trespasses, according to the riches of His grace. (Ephesians 1.7)

For, whosoever shall call upon the name of the Lord shall be saved. (Romans 10.13)

If thou shalt confess with thy mouth **Jesus** *as Lord, and shalt believe in thy heart that God raised Him from the dead, thou shalt be saved: for with the heart man believeth unto righteousness; and with the mouth confession is made unto salvation.* (Romans 10.9-10)

But as many as received Him, to them gave He the right to become children of God, even to them that believe on His name. (John 1.12)

If you understand you are a sinner in need of salvation because there is a real Hell, ask **Jesus** to save you right now. Tell Him that you are trusting in Him to save you and cleanse your sins by the blood He shed on the cross.

Once you have trusted in **Jesus**, and in Him alone to save you, find a good Bible teaching church to join. If you need help locating a church, call the World Bible Society (800.866.9673).

DISCIPLESHIP

Jesus commissioned His disciples to be His witnesses to His resurrection, and to make disciples of all nations:

> *Go ye therefore, and make disciples of all the nations, baptizing them into the name of the Father and of the Son and of the Holy Spirit: teaching them to observe all things whatsoever I commanded you: and lo, I am with you always, even unto the end of the world.* (Matthew 28.19-20)

> *But ye shall receive power, when the Holy Spirit is come upon you: and ye shall be my witnesses both in Jerusalem, and in all Judaea and Samaria, and unto the uttermost part of the earth.* (Acts 1.8)

That commission applies to all true believers. Once a person is saved by trusting in **Jesus Christ** alone, he is to become a *disciple* of **Jesus**. One does that by engaging in several spiritual activities on a daily and a regular basis:

1-Prayer throughout the day (Ephesians 6.18; 1 Thessalonians 5.17)
2-Hearing Scripture daily (Prov. 8.34; Luke 8.15, 21; 11.28; James 1.22; Revelation 1.3)
3-Reading Scripture daily (Deuteronomy 17.19; Revelation 1.3)
4-Bible study on a daily basis (John 5.39; Acts 17.11; 2 Timothy 2.15)
5-Memorization of Scripture (Deuteronomy 6.6; Psalm 37.31; 40.8; 119.11; Proverbs 2.1; 3.1, 3; 4.1).
6-Meditation on Scripture (Joshua 1.8; Psalm 1.2)
7-Fellowship with the brethren (Acts 2.42, 46-47; Hebrews 3.13; 10.24-25)
8-Evangelism through living a holy life, and sharing your testimony as the Holy Spirit leads (Psalm 96.2; Acts 2.47; 1 Peter 3.15).
9-Make disciples (Matthew 28.19-20; 2 Timothy 2.2)

If a Christian develops a discipline in these basics of holy living he will become a *disciple* of **Jesus Christ**. It does not happen overnight. It takes many years to become a mature *disciple*, but it starts with the daily discipline of being in prayer, in the Word and in regular fellowship with other Christians.

Find a church and become an active member. Pray in the morning, throughout the day and before you go to sleep. Set up a daily Bible reading program. If you read three chapters a day you will read through the Bible in a year. Read two chapters in the Old Testament each day and one chapter in the New Testament. Buy an audio copy of the Bible, and listen to it at home and in the car. Buy DVDs of movies about the Bible and watch them often (*The Gospel of John, Peter and Paul, The Greatest Story Ever Told, King of Kings*, etc.). Memorize Scripture. If you memorize one verse a week you will have 52 verses memorized in one year. Meditate on Scripture and let the Holy Spirit teach you. Learn how to share the gospel. Ask your pastor to train you, and then share your personal testimony, and the gospel as the Lord leads.

APPENDIX C

BRIEF ARGUMENTS REFUTING IMMINENCE

1. Jesus said His disciples would not be alive when He returned (Luke 17.22).

2. Jesus said He would not return for a *"long time"* (Matthew 25.14-30; Luke 19.12-27).

3. Jesus said specific *signs* must precede the Rapture:

   A. Peter would die a martyr (John 21.18)
   B. The disciples would evangelize the entire Roman Empire (the known world) (Matthew 28.19)
   C. The Church would be built (Matthew 16.18)
   D. Paul would testify in Rome (Acts 23.11)
   E. The Temple would be destroyed (Matthew 24.1-2; Mark 13.1-2; Luke 21.5-6), and the city of Jerusalem would be taken and remain in Gentile control for an undisclosed period of time (Luke 21.20-24), which ended on June 7, 1967.

4. Jesus said the Rapture and the Tribulation would take place on the same 24-hour day (Luke 17.27, 29). This means the Antichrist must rise to power, and be in a position of authority to sign a covenant with Israel before the Rapture.

5. Peter knew he would be martyred (2 Peter 1.13-14).

6. Peter prophesied that in the *"last days"* mockers would say that Christ will not return (2 Peter 3.3-4). They obviously would rise up after Peter had died.

7. Paul knew that he would die before the Rapture, and that false teachers would come into the church after he died (Acts 20.28-30; 2 Timothy 4.6-7).

8. Paul said there would be a period of worldwide *"peace and safety"* before the Rapture (1 Thessalonians 5.3).

9. Paul said there would be a massive apostasy *(falling away)* from the faith by Christians before the Rapture (2 Thessalonians 2.3).

10. Paul said the Antichrist would rise to power before the Rapture (2 Thessalonians 2.3).

11. The myriad passages concerning the Antichrist were not given so the unsaved can identify him during the Tribulation. They were given for Christians to identify him before the Rapture so they can warn the lost about him before they are raptured.

12. The early Church fathers believed that *signs* would be fulfilled and the Antichrist would rise to power before the Rapture.

13. Some of the Reformers looked for *signs* of the Rapture, and believed the Rapture would occur in their lifetime because they saw *signs* they believed heralded Christ's return.

14. There are 27 major prophecies that will be fulfilled before the Rapture; 7 have been fulfilled, 5 are being fulfilled and 15 more will be fulfilled before that blessed event (Appendix A).

15. All of the prophecies in Appendix A must be fulfilled before the Tribulation starts. Since there is no *gap* between the Rapture and the start of the Tribulation, the Rapture cannot take place at *any moment*. All of the *warning signs* of the Tribulation must be, and will be fulfilled before the Rapture. Therefore, the Rapture is not an *imminent* event!

16. Teachers of *imminence* say Christians must believe it to keep them alert and to live holy lives. Every Christian should serve Jesus Christ to full capacity every day because of their love for what He did on the cross, and what He has given them – eternal life. Christians should also be holy because one can be called home at *any moment*. The knowledge of the *imminence* of death is a greater incentive for holiness than to believe in the *imminent* return of Christ. James said our lives are just a *"vapor"* (4.14).

17. The Holy Spirit is omniscient, and He knew that Christ was not scheduled to return for over 1900 years when He inspired James, Paul, Peter and John to write their letters. The Holy Spirit did not deceive the disciples into thinking Christ could return in their lifetime, and in no way did He seek to have millions of Christians misled into believing Christ could return at *any moment* with no *warning signs* preceding His return!

18. To say the Holy Spirit deliberately deceived the apostles, and that He has deceived millions of Christians for the last 1900 years into believing Christ could return at *any moment* would be accusing Him of Jesuit casuistry (the end justifies the means). The Holy Spirit is incapable of sinning just as the Father and Son are.

19. Jesus gave a warning to look for His immediate return when the *signs* He mentioned (the ones that take place on the day of the Rapture – Luke 21.25) begin to take place (Luke 21.28). He also said to remember Lot's wife. If there are no *warning signs* to look for on the day of the Rapture, the warning to remember Lot's wife would make no sense. Since there are two significant *warning signs* on that day the Rapture cannot take place at *any moment*.

APPENDIX D

REJECTION OF OTHER RAPTURE POSITIONS

We reject the Mid-Tribulation and the Post-Tribulation Rapture positions, along with the Pre-Wrath Rapture position, for several reasons. For the sake of brevity, we present a few key reasons.

Mid-Tribulation Rapture

Scripture clearly teaches that Christians are not destined for wrath:

For God appointed us not into wrath, but unto the obtaining of salvation through our Lord Jesus Christ. (1 Thessalonians 5.9)

The context of the passage is not the wrath of Hell, but of some other form of wrath. The only other form of wrath is what God pours out on the unsaved during the Tribulation. If Christians went through the first half of the Tribulation or beyond, they would suffer the wrath of God. His wrath is poured out with the breaking of the Sixth Seal (Revelation 6.12-17). This would mean that there would be a clear contradiction in the Bible.

There would be no reason to commission 144,000 men of the twelve tribes of Israel to preach the gospel if Christians go into the Tribulation. The 144,000 witnesses are commissioned immediately after the wrath of God is poured out (Revelation 7.1-8), because all the Christians have been raptured off the planet, and there is no one to share the gospel with the lost.

Post-Tribulation Rapture

A major problem with this position is the same one noted above – if Christians go through the Tribulation they will suffer the wrath of God. Another major problem with the Post-Tribulation Rapture position is there will be no one to enter the Millennial Kingdom in mortal bodies. Paul said that the dead in Christ will be resurrected and given immortal bodies, and the living will have their mortal bodies changed into immortal ones (1 Corinthians 15.52). The unsaved are judged by Christ when He returns, and they are cast into the Lake of Fire (Matthew 25.31-46).

Some people must go into the Millennial Kingdom with mortal bodies, because Scripture says that some of them will die during that age (Isaiah 65.20). The people who were saved during the Tribulation are the ones who will enter that kingdom.

Another proof that people will go into the Millennial Kingdom in mortal bodies is the rebellion at the end of that age. A great number of people will rebel, and be executed by God (Revelation 20.7-9). If Christians enter the

Millennial Kingdom with immortal bodies, some of them must reject their belief in Jesus Christ, and join the Devil in his final rebellion. If that is true, it would mean that the doctrine of eternal security of believers is not biblical. It would also mean that a great number of Christians will lose their salvation and be cast into the Lake of Fire. We must reject that belief.

If the Post-Tribulation Rapture doctrine is biblical, there are clear contradictions in the Bible. We have many passages that say once we believe in Jesus Christ we have eternal life (Matthew 25.46; John 3.16, 36; 5.24; 1 John 5.11-13); there is no condemnation for us (John 5.24; Romans 8.1); and we will reign with Jesus Christ forever (Revelation 22.5). Those promises would not be true if some Christians lose their salvation at the end of the Millennial Kingdom, when, as the Post-Tribulationists say, they join the Devil in his final rebellion. God forbid!

Pre-Wrath Rapture

We also reject the Pre-Wrath Rapture position because its proponents say the wrath of God is poured out in the last few months of the Tribulation. The Bible is clear that God's wrath is poured out early in the Tribulation with the breaking of the Sixth Seal:

And I saw when he opened the sixth seal, and there was a great earthquake; and the sun became black as sackcloth of hair, and the whole moon became as blood; and the stars of the heaven fell unto the earth, as a fig tree casteth her unripe figs when she is shaken of a great wind. And the heaven was removed as a scroll when it is rolled up; and every mountain and island were moved out of their places. And the kings of the earth, and the princes, and the chief captains, and the rich, and the strong, and every bondman and freeman, hid themselves in the caves and in the rocks of the mountains; and they say to the mountains and to the rocks, Fall on us, and hide us from the face of him that sitteth on the throne, and from the wrath of the Lamb: for the great day of their wrath is come; and who is able to stand? (Revelation 6.12-17)

The wrath of God and Jesus Christ is poured out on the unsaved with the breaking of the Sixth Seal. The wrath that is mentioned later in Revelation is merely more wrath:

And I saw another sign in heaven, great and marvellous, seven angels having seven plagues, which are the last, for in them is finished the wrath of God. (Revelation 15.1)

The 7 bowl judgments are not the total wrath of God; they are the final judgments of the wrath of God. The premise of the Pre-Wrath Tribulation Rapture doctrine, that Christians will be raptured out just before the bowl judgments are poured out, is not biblical. It also contradicts Scripture, because it says that millions of Christians will endure most of the wrath of God (Revelation 6.12-17; 8.1-12; 9.1-21; 11.4-6). Scripture is clear that no Christian of the Church Age will suffer the wrath of God (1Thessalonians 5.9).

The men who teach the Pre-wrath Tribulation Rapture can argue that the Rapture will take place just before the breaking of the Sixth Seal (Revelation 6.12), when the wrath of God is first poured out on the world, but to argue for a later time is not biblical.

Amillennialism

This doctrine denies that there will be a literal kingdom over which Jesus Christ will rule on earth for 1000 years. It teaches that the 1000 years mentioned 6 times in Revelation 20 is a symbolic number. Augustine wrote in his book, *The City of God*, that the book of Revelation is a spiritual allegory. The Millennial Kingdom began with the Church, and Christ's reign on Earth is spiritual in nature. Jesus Christ will return at the end of the Church Age, and establish an eternal kingdom. This erroneous theology was adopted by the Roman Catholic Church and also by most of the Reformers who could not reject all of the nonsensical doctrines of the Church of Rome.

A few of the early Church fathers of the 1st and 2nd centuries believed in Amillennialism, but none of their writings are extant. There are a few references to their beliefs in the writings of Justin Martyr (100-165 AD). As noted previously in this book (p. 294), the vast majority of the early Church fathers taught that there would be a Millennial Kingdom. Only a handful of them rejected a literal kingdom – Clement of Alexandria, Caius, Origen and Dionysius. The latter two are considered to have been heretics. It was not until Augustine (354-430 AD), a Catholic Church bishop, began to write on eschatology that the belief in a spiritual Millennial Kingdom took hold. He was a faithful Roman Catholic priest who held to all of the false doctrines of the church, including the damnable doctrine of Purgatory. The Roman Catholic Church, the Eastern Orthodox Church, and most of the Reformed denominations teach that doctrine.

We reject it because it denies the literal fulfillment of Bible prophecy. It is inconceivable that God would fulfill all the prophecies of the Messiah's First Coming in a literal manner, and then have most of the prophecies of His Second Coming fulfilled in an allegorical manner. As we noted before, "*Jesus Christ is the same yesterday and today, yea and forever*" (Hebrews 13.8).

One must ask who is more trustworthy concerning doctrine: the false Roman Catholic Church, which invented Amillennialism, or the Holy Spirit, the apostles and the early Church fathers? The Reformers merely held on to that doctrine when they split from the Catholic Church just as some did with other false doctrines such as infant baptism.

We must note that the understanding by Amillennialists of the identity of the prince of Daniel 9.25-27 is not biblical. They argue that the "*anointed one, the prince*" in verse 25 and the "*anointed one*" in verse 26 is Jesus (which is correct), but the "*prince*" in verse 26 was Titus. The "*he*" in verse 27 is Jesus who made a covenant with Israel at the beginning of His ministry and broke it after 3½ years. The *"one that maketh desolate"* in verse 27 was Titus.

It is creative exegesis, but it is not correct. It is impossible, by all rules of grammar, for the *"he"* in verse 27 to refer back to the *"anointed one"* of verses 25 and 26. It can only refer back to the *"prince"* of verse 26. Another insurmountable problem with this clumsy eisegetical trick is that Jesus did not make a covenant with Israel when He began His ministry. Titus did not make a covenant with Israel, and neither did anyone else in the 1st century AD that could be a fulfillment of this prophecy. The Antichrist who is to come in the future will make that covenant.

Amillennialists think the false Catholic religion got it right, while the Old Testament prophets, Jesus Christ, the apostles and the early Church fathers got it wrong. The Church fathers who taught that there will be a literal Millennial Kingdom were: Clement of Rome, Barnabas, Hermas, Polycarp, Ignatius, Papias, Pothinus, Justin Martyr, Melito, Hegisippus, Tatian, Irenaeus, Tertullian, Hippolytus, Apollinaris, Cyprian, Commodian, Nepos, Coracion, Victorinus, Methodius and Lactantius (Chafer, Lewis Sperry, *Systematic Theology*, Vol. 4, p. 271-274). At the Nicene Council, "318 bishops from all parts of the earth placed themselves on record" in believing in a literal Millennial Kingdom (Ibid., p. 275). The teaching of the Catholic Church on this matter is wrong. The Old Testament prophets, Jesus Christ, the apostles and the early Church fathers are right that there will be a Millennial Kingdom.

Those who hold to Amillennialism must consider carefully where the doctrine came from. Did it come from the Holy Spirit who gave it to bishops of the Roman Catholic Church or was it given to the Old Testament prophets, the apostles and early Church fathers? They must also consider why Jesus taught a literal Millennial Kingdom. Was He mistaken?

Postmillennialism

Postmillennialism teaches Christians will create a Golden Age on Earth, gradually defeating the forces of evil. After they have established a Utopian Paradise, Jesus Christ will return and establish His eternal kingdom. Some who believe this call themselves Reconstructionists and label it Dominion Theology. Some of them accept certain ideas within Preterism, believing that many of the prophecies of the "last days" have already been fulfilled.

This doctrine must also be rejected, because it denies the literal fulfillment of the myriad prophecies of the Rapture, Tribulation and Second Coming. It also rejects a literal Millennial Kingdom. The belief that Christians will someday establish a theocracy on Earth is absurd to say the least. For the last 100 years the influence of Christians has waned greatly. The power of the major false religions (Roman Catholicism, Islam, Hinduism, Buddhism) has increased significantly along with atheism and humanism. The forces of darkness have also strengthened their control over the nations of the world. There was a rapid movement in the last century to consolidate the power of

Satan's minions among governments with the creation of numerous political and economic unions as shown in Chapters 15 and 16 of this book. That effort is growing stronger in this century with no signs of slowing. A world government, economy and religion under the power of Satan is inevitable just as the Bible says (Revelation 13 and 17).

Postmillennialists, Preterists and Amillennialists use the same method of study. They insert into the text a meaning that is not there. They make the text say what they want it to say, rather than accepting what the text says.

APPENDIX E

PETER'S BONES

Scripture says the coming World Church will move its headquarters to the rebuilt city of Babylon:

Then the angel that talked with me went forth, and said unto me, Lift up now thine eyes, and see what is this that goeth forth. And I said, What is it? And he said, This is the ephah that goeth forth. He said moreover, This is their appearance in all the land (and, behold, there was lifted up a talent of lead); and this is a woman sitting in the midst of the ephah. And he said, This is Wickedness: and he cast her down into the midst of the ephah; and he cast the weight of lead upon the mouth thereof. Then lifted I up mine eyes, and saw, and, behold, there came forth two women, and the wind was in their wings; now they had wings like the wings of a stork; and they lifted up the ephah between earth and heaven. Then said I to the angel that talked with me, Whither do these bear the ephah? And he said unto me, To build her a house in the land of Shinar: and when it is prepared, she shall be set there in her own place. (Zechariah 5.5-11)

The archeological find of the last two millennia will be made while the ancient city of Babylon is being rebuilt. Excavators will find the bones of the apostle Peter. This sensational discovery will compel the Roman Catholic Church to move its headquarters to that city, as described above.

The ancient city of Babylon was located in the land of Shinar. The woman is the World Church, which will be led by the Roman Catholic Church. After Peter's bones are found, the World Church will move from Jerusalem to Babylon. Some time before the Tribulation starts the Roman Catholic Church will move its headquarters from Rome to Jerusalem.

Currently the Roman Catholic Church claims they have the bones of Peter and that they are in a tomb beneath St. Peter's Basilica, but their claim is not supported by evidence. Antonio Ferrua, a Vatican archeologist who died in 2003, at the age of 102, was a dedicated Jesuit priest. He was the first archeologist to look for the bones of Peter in the cemetery under St. Peter's Basilica. He discovered a pagan cemetery there with some 20 pagan mausoleums. One of them was thought to be Peter's.

In 1939, workmen who were preparing a tomb for the recently deceased Pope Pius XI in St. Peter's Basilica unearthed ancient Roman masonry. Pope Pius XII commissioned Ferrua and 3 distinguished colleagues to excavate the site in total secrecy.

274

Their report on what they had found was issued, in 1951, causing a world-wide uproar. They said they found no trace of Peter and no inscriptions of his name anywhere. The bones of Peter, that were supposed to be in his tomb, were not there. Pope Pius XII called in Margherita Guarducci, a classical epigraphist. After several years of searching she found a box of bones and claimed they were the bones of Peter. She wrote a book about her work which was ridiculed by Ferrua. After thoroughly refuting her work, he wrote a memorandum to Pope Paul VI (reigned from 1963-1978). He noted that Guarducci's work was seriously flawed, and the box that allegedly contained the bones of Peter also contained the bones of sheep and pigs, along with a complete skeleton of a mouse. Mice and pigs are unclean animals. Pope Paul VI rejected Ferrua's proof, and declared that Peter's bones had been found. The "bones of Peter" were examined by orthopedists and were found to be those of a woman. Guarducci was banned from the Necropolis and the Basilica archives. The presumed bones of Peter were removed from their resting place.

Here is more evidence that Peter's bones had not been found in Rome, and that Peter never travelled to Rome:

1. In his letter to the church in Rome, Paul greeted 27 people and Peter was not one of them.
2. In Paul's last letter from Rome to Timothy (67 AD) he says, *"only Luke is with me"* (2 Timothy 4.11). If Peter was in Rome, as the Catholic Church claims, he had abandoned Paul.
3. Paul was the apostle to the Gentiles (Acts 9.15) and would obviously go to the headquarters of the Gentile world, Rome. Peter was the apostle to the circumcision (Galatians 2.8), and would have gone to Babylon, the location of the largest Jewish population outside of Israel.
4. In Peter's first letter he said he was in Babylon with Mark (1 Peter 5.13). Paul wrote to Timothy, who was a pastor in Ephesus, and asked him to bring Mark with him to Rome.
5. Paul's grave was found in Rome outside the city walls. (All Christians were buried outside the city walls.)
6. The traditional site of Peter's grave is inside the city walls of Rome. It is highly unlikely that he would be the only Christian buried inside the city walls.

Little archeology has been done in Babylon, but after the destruction of Islam (Ezekiel 38-39) there will be renewed efforts and we believe that Peter's bones will be discovered. That incredible discovery will cause the Vatican to move its headquarters to Babylon. The rebuilt city of ancient Babylon will become the capitol of the world by the mid-point of the Tribulation.

APPENDIX F

Incorrect Predictions of Christians

We expect the cults to make false predictions for the Second Coming, but it is something that no true believer should do. We are not commanded to predict the time the Rapture or Second Coming will take place. Instead, we are commanded to be *"looking for"* the *"blessed hope"* (Titus 2.13). Making predictions can only harm the faith of Christians. It can never increase their faith. This appendix has been included to emphasize the importance of not making predictions. Some great pastors and Bible teachers have fallen into the trap of making incorrect predictions. We can all learn from their mistakes and not make the same mistake.

Dr. Thomas Ice noted on his website that those who believe the doctrine of imminence should never set a date for the Rapture or Second Coming. We share this with you again to emphasize the importance of not setting dates:

Third, imminency **eliminates any attempt at date setting. Date setting is impossible** since the rapture is signless (i.e., providing **no basis for date setting**) and if imminency is really true, the moment a date was fixed then Christ could not come at any moment, destroying imminency.

Fourth, Renold Showers says, "A person **cannot** legitimately **say** that **an imminent event will happen soon.** The term 'soon' implies that an event must take place 'within a short time (after a particular point of time specified or implied).' By contrast, an imminent event may take place within a short time, but it does not have to do so in order to be imminent. As I hope you can see by now, **'imminent' is not equal to 'soon.'**" A. T. Pierson has noted that, "Imminence is the combination of two conditions, viz.,: certainty and uncertainty. By an imminent event we mean one which is certain to occur at some time, uncertain at what time." ("Imminency And The Any-Moment Rapture")[1]

Early Church fathers

Some of the early Church fathers believed that most of the prophecies concerning the end times had been fulfilled in their time as noted previously in Chapter 5. They eagerly awaited the return of Jesus Christ because they did not know that there were many more prophecies that had to be fulfilled before the Lord's return. Here are some of their statements:

Clement of Rome said around 100 AD, "Soon and suddenly shall his will be accomplished."

Ignatius said around 100 AD, "The last times are upon us."
Montanus, Priscilla and **Maximilla** (Montanism movement leaders) predicted that the world would end in their lifetime (2nd Century).

Cyprian said around 250 AD, "The kingdom of God, beloved brethren, is beginning to be at hand."

Martin of Tours said around 400 AD, "There is no doubt that the Antichrist has already been born. Firmly established already in his early years, he will, after reaching maturity, achieve supreme power."

Hippolytus predicted the end of the age would come in 500 AD.[1]

Middle Ages

Millennial Madness

On December 31, 999 A.D. millions of people thought the Lord was about to return. Thousands crowded into the old basilica of St. Peter's Church in Rome awaiting the return of Jesus Christ. Many gave their land, homes and personal possessions to the poor as an act of contrition. Some traveled to Palestine believing the Lord would return there. Everyone was disappointed. Many Europeans made the same mistake in December of 1099 and 1199. They also thought Christ would return 1000 years after His resurrection in 33 AD.

Joachim of Fiore
(1135-1202)

Joachim of Fiore, founder of the monastic order of San Giovanni in Fiore, Italy, predicted that the Antichrist would rise to power in 1260 AD. (Abanes, Richard, *End-Time Visions*, p. 338)

Renaissance

Nicolas of Cusa
(1401-1464)

Cardinal Nicholas of Cusa predicted that doomsday would take place between 1700 and 1734. (McIver, Tom. *The End of the World: An Annotated Bibliography*, #73)

Melchoir Hofmann
(1495-1544)

Melchoir Hofmann announced in 1531 that the Second Coming would take place in the year 1533. (DeMar, Gary, *Last Days Madness*, p. 13).

Christopher Columbus
(1451-1506)

The great explorer Christopher Columbus is said to have predicted the world would end in 1656. (*End-Time Visions*, p. 338)

Reformation

Martin Luther
(1483-1546)

Martin Luther considered the year 2000 AD as a possible end-time date before finally settling on 1600 AD (Kyle, Richard, *The Last Days are Here Again*, p. 192). His belief that the Second Coming would take place around 1600 is seen in this comment:

I believe that **all the signs** which are to precede the last days **have already appeared**. Let us **not think that the Coming of Christ is far off**; let us look up with heads lifted up; let us expect our Redeemer's coming with longing and cheerful minds. (*Systematic Theology*, vol. 4, p. 279, emphasis mine)

Luther knew to "look" for *signs*, and he thought all of the *warning signs* of the Rapture had been fulfilled. He was mistaken as were other Reformers, and some of the early Church fathers. They did not know all of the *warning signs*. We have the advantage of knowing those *signs*, (Appendix A), and we have no excuse to not be "watching" and to not be ready.

Hugh Latimer
(1485-1555)

Hugh Latimer who was burned at the stake believed the Second Coming would take place in his or that of his children's lifetime:

All those excellent and learned men whom, without doubt, God has sent into the world in these **latter days** to give the world **warning**, do gather out of the Scriptures that the **last days can not be far off**. Peradventure it may come in my day, old as I am, or in my children's days. (*Systematic Theology*, vol. 4, p. 279, emphasis mine)

Johann Heinrich Alsted
(1588-1638)

Johann Heinrich Alsted, a German Calvinist, predicted that Jesus Christ would return in 1694. He was convinced that the Thirty Years War (1618-1648) would lead to the end of the world. He came up with 1694 by taking 69 AD as the start of the time that the regular sacrifice is abolished. He then added 1,290 day-years (Daniel 12.11) to come up with 1359 AD and then he added 1,335 day-years (Daniel 12.11) to arrive at 2694 AD. He subtracted 1000 years for the Millennial Kingdom to arrive at the year 1694 AD as the year of the Second Coming of Jesus Christ. (Armerding, Carl Edwin and Gasque, W. Ward. *Handbook of Biblical Prophecy*, pp. 30-32).

Using numbers found in the Bible to calculate the date of the Rapture and the Second Coming is a futile effort as those who have done so understand. The key to knowing the **When** (Rapture) is not numerology or the calculation of numbers. The only way to know when the Rapture will take place, and subsequently the Second Coming is to diligently "watch" the *warning signs* be fulfilled that Jesus, the prophets and the apostles gave us.

Modern Era

Cotton Mather
(1663-1728)

The Puritan preacher Cotton Mather predicted the Lord would return in 1697 and then in 1716 and finally in 1736. (*End-Time Visions*, p. 338)

John Wesley
(1703-1791)

Methodist Church founder John Wesley foresaw the Millennium beginning in 1836, the same year that the Beast of Revelation was supposed to rise from the sea. (*The End of the World: An Annotated Bibliography*, #269)

The Shakers
(1747-Present)

The Shakers, United Society of Believers in Christ's Second Appearing, sprang from the Protestant denomination the Quakers. They believed in celibacy and could not attract many followers. They predicted the world would end in 1792.

Hatley Frere
(1779-1866)

Hatley Frere, who brought Edward Irving into the premillennial fold, thought Louis Napoleon was the Antichrist. He also predicted that the Jews would return to Palestine and rebuild their temple in 1865 and that the Roman Catholic Church would become defunct by 1864 (*Handbook of Biblical Prophecy*, pp. 54-55).

Michael Baxter
(1834-1910)

The Anglican minister Michael Paget Baxter was an ardent date setter, a veritable Charles Taylor of the 19th century. In one of his earliest publications he predicted the end of the world for 1861-1867. (*The End of the World: An Annotated Bibliography,* #348)

He also predicted the end to come in 1868 and 1869. He continued to make predictions picking the years 1871-1872. He took some time off from predicting, and then chose 1896. He did not stop. He foresaw the end of the world in 1901 in his book, *The End of This Age About the End of This Century*. He refused to quit, and in another book, *Future Wonders of Prophecy*, he predicted that the Rapture would take place on March 12, 1903, between 2-3pm. (*The End of the World: An Annotated Bibliography*, #353)

Leonard Sale-Harrison
(1875-1956)

Leonard Sale-Harrison was a solid Pre-Tribulationist. He thought Mussolini was the Antichrist and predicted the Rapture would take place in either 1940 or 1941. He made the fatal mistake that most of the modern Pre-Tribulationists make who believe that there are no *signs* for the Rapture. Robert Clouse commented on this prognosticator saying, "Like many pretribulation premillennialists, Sale-Harrison was rather inconsistent. If there are no signs required before the coming of the Lord to rapture His church, then why is so much time spent in reading current events into the Bible?" (*Handbook of Biblical Prophecy*, pp. 30-32).

Henry "Harry" Ironside
(1876-1951)

Dr. Henry Ironside thought, in 1915 when he wrote the book *The Midnight Cry*, that he was living in the "last days" and the Lord would return in his lifetime:

Reader, let me press my point again. – The world-wide Gospel proclamation and world-wide apostasy at the same time are **clear proofs** that **the end is close upon us**. (*The Midnight Cry*, p. 28, citing Lindsell, *The Gathering Storm*, p. 123, emphasis mine)

Laodicea is the closing period of the Church's history, and who can doubt that we have now reached the very time predicted? It behooves us to act as men who wait for their Lord, knowing that **His coming cannot be much longer delayed** (Ibid. p. 35, citing Lindsell, p. 124, emphasis mine)

It has been 95 years since he wrote that the return of Christ "cannot be much longer delayed." He saw some *warning signs*, but not all of them. No one can know the **When** (time of the Rapture) without knowing all of the **What** (major *warning signs*).

William Branham
(1909-1965)

William Branham, founder of the post World War II faith healing movement, proclaimed himself to be the angel of Revelation 3.14 and 10.7. He prophesied that by 1977 all denominations would be consumed by the World Council of Churches under the control of the Roman Catholics, that the Rapture would take place and that the world would be destroyed.[1]

Lester Sumrall
(1913-1996)

Lester Sumrall predicted the end of the world in his book, *I Predict 1985*. When that prediction failed he wrote another book. In his book, *I Predict 2000 A.D.*, he argued that the Lord would return by the year 2000 at the latest to set up His Millennial Kingdom. "I predict the absolute fullness of man's operation on planet Earth by the year 2000 A.D. Then Jesus Christ shall reign from Jerusalem for 1000 years." (*End-Time Visions*, p. 99, 341)

Kenneth Hagin
(1917-2003)

Kenneth Hagin predicted the Rapture would take place in October of 1997. This is what he said at revival meeting in July 1997:

It shall **come to pass this year!** It shall come to pass at last. That which has hindered shall be taken out of the way. The last vestige shall be removed! And it shall come. What is that I see? Shining so bright coming from heaven. Awesome; you want to weep, yet shout, cry yet laugh. I see it coming, nearer and nearer. Blinding light. **The fall of this year - October.**

As the people walk in the light of what they have, the rest shall come to pass.

We are going with God. We'll go off and leave some, but we are going with God. Going with God! In the spirit he speaketh mysteries, secrets. Things which are and shall be. When it comes to pass you will know.

In **October** in St. Louis, the center and heart of the nation, it shall come. It shall spread all over the nation. **Manifestations everywhere.** That which has frustrated will be removed. Then you will know the full meaning of the Divine glow. And others will be invited to walk in the light of it, and so they shall. The glory of the Lord shall shine upon His people. (Hagin Holy Ghost Meeting, Oct. 12-24 or longer, St. Louis Family Church, Jeff C. Perry, Pastor, with satellite broadcast, emphasis mine)

Charles Taylor

End-time preacher Charles Taylor made several predictions for the date of the Rapture. The first year he picked was 1975. When 1975 failed he picked 1976. He didn't stop and went on to pick 1980, 1981, 1982, 1983, 1985, 1986, 1987, 1988, 1989, 1992 and 1994. He quit predicting the Rapture due to an untimely ailment called death (*End-Time Visions*, p. 99).

Edgar Whisenant
(1932-2001)

Edgar Whisenant and Greg Brewer wrote a book, *88 Reasons Why the Rapture Is in 1988*, in which they predicted the Second Advent would take place in 1988. When the Lord did not return in 1988, Whisenant wrote another book, *The Final Shout: Rapture Report 1989*. When the Lord failed to return in 1989 he stopped making predictions.

Jerry Falwell
(1933-2007)

Dr. Jerry Falwell, founder of the "Moral Majority," Liberty University and senior pastor of Thomas Road Baptist Church, made a prediction that did not come true. He predicted on his TV show (December 27, 1992) that the Rapture would take place before the end of 1999. Even though he expected the Rapture in seven years or less he said he expected to live as long as W.A. Criswell, who was 83 at the time. He was 59 years of age in 1992. (North, Gary, *Rapture Fever,* p. 200).

In 1999 Falwell said the Antichrist was probably alive, and that the Second Coming will probably be within 10 years. He also told about 1500 people at a conference on evangelism at Kingsport, Tennessee, that the Antichrist is a male Jew. "Who will the antichrist be? I don't know. Nobody else knows," he said.[2]

Billy Graham

In 1950, a young Billy Graham stated, "We may have another year, maybe two years. Then I believe it is going to be over." (Hugo McCord, *Date Setting*, article[3])

Doug Clark

Doug Clark self-published a book in the 1970s, in which he said the "Rapture could take place in the 70s. Yes it could!" (*Amazing Prophecies of the 70's!*, p. 57). He gave 51 prophecies that he said could be fulfilled in the 1970s. In that book he also speculated that Henry Kissinger could be the Antichrist, and he gave ten reasons for his choice (pp. 13-17).

On April 26, 1989, Doug Clark announced on Trinity Broadcasting Network's show, *Praise the Lord*, that World War III would begin within 3 years. (*End-Time Visions*, p. 92)

Pat Robertson

Pat Robertson, founder of the 700 Club television show, predicted the end of the world would occur in 1982. "I guarantee you by the end of 1982 there is going to be a judgment on the world," he said in a May 1980 broadcast of the 700 Club. (Boyer, Paul S., *When Time Shall Be No More*, p. 138)

Salem Kirban

In his 1968 book, *Guide to Survival*, Salem Kirban used Bishop Ussher's calculations to speculate that 1989 would be the year of the Rapture (p. 136).

Mikkel Dahl, Reginald Duncan & Emil Gaverluk

Mikkel Dahl predicted in "The Midnight Cry" that the present era would end by 1980. Reginald Edward Duncan predicted in "The Coming Russian Invasion of America" that the Millennium would begin in 1979. Emil Gaverluk, of the Southwest Radio Church, predicted that the Rapture would occur by 1981. (DeMar, Gary, *Last Days Madness*, p. 14)

Kenneth Copeland

On his broadcast on the morning of February 7, 2000, televangelist Kenneth Copeland claimed that a group of scientists and scholars had studied the Bible in great detail, and had determined that February 11, 2000, would be the last day of the 6000th year since Creation, a date when the Apocalypse would presumably happen. Copeland did not imply he believed this to be accurate yet he went on to say that the Rapture will come soon.

David Webber & Noah Hutchings

David Webber and Noah Hutchings, of the Southwest Radio Church, published a booklet in 1978 in which they speculated that the Second Coming of Jesus Christ might be in 2001. This is what they wrote:

A vital question that affects every man, woman and child living today is: "Will Christ come by 2001?" This impending possibility looms ominously on the human horizon and confronts each of the nearly 42 billion people on this planet. A time of unparalleled affliction, tyranny, and destruction must occur before the most shattering event in all history of man – the physical return of Christ to the earth, in real, visible, and overwhelming power.

The irrefutable evidence of prophetic Scripture indicates that Jesus **Christ may very well be here by 2001!** The **general signs** in the heavens and on earth, plus the **specific signs** occurring in Israel (God's dramatic timepiece), all point to **His soon return.** (*Will Christ Come by 2001?*, p. 2, emphasis mine)

They opened their booklet with a chart of past and future dates:

A.D. 1917-1921 - Balfour Declaration
A.D. 1918-1922 - The Beginning of Sorrows
A.D. 1948-1952 – Israel's Rebirth After the Flesh
A.D. 1967-1971 - Jerusalem Restored
A.D. 1974-1978 - Jewish Temple Rebuilt?
A.D. 1981-1985 - Beginning of the Tribulation
A.D. 1985-1989 - Middle of Tribulation
A.D. 1988-1992 - End of the Tribulation
A.D. 1995-1999 - Completion of Millennial Temple
A.D. 1996-2000 - The Jubilee, a rest
A.D. 1997-2001 - Beginning of the Kingdom Age (p. 3)

Needless to say they missed by a long shot. We must note that Webber and Hutchings are Pre-Tribulationists. That means the Rapture must take place before the start of the Tribulation. According to their chart the Rapture should have taken place in 1985 by the latest.

Webber and Hutchings teamed up with Emil Gaverluk and published a transcript of a radio program in 1978 in which they predicted the Rapture would take place in the 1980s. Here are a few of the things they predicted would take place in that decade:

1980: New World Monetary System emerges
1981: Great Synagogue completed
1982: Parade of Planets
1983: Russian invasion of the Middle East
1984: George Orwell's world of 1984 (World government)
1985: Treaty with Israel aborted
1986: Halley's Comet reappears
1987: Massive storms, earthquakes, extreme heat from the sun
1988: Comet Kohoutek reappears 1989: A great invasion from outer space. Jesus Christ institutes a new government on earth. *(God's Timetable for the 1980's, p. 2)*

These Pre-Tribulationists firmly believe the Rapture will take place at least seven years prior to the start of the Tribulation. The Tribulation starts with the signing of the covenant between the Antichrist and Israel. Since they place the breaking of the covenant in 1985, they believed the Rapture would take place by 1982 at the latest. The Antichrist breaks his covenant with Israel 3.5 years after signing it (Daniel 9.27). They missed the date of the Rapture by 28 years and counting.

Grant Jeffrey

In 1990 Dr. Grant Jeffrey wrote *Armageddon: Appointment with Destiny*. He predicted that the year 2000 A.D. "is a probable termination date for the 'last days'" (p. 193). He used an elaborate argument based on the jubilee years. He cited the start of the Lord's ministry where He read Isaiah 61.1 and the first line of verse two. The Lord's ministry began in a jubilee year:

The year when this occurred, the fall of A.D. 28, was, in fact, not only a Jubilee Year, but was also the thirtieth Jubilee since the Sabbatical-Jubilee system of years began when Israel crossed the Jordan River in 1451 B.C. Thus, Jesus Christ precisely fulfilled "the acceptable year of the Lord" on the exact year of Jubilee – the year of liberty and release.

Please note that He stopped reading at "the acceptable year of the Lord" because He knew that the next phrase of the prophet's sentence, "and the day of vengeance of our God," which refers to Armageddon, would be postponed exactly 2,000 biblical years (2000 biblical years times 360 days equals 720,000 days divided by 365.25 equals 1971.25 calendar years).

If we add 2000 biblical years (1971.25 calendar years) to the beginning of Christ's ministry on a Jubilee Year when He read the prophecy about "the acceptable year of the Lord" in the fall of A.D. 28; we arrive at the year A.D. 2000, forty Jubilee Cycles later.

The next Jubilee Year will occur in A.D. 2000, completing the Sabbatical-Jubilee system of years – the seventieth Great Jubilee.

In the thirtieth Jubilee Year, Christ commenced His ministry in A.D. 28. In the seventieth Jubilee Year, Christ may commence His kingdom in A.D. 2000. It is also interesting that both the First and Second Temples were dedicated to the Lord on the Feast of Tabernacles in a Year of Jubilee. (pp. 192-193)

Jeffrey went on to argue that his calculations were being confirmed by "thousands of pastors and believers around the world that are **receiving a quiet assurance in their own spirit** that the Second Coming of the Lord is quickly approaching." (Ibid., p. 193, emphasis mine)

It is obvious that his calculations were wrong. If Christ was scheduled to return in 2000 AD, the Rapture should have taken place in 1993. It's been 16 years since Jeffrey predicted the Lord should have returned, and it may be another decade before He does.

Those thousands of pastors and believers who had "a quiet assurance in their own spirit that the Second Coming of the Lord is quickly approaching" were also wrong. That assurance did not come from the Lord or from the Bible; it came from wishful thinking. The key to understanding when the Rapture will take place is not elaborate calculations or quiet assurances. The key is to know what *warning signs* will take place before the Rapture. Once you know them you can diligently look for them to be fulfilled, and watch as the Rapture approaches.

Everyone who has made a prediction based on Biblical calculations has been wrong. We do not believe anyone can use mathematical calculations to determine the exact or approximate date of the Rapture and Second Coming. The possible exception might be Sir Isaac Newton who has predicted that the Second Coming will take place in 2060 AD. We will have to wait to see if his calculation was divinely inspired. The way to determine the approximate time of these events is to know what *signs* have yet to be fulfilled, and then keep diligent watch for them to be fulfilled.

Jeffrey decided to give up date-setting a few years later. In his 1994 book, *Prince of Darkness*, he had this warning for all date-setters:

We should emulate Paul's attitude of watching expectantly for the Lord's return but refuse to set a date for it... **Attempts to calculate the exact timing are doomed to failure** and **are in direct disobedience to the words of Christ**. (p. 212, emphasis mine)

It is a shame he did not come to this conclusion before he predicted in 1990 that the Rapture would take place in 2000.

Timothy LaHaye

In Dr. Timothy LaHaye's first book on prophecy published in 1972, *The Beginning of the End*, he stated succinctly that one of the primary *signs* of the last days was the fulfillment of Matthew 24.7:

For nation shall rise against nation, and kingdom against kingdom; and there shall be famines, and pestilences, and earthquakes, in various places. (NKJV)

What war was the fulfillment of that prophecy? LaHaye had this to say:

Now we are ready to ask: Has there ever been a war, started by two nations, which grew into a worldwide war by the kingdoms of the world, followed by unprecedented famines, pestilences, and earthquakes in various places (perhaps simultaneously)? I am of the opinion that we can discern such. Though reluctant to be dogmatic on the subject, I believe there is one event that fulfills all four parts of this prophecy. That terrible event has been labeled by historians as World War I, which took place between 1914 and 1918. (Ibid., pp. 35-36)

Jesus said, *"Verily I say unto you, This generation shall not pass away, till all these things be accomplished"* (Matthew 24.34). How long is a generation according to LaHaye? Here is what he had to say about the length of a generation:

We may logically inquire next, "How long is a generation?" Psalm 90:10 provides insight into this subject. "The days of our years are three-score years and ten; and if, by reason of strength, they be four-score years, yet is their strength labor and sorrow...." This does not mean that the final generation is limited to seventy or eighty years; the psalmist is acquainting us with the general length of a generation.

How many people make up a generation? No particular number; just one person who comprehended the four parts of the 1914-1918 sign could represent the "generation." (Ibid., p. 168)

He argues that just one person needs to be alive, who was old enough to understand that World War I was a *sign*, for the prophecy of Jesus to be fulfilled. If we say a four-year-old child could understand that World War I was a *sign* that means the Lord must return before the last person dies who was born in 1910 or before. According to his argument if a person lives to 120 who was born in 1910, the Lord would have to return by 2030. The rapture would have to take place seven years early in 2023.

The longest period of time for a generation in the Bible is 100 years (Genesis 15.13, 16). Using that period of time as the longest period for a generation the Lord must return by 2014 at the very latest. The start of World War I was the first *sign* according to LaHaye:

> The uniqueness of this prophetic book is the basing of these signs in the first great sign, World War I. Admittedly, some appeared prior to 1914, just as the conditions that produced the tragic war rumbled long before the opening Serbian shot was fired. (Ibid., p. 161)

In a later book, *Are We Living in the End Times?*, he pinned down a generation:

> As my friend and prophecy scholar Dr. Arnold Fruchtenbaum has written, "The Bible nowhere limits the period of a generation simply to forty years. The one place where the term generation is given a specific time length, it is reckoned to be 100 years (Genesis 15:13-16). Actually, the term generation can mean 20, 40, 70, 80, or 100 years." (p. 60)

The longest a generation can possibly be is 100 years! He teaches the Rapture will take place seven years earlier. Therefore, that "*blessed hope*" must take place by 2007 at the very latest. That year has passed without the Rapture taking place.

In *The Beginning of the End*, published in 1972, he had this to say about how close the Rapture was:

> No one knows how long we have before we see the fulfillment of these things, but as we shall see in future studies, it seems that it cannot be much longer before our Lord comes for his Church. As the Lord Jesus said, although we cannot predict the "day or the hour" (Matthew 24:36) when He shall return, **we can know the season**. This book is dedicated to showing that **we are not only in the season**, but the **twilight of the season**. (p. 84, emphasis mine)

If a season is 100 years long and the twilight is 20 years long, it means he made another prediction that did not come to pass as he said it would. It all depends on how long a "season" is and how long the "twilight" is.

He listed the 12 most important *signs* of the Second Coming, and described them in that same book, *The Beginning of the End*. He signified how close we were to the Rapture in 1972 by giving the time of the night for each *sign*:

World War I (10:30 pm)
Rebirth of Israel (10:35 pm)
Russia and the Middle East (10:40 pm)
Capital and Labor Conflicts (10:45 pm)
Skyrocketing Travel (10:50 pm)
Explosion of Knowledge (11:00 pm)
Apostasy (11:15 pm)
Occult Shadows and Realities (11:20 pm)
Perilous Times (11:30 pm)
A Flood of Wickedness (11:30 pm)
Scoffers Have Come (11:40 pm)
The Ecumenical Church 11:50 pm)
The Disunited Nations/World Government (11:58 pm) (pp. 162-163)

LaHaye implied by this clock that in 1972 the world was at 11:40 pm. All of the *signs* had been fulfilled except the last two – the ecumenical church and world government. If we divide 4200 seconds (70 minutes X 60 seconds) by 58 years (1914 to 1972) we come up with approximately 71 seconds per year. Since the last *sign* was fulfilled by 1972 (the time that the book was published) at 11:40 there were 20 minutes remaining on the countdown clock. There are 1200 seconds remaining (20 minutes X 60 seconds), which means the Second Coming of Jesus should have taken place in 1989 (1200 seconds divided by 71 seconds for each year, equals 17 years. 1972 plus 17 equals 1989). It's obvious that he was working off of a generation as being 70 to 80 years (Psalm 90.10). If we add 80 years to 1914 we come to 1994. If we take away seven years for the Pre-Tribulation Rapture that event should have taken place in 1987, which corresponds to his countdown clock. That is also very close to the year (1981) that Hal Lindsey predicted for the Rapture.

Chuck Smith

Chuck Smith made a clear statement in his book, *Future Survival,* that the Lord would Rapture the Church before the end of 1981:

From my understanding of biblical prophecies, **I'm convinced that the Lord is coming for His Church before the end of 1981. I could be wrong,** but it's a **deep conviction in my heart,** and **all my plans are predicated upon that belief.** (p. 20, emphasis mine)

Deep convictions should not be the basis for doctrine. Scripture is the only basis for doctrine, never feelings or convictions. If he truly believes the Rapture can take place at *any moment* all of his plans should have been predicated upon that belief.

We do not know why he chose 1981 for the date of the Rapture, but it's possible that he believed the teaching of Hal Lindsey. In his book, *The Late Great Planet Earth,* Lindsey speculated that a generation was 40 years. He believed the Lord would return 40 years after the establishment of the nation of Israel in 1948 because the Lord said that everything mentioned in the Olivet Discourse would take place before the *"generation"* that sees Israel become a nation again passes away (Matthew 24.32-34). Since the Rapture takes place seven years earlier it should have taken place in 1981.

Besides thinking 40 years was the Biblical length of a generation, he thought the return of Haley's comet might be a fulfillment of prophecy. He speculated that the return of Haley's comet might be one of the "signs in heavens" that Jesus spoke of:

And there will be signs in sun and moon and stars, and upon earth dismay among nations, in perplexity at the roaring of the sea and the waves, man fainting from fear and the expectation of the things which are coming upon the world; for the powers of the heavens will be shaken. And they will see the Son of Man coming in a cloud with power and great glory. (Luke 21.25-27)

Smith went on to speculate that the tail of Haley's comet could "affect the balance of the earth's ozone blanket" and "the sun's ultraviolet rays would begin to scorch people upon the earth" (Ibid., p. 20). Then he wrote:

The Lord said that towards the end of the Tribulation period the sun would scorch men who dwell upon the face of the earth (Rev. 16). The **year 1986 would fit just about right!** We're getting **close to the Tribulation** and the return of Jesus Christ in glory! (Ibid., p. 21, emphasis mine)

We are 30 years further down the road from when Smith wrote his book, *Future Survival* (1980), and there are still many things that must happen before the Rapture takes place. He continued to exhort the Church to be ready for the Rapture:

All the pieces of the puzzle are coming together. God is warning you. (Ibid., p. 21)

Smith did not stop there. He noted how Jesus had rebuked the Pharisees for not knowing *"the signs of My coming."* He also quoted Paul's exhortation that Christians are not *"children of darkness that that day should overtake you as a thief"* (1 Thessalonians 5.4). He concluded that chapter by saying:

Christ's return shouldn't come as a surprise to the child of God. God has given us **plenty of evidence to look for** – and **that evidence is here now! We can see it!** And so, with Paul the apostle I say to you that all of our futures are foreshortened. We don't have time to be involved in nonessential things. The time has come to let out all the stops and go for it

– because our **Lord is coming very soon!** (Ibid., pp. 21-22, emphasis mine)

The Rapture should not come as a surprise to Christians who know what *warning signs* to look for. The problem is that too many Christians do not know the specific *warning signs* that we should be looking for to know when the Rapture is near. We encourage every Christian to memorize the **What** (those *warning signs*), and to diligently look for them to know the **When** (time of the Rapture).

Smith made another prediction of sorts in 2010 on his "Pastor's Perspective" radio program:

I do think that the Antichrist is in the world. I think that he is alive, and I think that he is **chomping at the bit to take over the reins of the world.** (1.14.2010, emphasis mine)

When the Antichrist is revealed and it is shown that he was not an adult in 2010, it will mean Smith was wrong in his belief that the Antichrist was ready to take rulership of the world.

Jack van Impe

Jack van Impe has made several predictions for the date of the Rapture. He claimed in his video entitled, "AD 2000 – the End?" that the Rapture could possibly take place in September 1999. He based it on generations listed in the Gospel of Matthew. He took the 3 divisions of 14 generations and determined that from Abraham to Christ there were 2160 years. He divided those years by the 42 generations to arrive at 51.4 years per generation. He took year 1948 (when Israel was reborn) and added one generation (51.4 years) to determine that Christ would most likely return in the autumn of 1999.

When that prediction failed he took a break from predicting. Now his latest date is 2012. As of 2008 he is selling a DVD entitled, "2012," in which he lays out myriad reasons why he believes the Rapture will take place in 2012. One of those reasons is that the Mayan calendar ends on December 21, 2012. This is what he said:

In Matthew 1.17, there are 42 generations from Abraham until Christ. What? 2,160 years divided by 42 is 51.2. In Luke chapter three, verses 23 to 38, there are 77 generations into 4,000 years from Adam to Christ and that comes out to 51.2 and if you add the extra six months because the Six Day War took place in June you're almost at 52 years. You add 52 to 1967 and you come out pretty close to 2018, 2019, subtract seven years from now, we're talking about 2012. Remember what I said two weeks ago? The Mayan calendar ends December 21st 2012. It's all there, ladies and gentlemen. **I don't believe in setting dates**, Matthew 24.36, but Jesus said,

"When you shall see all these signs (and they are here) *then you'll know it's near even at the door*, Matthew 24.33. (Emphasis mine)

We are living in the "times of the signs," but the Mayan calendar has nothing to do with the timing of the Rapture. The only *signs* that a true believer in Jesus Christ should "watch" for are the prophecies found in the Bible. Secular signs are not reliable, and they should be ignored. When 2012 ends it will mean that once again Van Impe has made a false prediction.

Hal Lindsey

Thousands of preachers have said during the last 39 years that Jesus Christ would "soon" return or that His return was "very near." This recent prophecy craze was started by Hal Lindsey in 1970. His book, *The Late Great Planet Earth*, was the foundation for most of the predictions since 1970. He speculated, but did not state emphatically, that the "last generation" started in 1948 with the establishment of the nation of Israel. He said that a generation was 40 years so the Second Coming should be in 1988. He believes the Rapture will take place seven years earlier which means he thought the Rapture would probably take place in 1981.

Lindsey quoted the Lord, *"Verily I say unto you, this generation shall not pass away, till all these things be accomplished"* (Matthew 24:34), and then he made this statement:

What generation? Obviously, in context, the generation that would see the signs – chief among them the rebirth of Israel. A **generation** in the Bible is something like **forty years**. If this is a correct deduction, then within forty years or so of 1948, **all these things could take place**. Many scholars who have studied Bible prophecy all their lives **believe that this is so**. (*The Late Great Planet Earth*, p. 54, emphasis added, R.W.K.)

He thought he was right when the Iraq-Iran War broke out in September 1980, but the Lord did not return. He was wrong about that prediction. Many scholars, who believed like him, and had "studied Bible prophecy all of their lives," were also wrong.

Since then Lindsey has said dozens of times that the Rapture would take place "soon," "very soon" and that it was "very near." An example of one of his predictions, that is not a prediction, is found in his 1981 book, *The 1980'S: Countdown to Armageddon*:

During the last 25 years I have been studying prophecy I have seen incredible events forecast 3,000 years ago happen right before my eyes. Especially in the past 10 years, I have watched current events push toward the climax of history the prophets foretold. I believe many people will be shocked by what is happening right now and by what will happen in the very near future. *The decade of the 1980's could very well be the last decade of history as we know it.* (pp. 7-8, emphasis added, H.L.)

He missed that prediction also. The 1980's was not the "last decade of history as we know it." He was not even close.

Lindsey has also said the Lord would return to rapture the Church in his lifetime. If he dies it will mean that he missed it, no matter what excuse his defenders may make. He also said that the Rapture would take place by the time he reached the age of the life span of the average American male. That year has come and gone. He has made four clear predictions with three of them wrong. When he dies that will be his fourth inaccurate prediction.

He made a prediction dealing with the Soviet Union in his book, *The Late Great Planet Earth*. He said the Russians were "seeking to gain footholds in Iran by various overtures of aid. In order to mount a large-scale invasion predicted by Ezekiel, Russia would need Iran as an ally." He then wrote:

Watch the actions of Iran in relation to Russia and the United Arab Republic. This writer believes that significant things will soon be happening there. (p. 68)

Russia and her allies use this occasion to launch an invasion of the Middle East, which Russia has longed to do since the Napoleonic wars. (Ibid., p. 154)

In his second book, *The 1980'S: Countdown to Armageddon*, Lindsey said that he predicted, in his first book, that Russia would invade the Middle East:

In *The Late Great Planet Earth* I predicted that the Soviets would begin their Middle East campaign with a sweep through the Persian Gulf area into Iran. The recent Russian invasion of Afghanistan was a first step in that direction. Once the **Middle East falls to Russia**, the communists will withhold their newly-gained oil to cripple the west. Just how close the Soviets are to making this bold move will be discussed in a later chapter. (p. 13)

He also made this prediction about Russia's plans for the Middle East:

The Russian invasion of Afghanistan has telegraphed the **Soviet intention to take over the entire Middle East**. Russian troops are already present in South Yemen and Ethiopia, and the fall of the Shah in nearby Iran has opened the door for a **Soviet conquest of the strategic Persian Gulf area**. The rest of the Middle East – including **Saudi Arabia**, which sits on one-quarter of the world's known oil reserves – appears to be an **easy target for a Soviet takeover**.

This area has now **fit precisely** into the **pattern predicted** for it. All that remains is for the Russians to make their predicted move. (Ibid., p. 63, emphasis added, R.W.K.)

In 1980, when he wrote his second book, it looked as though the Soviets would take over the Middle East. Their invasion of Afghanistan in December of 1979, made him and most eschatologians think the end was very near. He made a prediction, on Paul Crouch's TBN network, that the Soviet invasion of Afghanistan was the beginning of the end. He said the Soviets would soon attack Israel, and that Christians should pack their bags.

Lindsey and most prophecy teachers did not foresee al-Qaeda, led by Usama bin Laden, defeating the Soviets, and running them out of Afghanistan with their tails tucked between their legs. Instead of the Soviets taking over the Middle East, and holding the world to ransom with oil, the United States has done that.

On October 7, 2001, George Bush invaded Afghanistan in response to the September 11 attacks, and then invaded Iraq in 2003. He captured Saddam Hussein, and had him hung. Before the invasion of the Middle East by Bush the price of oil was around $25.00 per barrel. It climbed to over $140.00 a barrel in 2008 before falling back. Lindsey should have predicted that the United States would invade the Middle East, and hold the world to ransom with oil.

On September 25, 1997, he predicted on his TV show, *International Intelligence Briefing,* that Russia would invade Israel within 18 months (*End-Time Visions*, p. 286).

The false prediction by Lindsey concerning the Soviet Union is to be expected because he does not speak for God as the Old Testament prophets did. We must all be knowledgeable about the political machinations of the families who run the world – Rothschilds, Rockefellers, Bronfmans, DuPonts, Habsburgs, Sassoons, Schiffs, Thyssens, Vanderbilts and Witten-Saxe-Coburg-Gotha-Windsors, and the organizations – Bilderberg Group, Royal Institute of International Affairs, Council on Foreign Relations, Trilateral Commission, Bohemian Club, Club of Rome, Skull and Bones Society, Fabian Society, New York Century Association, Cosmos Club, Twentieth Century Fund, United Nations, Federal Reserve Corp., Council of Nine, Freemasons, Roman Catholic Church, Society of Jesus, Knights of Malta, Knights Templar, Illuminati Order and hundreds of other groups – or we may also make similar mistakes.

In his second book, *The 1980'S: Countdown to Armageddon,* Lindsey said that the False Prophet was alive in 1980 when the book was written:

I believe the false prophet is in the Middle East today, awaiting his fateful hour. (Ibid., p. 48)

When the False Prophet is identified, and it is learned that he was born after 1980, it will mean that Hal Lindsey made another false prediction.

In his book, *Planet Earth 2000 A.D.,* Lindsey predicted the Rapture would take place in the year 2000. However, he left himself a face-saving outlet:

"Could I be wrong? Of course. The Rapture may not occur between now and the year 2000." (p. 306)

Lindsey has been wrong about every prediction he has made. Why? He has been unduly influenced by the doctrine of *imminence*, and he does not understand what the **What** is.

Texe Marrs

Texe Marrs suggested in a 1992 essay, "Night Cometh!" the Rapture could take place by the year 2000. He wrote that Satan's "New Age occult kingdom will be fully in place on planet earth and the New Age messiah will be in charge of this world. But, that's the Devil's timetable, not God's" (James, William T., *Storming Toward Armageddon*, p. 130).

The devil has wanted to establish his final world order for decades, but he has been hindered by the Holy Spirit.

Joe VanKoevering

Dr. Joe VanKoevering, president of "God's News Behind the News" and pastor of the Gateway Christian Center in St. Petersburg, Florida, with his wife Kaye Brubaker VanKoevering, made a DVD *Unveiling the Man of Sin* in which he identified the Antichrist as being Prince El-Hassan bin Talal. He is the son of King Talal of Jordan and Queen Zein al-Sharaf. He is the brother of the late King Hussein, and was Crown Prince from 1965 to 1999. He is also uncle to the present King Abdullah II of Jordan.

It is impossible for El-Hassan to be the Antichrist because he is far too old. He was born in 1947 and is 63 as of 2010. Even if the Tribulation were to begin this year he is too old. It would seem more reasonable the Antichrist will be a young man in his thirties because he comes as one in place of Jesus. We also know that no one will be able to identify the Antichrist until the world government is formed (Daniel 7.23) and it breaks into ten divisions (Daniel 7.24). Once those two prophecies are fulfilled Christians will be able to identify the Antichrist.

Benny Hinn

Toufik Benedictus "Benny" Hinn, Palestinian born televangelist, founder of the Orlando Christian Center and host of the television program "This is Your Day," has made numerous false prophecies with some of them concerning the Antichrist and the Rapture:

"A **world dictator** is coming on the scene. My! He's a **short man**. He's a short man. I see a short man who's a perfect incarnation of Satan.

[Hinn speaks in tongues.] Never in my life have I had anything happen like what's happening to me now! 'This man will rule the world. In the **next few years you will see him**. But not long after that you will see Me.'" (Orlando Christian Center, 12.31.1989, emphasis mine)

"We may have **two years before the rapture**. Can I be blunt with you? I don't know if we have **two years left**. I'm going to prove to you from the Word tonight, that **we have less than two years**." (Trinity Broadcasting Network, 11.9.1990, emphasis mine)

"**Jesus is coming again** within the **next two years**." (July 1997, fundraising telethon on TBN, emphasis mine)

Harold Camping

Harold Camping wrote a book, "1994?" in which he decided the end of the world when no one could be saved any longer would be September 6, 1994 (1994?, pp. 526-7, p.531). During that year he said emphatically that the Lord would return between September 15-27. He went on to predict September 29, and then October 2 for the end. Camping made another prediction a few years later picking March 31, 1995. When the Lord failed to return on those dates he said he did not predict the Lord's Second Coming. He said it was highly probable the Lord would return on those dates. Since then he has made another prediction for the Lord's return. That lucky year is 2011. Here is the warning posted on his website:

In 2 Peter 3:8, which is quoted above, Holy God reminds us that one day is as 1,000 years. Therefore, with the correct understanding that the seven days referred to in Genesis 7:4 can be understood as 7,000 years, we learn that when God told Noah there were seven days to escape worldwide destruction, He was also telling the world there would be exactly 7,000 years (one day is as 1,000 years) to escape the wrath of God that would come when He destroys the world on Judgment Day. Because Holy Infinite God is all-knowing, He knows the end from the beginning. He knew how sinful the world would become.

Seven thousand years after 4990 B.C. (the year of the Flood) is the year 2011 A.D. (our calendar). 4990 + 2011 − 1 = 7,000 [*One year must be subtracted in going from an Old Testament B.C. calendar date to a New Testament A.D. calendar date because the calendar does not have a year zero.*]

Thus Holy God is showing us by the words of 2 Peter 3:8 that He wants us to know that exactly 7,000 years after He destroyed the world with water in Noah's day, He plans to destroy the entire world forever. *Because the year 2011 A.D. is exactly 7,000 years after 4990 B.C. when the flood began, the Bible has given us absolute proof that the year 2011 is the end*

296

of the world during the Day of Judgment, which will come on the last day of the Day of Judgment.

Amazingly, May 21, 2011 is the 17th day of the 2nd month of the Biblical calendar of our day. Remember, the flood waters also began on the 17th day of the 2nd month, in the year 4990 B.C.

The Holy Bible gives several additional astounding proofs that May 21, 2011 is very accurate as the time for the Day of Judgment. For more information on this subject, you may request a copy of *We Are Almost There*, available free of charge from Family Radio.

God is proving to us that we have very accurately learned from the Holy Bible God's time-plan for the end of the world.

Sadly, the Holy Bible tells us that only a small percentage of today's world will turn from their evil ways, and with great humility and fear will cry to God for mercy. Nevertheless, the Bible assures us that many of the people who do beg God for His mercy will not be destroyed. We learn from the Bible that Holy God plans to rescue about 200 million people (that is about 3% of today's population). On the first day of the Day of Judgment (May 21, 2011) they will be caught up (raptured) into Heaven because God had great mercy for them. This is why we can be so thankful that God has given us advance notice of Judgment Day.[4] (Emphasis added, H.C.)

His date for the flood of Noah's time (4990 BC) is off by over 2500 years. The major dates for the flood are – Martin Antsey 2386, the Chinese 2348, Bishop Ussher 2348, the Great Pyramid 2343, Judaism 2105.

Camping teaches that May 21, 2011, will be the day that Christians are raptured and the Tribulation begins. He believes the Tribulation will last 5 months (Genesis 7.24), and Jesus Christ will return in person on October 21, 2011. On that day the unsaved will be judged.

He is also wrong in the number of people who will be saved. He gets that number from Revelation 9.16. The 200,000,000 is the number of the demonic creatures that will terrorize the world during the Tribulation with the blowing of the sixth trumpet. The number of people who will be raptured before the start of the Tribulation will be more than 200 million, and there may be that many or more saved during the Tribulation (Revelation 7.9). Most of those saved during the Tribulation will be martyred.

He confirmed his belief that Jesus will return on May 21, 2011 on his "Open Forum" program. He said he is positive that his date is correct:

I have no option, I can't say as I did a few years ago there is a high likelihood it'll be this or that. Now **I have to say it is absolutely certain** this is going to happen. ("Open Forum," 10.09.2009, emphasis mine)

It is hard to believe that Camping is right about his date for creation and everyone else is off by 6000 years. If his date for creation (11,013 B.C.), and the flood (4990 B.C.) are wrong, then his date for the Second Coming is also wrong. When May 22, 2011 roles around, it will mean that Camping has made another false prediction. Let's hope it will be his last.

Camping uses two verses – *"And it came to pass after the seven days, that the waters of the flood were upon the earth"* (Genesis 7.10), and *"But forget not this one thing, beloved, that one day is with the Lord as a thousand years, and a thousand years as one day"* (1 Peter 3.8) – to determine that the statement in Genesis is a prophecy that after 7000 years (7 days) the Earth will be destroyed. He chooses 4990 as the year of the flood, and counts 7000 years from that date to arrive at 2011. He also claims the flood started on May 21 of 4990 so the destruction of the world will begin on May 21, 2011. Jesus will return 5 months later (Genesis 7.24) to judge the wicked on October 21, 2011.

Arnold Murray

Arnold Murray, pastor of the Shepherd's Chapel teaches numerous false doctrines. He also made a few false predictions. In 1980 he said we were living in the last 3½ years of the Tribulation. He predicted that "one-worldism shall come to pass, and it shall receive a deadly wound about the end of this year." He also predicted the Millennial Temple would start to be built in 1981, and the Antichrist would appear in the same year.[5]

What God Says Concerning False Prophets

"When a prophet speaks in the name of the Lord, if the thing does not come about or come true, that is the thing which the Lord has not spoken. The prophet has spoken it presumptuously; you shall not be afraid of him." (Deuteronomy 18.22)

Conclusion

The only people who make incorrect predictions concerning the timing of the Rapture and Second Coming are those who think the Lord can return at *any moment*. Those who clearly understand that specific prophetic *warning signs* must be fulfilled before the Rapture can take place never make false predictions. They simply *"wait"* and *"watch"* for those prophecies to be fulfilled just as Jesus commanded us to do:

"Take heed, watch and pray: for you know not when the time is. For the Son of Man is as a man taking a far journey, who left his house, and gave authority to his servants, and to every man his work, and commanded the porter to watch. Watch ye therefore: for you know not when the master of the house cometh, at even, or at midnight, or at the cockcrowing, or in the morning: Lest coming suddenly he find you sleeping. And what I say unto you I say unto all, Watch." (Mark 13.33-37)

And what do we "*watch*" for? The only things that we can "*watch*" for are the prophetic *warning signs* (the **What**) that the Old Testament prophets, Jesus, Paul and Peter gave so we would know the **When** (time of the Rapture)!

STUDY QUESTIONS

Appendix F

1. Does the Bible encourage Christians to predict the time of the Rapture and Second Coming?

2. Can someone predict the timing of the Rapture based on numerology or numbers found in the Bible?

3. How does a student of Bible prophecy determine how near the Rapture/ Tribulation is?

4. Should Christians keep "watch" to know when the Rapture will take place?

5. What should Christians be "watching" for to know when the Rapture will take place?

6. What two things have all of the false prophets listed in this appendix have failed to understand concerning the Rapture and the start of the Tribulation?

APPENDIX G

NEW WORLD ORDER GANG

Shadow organizations

Some "shadow" organizations are the: Holy See (325), Knights of Malta (1080), Knights Templar (1118), City of London Corporation (1141), Military Order of Christ (1318), Order of the Garter (1348), Rosicrucian Society (1407), East India Company (1600), Freemasons (1314 or 1717), Society of Jesus (1534), Illuminati Order (1776), Cambridge Apostles (1820), Skull and Bones Society (1832), Bohemian Club (1872), Theosophical Society (1875), Fabian Society (1884), Martinist Order (1884), Society of the Elect (1891), Pilgrims Society (1902), Round Table Groups (1909), Thule Society (1911), Federal Reserve Corporation (1913), Royal Institute for International Affairs (1920), Vril Society (1921), Council on Foreign Relations (1921), Family (1935), Bilderberg Group (1954), Club of Rome (1968), the Trilateral Commission (1973), Al-Qaeda (1988), Belizean Grove (1999).

Conspirators

Thousands of people in key positions in politics, law enforcement, finance, business, religion, education and the military have been members/attendees of "shadow" organizations. Most have worked to create a "New World Order" while others are ignorant of the end game. The more notable members or attendees of a "shadow" organization (with a key at the end of this list) are:

Kings, Queens, Princes: Kings of England: Edward VII (M), Edward VIII (M), George IV (M), George VI (M) and William IV (M); King Juan Carlos I of Spain (B), Queen Elizabeth II (PS), Queen Beatrix of the Netherlands (B), Queen Sophia of Spain (B), Prince Philip of England (BC, M), Prince Bernhard of the Netherlands (B), Prince Willem-Alexander of the Netherlands (B).

Prime Ministers, Chancellors, Presidents: British PMs: Tony Blair (B), Winston Churchill (M), Edward Heath (B), Margaret Thatcher (B) and Harold Wilson (B); German Chancellors: Adolf Hitler (TS, VS), Helmut Schmidt (B, BC) and Angela Merkel (B); French Presidents: Jacques Chirac (B), Francois Mitterand (M) and Georges Pompiduo (B); Russian President Boris Yeltsin (CFR) and Mexican President Benito Juarez (M).

U.S. Presidents: George Bush (BC, SB), George H.W. Bush (B, BC, CFR, SB, TC), Bill Clinton (B, CFR, M, TC), Ronald Reagan (BC, M), James

Carter (CFR, TC), Gerald Ford, Jr. (B, BC, CFR, M), Richard Nixon (BC, CFR), Lyndon Johnson (M), John Kennedy (CFR), Dwight D. Eisenhower (BC, CFR), Harry Truman (M), Franklin Roosevelt (M), Herbert Hoover (BC, CFR), Calvin Coolidge (BC), Warren Harding (M), Theodore Roosevelt (BC, M), William Taft (BC, M, SB, PS), William McKinley (M), James Garfield (M), Andrew Johnson (M), James Buchanan (M), James Polk (M), Andrew Jackson (M), James Monroe (M), George Washington (M).

Vice Presidents: Richard Cheney (BC, CFR, PNAC, TC), George Clinton (M), Al Gore, Jr. (B, BC, TC), Richard Johnson (M), William Rufus King (M), Thomas Marshall (M), Walter Mondale (CFR, TC), Dan Quayle (B, M, PNAC), Nelson Rockefeller (BC), Henry Wallace (M).

Supreme Court Justices: Stephen Breyer (CFR), Ruth Bader Ginsburg (CFR), John Jay (M), Thurgood Marshall (M), Sandra Day O'Connor (CFR), Potter Stewart (SB), Earl Warren (BC, M).

Secretaries of State: Madeleine Albright (CFR), Hillary Clinton (B, CFR), Warren Christopher (CFR), Robert Gates (CFR), Alexander Haig (BC, CFR, KM), Henry Kissinger (B, BC, CFR, TC), Colin Powell (B, BC, CFR, KM), Elihu Root (CFR), George Shultz (BC, CFR, TC).

Secretaries of War/Defense: Frank Carlucci (CFR), William Cohen (CFR), Henry Knox (M), Robert McNamara (B, CFR, TC), Donald Rumsfeld (B, BC, PNAC), Caspar Weinberger (BC, CFR, PS).

Governors: Jeb Bush (BC, CFR, PNAC), John Hancock (M), George Pataki (B), Rick Perry (B), Arnold Schwarzenegger (BC), George Wallace (M), Christine Whitman (B).

Senators: Prescott Bush (CFR, SB), John Chafee (B, CFR, TC), Tom Daschle (B), Bob Dole (M), John Edwards (B), Diane Feinstein (B, CFR, TC), Chuck Hagel (B), Gary Hart (B, CFR), Robert Kennedy (BC, CFR), John Kerry (CFR, SB), John McCain, Jr. (B, CFR, M), Sam Nunn (B), John Rockefeller IV (B, CFR, TC), Robert Taft, Jr. (TC).

CIA/FBI/NSA/Military: Richard Helms (CIA – BC), Bobby Inman (DIA, NSA, ONI – BC, CFR, TC), William Webster (CIA, FBI – BC, CFR), Albert Wedemeyer (BC), Robert James Woolsey (CIA – BC).

Bankers: Roger Altman (CFR), Ben Bernanke (B), Arthur Burns (CFR), Alan Greenspan (BC, CFR, TC), Timothy Geithner (B), James Johnson (B, CFR, TC), Henry Paulson, Jr. (B), Jakob Meyer Rothschild (M), Robert Rubin (CFR), Paul Volker (B, BC, CFR, TC), James Warburg (CFR), Paul Warburg (CFR), James Wolfensohn (B, CFR), Robert Zoellick (B, CFR).

Billionaires: Francis David Astor (B), John Jacob Astor (M), Riley Bechtel (BC), Stephen Bechtel, Sr. (BC), Stephen Bechtel, Jr. (BC), John Kluge (BC), Daniel Ludwig (BC), David Rockefeller (B, BC, CFR, PS, TC), David Rockefeller, Jr. (BC, CFR, M), Edmond de Rothschild (B), Evelyn de Rothshild (B), Guy de Rothschild (B), Lionel Rothschild (B), George Soros (B), Kevin Trudeau (B).

Media: David Brinkley (CFR), Tom Brokaw (CFR), William Buckley (B, BC, CFR, SB), John Chancellor (CFR), Walter Cronkite (BC), Katherine Graham (B, CFR, TC), Donald Graham (B), William Randolph Hearst, Jr. (BC), Peter Jennings (B), Jim Lehrer (CFR), Henry Luce (CFR, SB), Irving Kristol (CFR), William Kristol (B, PNAC), Bill Moyers (B, CFR), Robert Novak (BC), William Paley (CFR), Dan Rather (CFR), Harry Reasoner (CFR), Diane Sawyer (CFR), George Stephanopoulos (B, CFR), Laurence Tisch (CFR), Barbara Walters (CFR), John Welch (CFR), Mort Zuckerman (B, CFR).

Preachers: Manly Hall (M), William Hamilton (M), Jesse Jackson (CFR, M), Peter Marshall (M), William Miller (M), Norman Vincent Peale (M), Joseph Smith, Sr. & Jr. (M), Rick Warren (CFR), Brigham Young (M).

Others: Elliot Abrams (CFR), Giovanni Agnelli (B), Benedict Arnold (M), Mikhail Bakunin (M) George Ball (B), José Barroso (B), Sandy Berger (CFR), Shirley Black (CFR), John Bolton (B, PNAC), Edgar Bronfman, Sr. (CFR), Zbigniew Brzezinski (BC, CFR, TC), McGeorge Bundy (CFR), Alessandro Cagliostro (I, M), Peter Carrington (B), Alexander Christakis (CR), Doug Coe (BC), Aleister Crowley (M), Étienne Davignon (B), Benjamin Franklin (M), David Gergen (B, BC, CFR, TC), Hermann Göring (TS,VS), Maurice R. Greenberg (B, CFR, TC), Richard Haass (CFR), Otto von Habsburg (B), Denis Healey (B), Heinrich Himmler (TS, VS), Alec Douglas-Home (B), J. Edgar Hoover (M), Erich Jantsch (CR), Vernon Jordan (B, CFR), Robert Kagan (PNAC), Alexander King (CR), Freiherr Knigge (I), Henry Mallon (SB), Giuseppe Mazzini (M), Alfred Milner (RT), Hasan Ozbekhan (CR), Richard Parsons (M), Aurelio Peccei (CR), Richard Perle (B, CFR, PNAC), Philip, Duke of Wharton (M), Albert Pike (M), George Robertson (B), Joseph Retinger (B), Cecil Rhodes (RT), Eric Roll (B), Karl Rove (BC), Walter Scheel (B), James Steinberg (B), Lawrence Summers (B, CFR), Mark Twain (BC, M), Voltaire (M), H.G. Wells (FS), Adam Weishaupt (I, M), Paul Wolfowitz (B, CFR).

Key: Bilderberg. (B), Bohemian Club (BC), Club of Rome (CR), Council on Foreign Relations (CFR), Fabian Society (FS), Masons (M), Illuminati (I), Knights of Malta (KM), Pilgrims Society (PS), Project for a New American Century (PNAC), Round Table Groups (RT), Skull and Bones (SB), Thule Society (TS), Trilateral Commission (TC), Vril Society (VS).

Conclusion to Part V

The easiest way to establish a "New World Order" is to make people believe there is no movement to create one. Eric Blair understood this and noted it in his most famous novel, *1984*:

> Until they become conscious they will never rebel, and until after they have rebelled they cannot become conscious. (p. 61)
> The masses never revolt of their own accord, and they never revolt merely because they are oppressed. Indeed, so long as they are not permitted to have standards of comparison they never even become aware that they are oppressed. (p. 171)

Deception is the name of the game. Blair knew that there was a group of "New World Order" conspirators, and he wrote *1984* to warn mankind about them. His book was published on June 8, 1949, and he died on January 21, 1950. Some conspiriologists speculate he was murdered for writing *1984*. This is a portion of the dialogue that a Party member, O'Brien, gives to the hero of the novel, Winston Smith, who wanted to be free of the Party:

> "The Party seeks power entirely for its own sake. We are not interested in the good of others; we are interested solely in power, pure power. What pure power means you will understand presently. We are different from all the oligarchies of the past in that we know what we are doing. All the others, even those who resembled ourselves, were cowards and hypocrites. The German Nazis and the Russian Communists came very close to us in their methods, but they never had the courage to recognize their own motives. They pretended, perhaps they even believed, that they had seized power unwillingly and for a limited time, and that just around the corner there lay a paradise where human beings would be free and equal. We are not like that. We know that no one ever seizes power with the intention of relinquishing it. **Power is not a means; it is an end.** One does not establish a dictatorship in order to safeguard a revolution; **one makes the revolution in order to establish the dictatorship. The object of persecution is persecution. The object of torture is torture. The object of power is power.**" (*1984*, p. 217, emphasis mine)

Blair tossed in some clever slogans that showed how evil the "New World Order" gang was (and still is):

WAR IS PEACE
FREEDOM IS SLAVERY
IGNORANCE IS STRENGTH

The conspirators have placed slogans and symbols of their conspiracy in public view. Some of these symbols are the fasci bundle of sticks; the "all-seeing eye" over the pyramid; and the pyramid. Some slogans are *"Novus Ordo Seclorum"* and *"Annuit Coeptis."*

Toward the end of his book Blair explained the significance of the middle slogan through the antagonist, O'Brien speaking to Smith:

> "Has it ever occurred to you that it is reversible? **Slavery is freedom.** Alone–free–the human being is always defeated. It must be so, because every human being is doomed to die, which is the greatest of all failures. But if he can make complete, utter submission, if he can escape from his identity, if he can merge himself in the Party so that he is the Party, then he is all-powerful and immortal. The second thing for you to realize is that power is the power over human beings. Over the body–but, above all, over the mind. Power over matter–external reality, as you would call it–is not important." (Ibid., p. 218, emphasis mine)

> "Obedience is not enough. Unless he is suffering, how can you be sure that he is obeying your will and not his own? **Power is in inflicting pain and humiliation. Power is in tearing down human minds to pieces and putting them together again in new shapes of your own choosing.** Do you begin to see, then, what kind of world we are creating? It is the exact opposite of the stupid hedonistic Utopias that the old reformers imagined. A world of fear, treachery, and torment, a world of trampling and being trampled upon, a world which will grow not less but more merciless as it refines itself. **Progress in our world will be progress toward more pain.** The old civilizations claimed that they were founded on love and justice. **Ours is founded on hatred.** In our world there will be no emotions except fear, rage, triumph, and self-abasement. Everything else we shall destroy– everything." (Ibid., p. 220, emphasis mine)

O'Brien went on to explain to Smith how the Party destroys civilization:
> "We have cut the links between child and parent, and between man and man, and between man and woman. No one dares trust a wife or a child or a friend any longer. But in the future there will be no wives and no friends. **Children will be taken from their mothers at birth**, as one takes eggs from a hen." (Ibid., emphasis mine)

> "There will be no loyalty, except loyalty to the Party. **There will be no love, except the love of Big Brother.** There will be no laughter, except the laughter of triumph over a defeated enemy. There will be no art, no literature, no science. **When we are omnipotent we will have no need of science.** There will be no distinction between beauty and ugliness. There will be no curiosity, no employment of the process of life. All competing pleasures will be destroyed. But always – do not forget this, Winston – always there will be the intoxication of power, constantly increasing and constantly growing subtler. Always, at every moment, there will be the thrill of victory, the sensation of trampling on an enemy who is helpless. **If**

you want a picture of this future, imagine a boot stamping on a human face–forever.

"And remember that it is forever. The face will always be there to be stamped upon. The heretic, the enemy of society, will always be there, so that he can be defeated and humiliated over again. Everything that you have undergone since you have been in our hands – all that will continue, and worse. The espionage, the betrayals, the arrests, the tortures, the executions, the disappearances will never cease. **It will be a world of terror** as much as a world of triumph. The more the Party is powerful, the less it will be tolerant; the weaker the opposition, the tighter the despotism. Goldstein and his heresies will live forever. Every day, at every moment, they will be defeated, discredited, ridiculed, spat upon–and yet they will always survive." (Ibid., pp. 220-221, emphasis mine)

O'Brien continued to explain that progress was only made to further the tyrannical power of the Party:

"And even technological progress only happens when its products can in some way be used for the diminution of human liberty. In all the useful arts the world is either standing still or going backwards." (Ibid., p. 159)

The two major goals of the Party was conquest and the elimination of independent thought:

The two aims of the Party are to conquer the whole surface of the earth and to extinguish once and for all the possibility of independent thought. (Ibid.)

Party members were expected to have a war-like mentality and wicked behavior was encouraged in the negative utopia that Blair depicted:

In other words it is necessary that he should have the mentality appropriate to a state of war. (Ibid., p. 158)

There were bribery, favoritism, and racketeering of every kind, there were homosexuality and prostitution, there was even illicit alcohol distilled from potatoes. **The positions of trust were given only to the common criminals, especially the gangsters and the murderers, who formed a sort of aristocracy. All the dirty jobs were done by the politicals**.

There was constant come-and-go of prisoners of every description; drug peddlers, thieves, bandits, black marketers, drunks, prostitutes. (Ibid., pp. 187-188, emphasis mine)

The insidious evil of this "New World Order" that Blair described was prophesied by Jesus and Paul:

"Then shall they deliver you up unto tribulation, and shall kill you: and ye shall be hated of all the nations for my name's sake. And then shall many

stumble, and shall deliver up one another, and shall hate one another. And many false prophets shall arise, and shall lead many astray. And because iniquity shall be multiplied, the love of the many shall wax cold." (Matthew 24.9-12)

"And brother shall deliver up brother to death, and the father his child; and children shall rise up against parents, and cause them to be put to death. And ye shall be hated of all men for my name's sake: but he that endureth to the end, the same shall be saved." (Mark 13.12-13)

But know this, that in the last days grievous times shall come. For men shall be lovers of self, lovers of money, boastful, haughty, railers, disobedient to parents, unthankful, unholy, without natural affection, implacable, slanderers, without self-control, fierce, no lovers of good, traitors, headstrong, puffed up, lovers of pleasure rather than lovers of God; holding a form of godliness, but having denied the power therefore. From these also turn away. (2 Timothy 3.1-5)

Some of the things that Blair described in his book are already being implemented. Scripture says the final world empire will be very evil, like that in *1984*. It will be Satan's last stand, and he will pull out every stop. It will be more demonic, destructive, devious, evil, hateful, hideous, insidious, oppressive, sinful, tyrannical and uglier than all the world empires before it.

This demonic empire will not arise overnight. It is being built brick-by-brick over centuries. The closer we come to the culmination of this satanic conspiracy, the worse things will be for Christians and everyone who cherishes freedom. They will be persecuted, imprisoned and killed. Once the Beast Kingdom is established, the reign of terror will be far greater than all the former reigns of terror. Christians, patriots and freedom lovers will be exterminated in large numbers (Revelation 6.9-11).

As we noted previously the Bible teaches us that the devil is the god of this world (2 Corinthians 4.4), the prince (ruler) of this world (John 12.31; 14.30; 16.11), the prince of the powers of the air (Ephesians 2.2) and the evil one (1 John 5.19). The devil also has a host of fallen angels and demons that serve him. Christians do not fight *"against flesh and blood, but against the "principalities, against the powers, against the world-rulers of this darkness, against the spiritual hosts of wickedness in the heavenly places* (Ephesians 6.12). These immortal beings rule over the nations of the world as Daniel was told by an angel:

Then said he, Knowest thou wherefore I am come unto thee? and now will I return to fight with the prince of Persia: and when I go forth, lo, the prince of Greece shall come. (Daniel 10.20)

The *"prince of Persia"* and the *"prince of Greece"* were high-ranking fallen angels that ruled over those kingdoms. Fallen angels still rule over nations and empires today. Now that we are getting close to the start of the

Tribulation when the devil and his gang of evil angels will have absolute control over the world, Christians will face much more persecution from them.

Christians must prepare for the worst period of persecution in the history of the Church. We can do this by putting on the full armor of God:

Finally, be strong in the Lord, and in the strength of his might. Put on the whole armor of God, that ye may be able to stand against the wiles of the devil. For our wrestling is not against flesh and blood, but against the principalities, against the powers, against the world-rulers of this darkness, against the spiritual hosts of wickedness in the heavenly places. Wherefore take up the whole armor of God, that ye may be able to withstand in the evil day, and, having done all, to stand. Stand therefore, having girded your loins with truth, and having put on the breastplate of righteousness, and having shod your feet with the preparation of the gospel of peace; withal taking up the shield of faith, wherewith ye shall be able to quench all the fiery darts of the evil one. And take the helmet of salvation, and the sword of the Spirit, which is the word of God: with all prayer and supplication praying at all seasons in the Spirit, and watching thereunto in all perseverance and supplication for all the saints. (Ephesians 6.10-18)

A Christian girds his loins with the truth by daily studying the Bible (Acts 17.11); he puts on the breastplate of righteousness by living a holy life (1 Peter 1.15-16); he shods his feet with the gospel of peace by learning how to share his faith in a gentle and reverent manner (1 Peter 3.15); he takes up the shield of faith by trusting in God in all things (Proverbs 3.5-6); he wears the helmet of salvation by trusting in the blood of Jesus to cleanse him of his sins (Ephesians 1.7; Revelation 1.5; 5.9); he takes up the sword of the Spirit by memorizing Scripture so he can quote it to defeat the enemy (Deuteronomy 8.3; Matthew 4.1-4). He also prays without ceasing (Ephesians 6.18; 1 Thessalonians 5.17). All Christians should prepare for the time of trouble ahead by fellowshipping with the brethren as often as possible (Hebrews 10.24-25) and by making disciples (Matthew 28.19-20; 2 Timothy 2.2).

Some pastors say there is nothing Christians can do or should do to oppose the efforts of the conspirators to create a "New World Order":

Inasmuch as the Scriptures tell us that it's going to come, how can you stave it off? I mean, it's part of God's plan... I think that we need to be wise to what's happening, but only inasmuch as we need to be preparing for the Lord to come, and rescue us from this corrupt system.

The New World Order is coming. We know that, Revelation 13. It seems to be happening at an exponential rate. Like we were talking yesterday with Gordon Brown, Barak Obama's idea of a new world economy is to globalize the economy. Basically to save everything, save jobs, to invest in that, and so it's here, you know, and just a matter of time before the final Antichrist takes over, but there are many antichrists running around now doing their bit. So what can you really do? We try to vote at the ballot box, but that seems to have not a whole lot of effect. You know it's common. So we just need to be aware of it... Let's be aware of what's going on, know the signs of the times in that way we won't be caught unaware like the Bible encourages us to be.[34]

I think as Christians we would be far better served to become biblically literate, to learn to read the Bible for all it's worth. So rather than spending endless hours in conspiracy theories let's do what we are called to do, and that is to change the hearts of individuals through the power of the Holy Spirit. And when we do that we affect our world in the way we are empowered to affect our world. But we cannot know what is coming tomorrow or the next day. Jesus said, "Do not worry about tomorrow. You do not know what a day will bring forth." Don't worry about tomorrow. Each day He said has enough trouble of its own. So let's not project on what can happen tomorrow, we don't know. What we know is the God we serve holds tomorrow in His hands. In the meantime we're called to be prudent, to be faithful, to live by biblical principles and not to engage in endless conspiracy theories about what might happen based on a paradigm, by the way, that has little basis in the text of Scripture.[35]

The "New World Order" is being built, and it is not a "conspiracy theory;" it is a conspiracy fact! Some secular talk show hosts say there is no conspiracy to create a "New World Order," but due to the economic crisis of 2008-2009 and the ascension of Barak Obama, some have changed their minds:

Dick Morris: There is a big thing that's going to happen at this thing in London, the G-20, and they're hiding it, they're camouflaging it, they're not talking about it. Coordination of international regulation. What they are going to do is put our Fed and FCC under control, in effect, of the IMF.

Sean Hannity: Oh, come on. You believe they're going to do this?

Morris: That's what is in the **draft agenda**. They call it coordination of regulation. What it really is, is **putting the American economy under international regulation**. And those people who've been yelling, oh, the UN is going to take over, **global government**.

Hannity: **Conspiracy theorists**.

Morris: They've been crazy, but **now they are right**.

Hannity: Well, what Geithner said he would be open to the idea of a **global currency** last week. Those **conspiracy people** had said, had suggested that for years.

Morris: **They're not wrong**.

Hannity: **They're not wrong**.

308

Morris: You know, what they always do at these conferences is they have the center show is here, and the side show they want you to pay attention to. The center show is the size of the stimulus package. **The real show is international regulation for financial institutions**, which is going to happen **under the IMF control**. And remember, the **IMF is run by Europeans**, the World Bank by Americans.[36] (Emphasis mine)

In a separate broadcast, Michael Savage had this to say about the possibility of the government creating a crisis for its benefit:

Very soon, **Obama will create a crisis along the lines of the Reichstag fire**, the Reichstag fire. I don't know what form it will take, but I believe that once the minions are seen for what they are, **Rahm Immanuel and his gang will set off a Reichstag fire in this country of some kind**, and they will recall the military dictatorship of Lincoln and Stanton during the Civil War, when civilian suspects were arrested without warrant. I will tell you as I sit here I fear that every night as I go to sleep. I put nothing past these agitators who have suddenly seized control of the most powerful economy and the most powerful military on Earth.[37] (Emphasis mine)

As we get closer to the formation of the Devil's "New World Order," it will become obvious that the prophecies in the Bible are being fulfilled. Christians need to be prepared to use fulfilled Bible prophecies as a springboard to share the gospel. They should also stand against the satanic "New World Order." As noted in the Preface, Scripture commands Christians to rebuke the wicked (Proverbs 24.24-25), keep the law to strive against the wicked (Proverbs 28.4) and expose their evil deeds (Ephesians 5.11). Most Christians in America have not shed blood in resisting sin (Hebrews 12.3-4). A Christian who is unwilling to take a stand against the wicked is like "*a troubled fountain, and a corrupted spring*" (Proverbs 25.26). You can oppose it by warning others about it.

Edmund Burke (1729-1797), the famous Anglo-Irish statesmen, philosopher, author, orator and political theorist said, "The only thing that is necessary for evil to triumph is for men of good will to do nothing."

Christians are people of good will, therefore we must oppose evil, including the "New World Order Gang" and their Old World Nightmare.

General George Washington (1732-1799) made this comment about the American Christian, "He will die on his feet before he will live on his knees."

Many Christians have died for Jesus Christ, and many more will die for Him as we race toward the Rapture and the start of the Tribulation. Some may even be martyred for their faith in America in the coming years.

General George S. Patton, Jr. told his soldiers to "Live for something rather than die for nothing." Christians should live for Christ.

We ask what the psalmist asked, "*Who will rise up for me against the evil-doers? Who will stand up for me against the workers of iniquity?*" (Psalm 94.16)

NOTES

Chapter 5, Warning signs that have yet to be fulfilled

1. www.rferl.org/content/Iraqs_Ancient_Babylon_To_Be_Restored/14920 06.html.
2. Georgia House of Representatives - 1995/1996 Sessions. HB 1274 - Death penalty; guillotine provisions.
1-21 "17-10-38. (Index)
1-22 (a) All persons who have been convicted of a capital
1-23 offense and have had imposed upon them a sentence of death
1-24 shall, at the election of the condemned, suffer such
1-25 punishment either by electrocution or by guillotine. If
1-26 the condemned fails to make an election by the thirtieth
1-27 day preceding the date scheduled for execution, punishment
1-28 shall be by electrocution.

Chapter 6, The Early Church Fathers

1. http://www.ccel.org/ccel/schaff/npnf207.ii.xix.html

Chapter 10, The Gap

1. http://www.stempublishing.com/authors/darby/PROPHET/11010E.html.
2. LaHaye, Tim. The Tim LaHaye Prophecy Study Bible, AMG Publishers, 2000. Page 1286.
3. www.pre-trib.org/article-view.php?id=63.
4. "Are You Rapture Ready?" www.hilton-sutton.org/view_acrobat%20files/rapture _ready_ outline.pdf.

Chapter 11, The Doctrine of Imminence

1. www.pre-trib.org/article-view.php?id=30.
2. http://www.stempublishing.com/authors/darby/PROPHET/11010E.html.
3. Pastor's Perspective, 6.18.2009.
4. www.joelrosenberg.com/ezekiel_q5.asp.

Chapter 15, The World Economy

1. "Gulf monetary pact enters into effect: Kuwait minister." Economic Times. 12.15.2009. http://economictimes.indiatimes.com/articleshow/5340052.cms.
2. Evans-Pritchard, Ambrose. "The G20 moves the world a step closer to a global currency." Daily Telegraph. 4.03.2009. www.telegraph.co.uk/finance/comment/ambroseevans_pritchard/509 6524/The-G20moves-the-world-a-step-closer-to-a-global-currency.html.
3. Sunday Times. "The special relationship is going global." 3.01.2009. www.timesonline. co.uk/tol/comment/columnists/guestcontributors/article5821821.
4. New York Times, 8.10.1973.
5. http://quotes.liberty-tree.ca/quote_blog/Louis.McFadden.Quote.8788.
6. New York Times. "Gen. Butler Bares a 'Fascist Plot.'" 11.21.1934, p. 1. The Philadelphia Record, 11.21-22.1934.

7. Council on Foreign Relations Press. "Building a North American Community." May 2005. Task Force Report No. 53 ISBN 0876093489. www.cfr.org/publication/7912/creating_a_north_american_community.html.

Chapter 16, The World Government

1. USA Today, 3.11.1993, page 2a.
2. "Baron David de Rothschild sees a New World Order in global banking governance." Aftermath News. 11.7.2008. http://aftermathnews.wordpress.com/2008/11/07/baron-david-de-rothschild-sees-a-new-world-order-in-global-banking-governance.
3. www.propagandamatrix.com/archive_new_world_order.html.
4. New York Times. 8.10.1973.
5. Front page of www.mauricestrong.net.
6. www.nationalcenter.org/DossierStrong.html.
7. www.youtube.com/watch?v=G8JTnLBkXy4 & www.youtube.com/results?search_query=cronkite+says+i%27m+glad+to+do+the+work+of+ satan.
8. http://usa-the-republic.com/illuminati/cfr_2.html.

Chapter 17, Big Brother

1. Pack, Dee W. "Civilian Uses of Surveillance Satellites." Crosslink. Volume 1, Number 1, Winter 1999/2000. Carl J. Rice, Barbara J. Tressel, Carolyn J. Lee-Wagner, and Edgar M. Oshika. www.aero.org/publications/crosslink/winter2000/01.html
2. Juliano, Nick. "DHS ignores civil liberties in domestic spy satellite plan, lawmakers say." 4.07.2008. http://rawstory.com/news/2008/DHS_domestic_spy_satellite_plan_lacks_0407.html & Shorrock, Tim. "Domestic Spying, Inc." CorpWatch. 11.27.2007. www.corpwatch.org/article.php?id=14821.
3. "Markey Demands Answers on Bush Administration's Plan to Turn Spy Satellites on Americans. 8.16.2007. http://markey.house.gov/index.php?option=content&task=view&id=3049&Itemid=125. & http://markey.house.gov/docs/privacy/Spy/%20Satellites%20Letter%20to%20Chertoff_081607.pdf.
4. http://en.wikipedia.org/wiki/Radar_gun
5. Barnes, Julian E. "Pentagon plans blimp to spy from new heights." LA Times. 3.13.2009. www.latimes.com/news/nationworld/nation/la-na-spyblimp132009mar13,0,4608400.story
6. Soller, Kurt. "Eye in the Sky: Raytheon's unmanned blimp at this year's Indy 500." Newsweek. 6.11.2009. www.newsweek.com/id/201697.
7. McCullagh, Declan. "Drone aircraft may prowl U.S. skies." CNET News. 3.29.2006. http://news.cnet.com/2100-11746_3-6055658.html4.
8. "Honeywell Wins FAA Approval for MAV." Flying Magazine, Vol. 135., No. 5, May 2008, p. 24.
9. La Franchi, Peter. "Flight International. UK Home Office plans national police UAV fleet." Flight Global. 7.17.2007. www.flightglobal.com/articles/2007/07/17/215507/uk-home-office-plans-national-police-uav-fleet.html
10. Albrecht, Chris. "Comcast Cameras to Start Watching You?" Newteevee.com. 3.18.2008. http://newteevee.com/2008/03/18/comcast-cameras-to-start-watching-you.
11. Lewis, Jason. "Big Brother CCTV to spy on pupils aged four - complete with CPS evidence kit." Daily Mail. 12.28.2008. www.dailymail.co.uk/news/article-1102205/Big-Brother-CCTV-spy-pupils-aged-complete-CPS-evidence-kit.html.
12. Levy, Andrew. "Council uses spy plane with thermal imaging camera to snoop on homes wasting energy." Daily Mail. 3.24.2009. www.dailymail.co.uk/news/article-1164091/ Council-uses-spy-plane-thermal-imaging-camera-snoop-homes-wasting-energy.html.
13. Pickard, Gabrielle. "The Mother of all Gadgets!" Russia Today. 1.19.2009. http://rt.com/prime-time/2009-01-18/_The_%E2%80%9Cmother%E2%80%9D_ of_all_gadgets!. html.

14. Byrne, John. "Google offers free software to track people." Rawstory. 2.04.2009. http://rawstory.com/news/2008/ Google_ offers_ software_to_ track_people_0204.html.

15. Court to FBI: No spying on in-car computers. ZDNet News. Declan McCullagh. 11.19.2003. http://news.zdnet.com/2100-9584_22-132934.html

16. Kage, Ben. "Big Brother is listening: Government can eavesdrop on your life by secretly listening through your cell phone." NaturalNews. 12.05.2006. www.natural news.com/021240.html.

17. www.tscmvideo.com/eavesdropping/hookswitch%20bypass.html#.

18. Fox News. "FBI DITCHES CARNIVORE SURVEILLANCE SYSTEM." 1.18.2005. www.foxnews.com/story/0,2933,144809,00.html.

19. http://en.wikipedia.org/wiki/NarusInsight & www.eff.org/cases/att & www.narus.com & Bamford, James, *The Shadow Factory: The Ultra-Secret NSA from 9/11 to the Eavesdropping on America*.

20. Schmid, Gerhard (2001-07-11). "On the existence of a global system for the interception of private and commercial communications (ECHELON interception system), (2001/2098(INI))" (pdf – 194 pages). European Parliament: Temporary Committee on the ECHELON Interception System. www.europarl.europa.eu/sides/getDoc.do?pubRef=-//EP//NONSGML+REPORT+A5-200 1-0264+0+DOC+PDF+V0//EN&language=EN.

21. http://en.wikipedia.org/wiki/Room_641A.

22. http://cryptome.org/echelon-nh.htm.

23. USA Today. 5.11.2006. Leslie Cauley, http://www.usatoday.com/news/washington/2006-05-10-nsa_x.htm.

24. Rood, Justin. "NSA Eavesdropping 'Outrageous' and 'Disturbing,' Critics Say – Insiders Told ABC News What NSA Really Heard." ABC News. 10.10.2008. www.abcnews.go.com/Blotter/story ?id=5998860&page=1.

25. http://www.icdc.com/~paulwolf/cointelpro/churchfinalreportIIa.htm & http://en.wikiped ia.org/wiki/COINTELPRO.

26. INTELLIGENCE ACTIVITIES AND THE RIGHTS OF AMERICANS, BOOK II, FINAL REPORT. www.icdc.com/~paulwolf/cointelpro/churchfinalreportIIa.htm.

27. Rothschild, Matthew. 2008-02-07. "Exclusive! The FBI Deputizes Business." The Progressive. www.progressive.org/mag_rothschild0308. www.infragard.net & www.infragard members.org.

28. http://en.wikipedia.org/wiki/Operation_TIPS

29. Eggen, Dan. "Ashcroft backs away from TIPS informant program, just slightly." Washington Post. 7.26.2002. Page A10. http://lists.jammed.com/politech/ 2002/07/0097.html.

30. "Truckers, Toll Takers, Bus Drivers Recruited For Homeland Security." Bucks County Courier Times. 9.30.2004. www1.phillyburbs.com/pb-dyn/login.cfm?continue=/pb-dyn/article. cfm?404%3Bhttp%3A%2F%2Fwww1%2Ephillyburbs%2Ecom%3A80%2Fpb%2Ddyn%2Fnews %2F111%2D09282004%2D373236%2Ehtml%3Femail%3Dreferrer.

31. "FBI Proposes Building Network of U.S. Informants." 7.25.2007. Brian Ross. http://blogs.abcnews.com/theblotter/2007/07/fbi-proposes-bu.html

32. Finley, Bruce. "Terror watch uses local eyes 181 TRAINED IN COLO." The Denver Post. 6.29.2008. www.denverpost.com/news/ci_9725077.

33. Dewan, Shaila and Goodman, Brenda. "As Prices Rise, Crime Tipsters Work Overtime." New York Times. 5.18.2008. www.nytimes.com/2008/05/18/us/18crimestopper.html?pagewant ed=2&_r=1&partner=rssnyt&emc=rss.

34. "Operation Bright Eyes." 7.22.2009. www.myfoxorlando.com/dpp/money/072209operat ion_bright_eyes.

35. Indy.com. "Indy to enlist citizens in terrorist watch program." 10.04.2009. www.indy. com/posts/indy-to-enlist-citizens-in-terrorist-watch-program. - Los Angeles iWatch Web site: www.iWatchLA.org.

36. Lobe, Jim. "Congress Defunds Controversial 'Total Information' Program." OneWorld.net. 9.26.2003. www.commondreams.org/headlines03/0926-02.htm.

37. Shachtman, Noah. "A Spy Machine of DARPA's Dreams." Wired Magazine. 5.20.2003, www.wired.com/techbiz/media/news/2003/05/58909.

38. http://en.wikipedia.org/wiki/MATRIX

39. Weissert, Will. "Mexican attorney general personally goes high-tech for security." AP. 7.14.2004. www.usatoday.com/tech/news/2004-07-14-mex-security-implant_x.htm.

40. Croft, Jane. "Sorry, we don't take cash. Have you an arm or a leg?" Financial Times. 5.19.2007. www.ft.com/cms/s/0/6fd682a4-05a5-11dc-b151-000b5df10 621.html?nclick_check=1.

41. Unruh, Bob. "Radio chip coming soon to your driver's license?" WorldNetDaily. 2.28.2009. www.worldnetdaily.com/index.php?pageId=90008.

42. Impact Lab. "Human tracking chip created by Xega." 8.23.2008. www.impactlab.com/2008/08/23/human-tracking-chip-created-by-xega.

43. Daily Mail. "Met Police officers to be 'microchipped' by top brass in Big Brother style tracking scheme." 4.10.2008. www.dailymail.co.uk/pages/live/articles/news/news.html?in_art icle_id=558597&in_page_id=1770.

44. Black, Jeffrey and Denning, Jeffrey. "Want some torture with your peanuts?" Washinton Times. 7.01.2008. www.washingtontimes.com/weblogs/aviation-security/2008/Jul/01/want-some-torture-with-your-peanuts. & "Air safety proposal: shock-bracelets controlled by flight attendants." Boing Boing. 3.20.2008. www.boingboing.net/2008/03/20/air-safety-proposal.html.

45. http://www.sourcewatch.org/index.php?title=Rex-84.

46. www.sourcewatch.org/index.php?title=American_concentration_camps.

47. www.nationalguard.com/careers/mos/description.php?mos_code=31E.

48. http://en.wikipedia.org/wiki/List_of_United_States_Army_careers#Strategic_Plans_and_P olicy_FA.

49. Georgia House of Representatives - 1995/1996 Sessions. HB 1274 - Death penalty; guillotine provisions.
1-21 "17-10-38. (Index)
1-22 (a) All persons who have been convicted of a capital
1-23 offense and have had imposed upon them a sentence of death
1-24 shall, at the election of the condemned, suffer such
1-25 punishment either by electrocution or by guillotine. If
1-26 the condemned fails to make an election by the thirtieth
1-27 day preceding the date scheduled for execution, punishment
1-28 shall be by electrocution.

ABOUT THE AUTHORS

Dr. F. Kenton Beshore

"Doc," as he is affectionately known, was saved at the age of 5 and called to preach at age 8. While growing up, he listened to, and read books, by several great dispensational teachers – Donald Grey Barnhouse, William Pettingill and Harry Ironside.

At the age of 17, Doc was licensed to preach, and his first sermon was on the Second Coming of Jesus Christ. In that sermon, he spoke of the promise, the plan, the purpose, the power and the person of His coming. Throughout his life, beginning at a very early age, he studied prophecy, and frequently sees something new.

Doc pastored his first church at age 18, and was ordained at 19, at Bellview Baptist Church, Memphis, Tennessee, by his pastor, Dr. Robert G. Lee. He pastored churches most of his life, and much of his preaching, teaching and writing has been on Bible prophecy. He taught through the entire Bible verse-by-verse before age 40.

Dr. David L. Cooper was the Doc's mentor for ten years at the Biblical Research Society, and he became its president when Dr. Cooper went home to be with the Lord. He was also the editor of the Biblical Research Monthly. Possessing several earned degrees – D.D., Litt. D., D. Sac. Th., Ph. D., Th. D. – Doc has taught at Faith Seminary and Louisiana Baptist Seminary.

The Lord enabled Doc to begin a daily radio ministry in 1954. That program, the Bible Institute of the Air, has grown through the years to cover most of the world. He has produced more than 14,900 radio broadcasts. He has also taught his six-hour prophecy seminar in almost every state of the Union.

Today, Dr. Beshore is President of the World Bible Society, which has printed and distributed Bibles in 65 countries (10 million in Russia since 1989 on the former Communist Party propaganda presses). He is the author of *The Millennium the Apocalypse and Armageddon*, and has written dozens of booklets that have been translated into more than 40 languages. He also has dozens of Bible studies available on CD and DVD formats.

Doc and Lois, his wife of 62 years, have three children, Kenette, Kenton and Kandis. Kenton is pastor of Mariners Church in Irvine, California, one of the largest churches in America, where Doc teaches a large class each Sunday. His sons-in-law are active in Ministry: Kenette's husband, Gene Mollway, is a pastor, and Kandis' husband, David Arnold, serves as vice-president of the World Bible Society in a volunteer capacity. Doc and Lois have 11 grandchildren and 5 great-grandchildren. Two of their grandsons are youth pastors.

R. William Keller

William's father shared the gospel with him and his older brother after the Sunday night service on July 13, 1958. They both asked Jesus to be their Savior. He was reared in a strong Christian home, and a solid Bible-teaching church. At the age of 14, he began to study the Bible diligently. He joined the Air Force at age 20, and worked with the Navigators during his tour of duty stateside and overseas. After leaving the Air Force, he dedicated his life to the study and teaching of Scripture. He has taught in several churches, and has led several home Bible studies.

He has a degree in Religious Studies, and became the director of research for the World Bible Society in 1992. Through the teaching of the Holy Spirit (1 John 2.27), his personal library of more than 20,000 volumes and the teaching of Dr. Beshore, God gave him more wisdom.

To order more copies of this book, or other books, DVDs, and CDs by Dr. Beshore, contact the:

WORLD BIBLE SOCIETY
P.O. Box 5000
Costa Mesa, CA 92628
714.258.3012 - 800.866.WORD
www.worldbible.com

BIBLIOGRAPHY

Allen, Gary. *The Rockefeller File.* Seal Beach, California: '76 Press, 1976.

Bernays, Edward L. *Propaganda.* New York, New York: H. Liveright, 1928

Breese, Dave and James, William T. *Storming Toward Armageddon.* Green Forest, Arkansas: New Leaf Press, 1992, (Second printing) 1993.

Butler, Smedley. War is a Racket." Torrance, California: The Noontide Press, 1984.

Chafer, Lewis Sperry. *Systematic Theology.* Dallas, Texas: Dallas Seminary Press, 1947, (Twelfth Printing) 1974.

Ferguson, Niall, *The House of Rothschild: Money's prophets, 1798-1848.* New York City, New York: Penguin, 1999.

Fruchtenbaum, Arnold G. *The Footsteps of the Messiah.* Tustin, California: Ariel Ministries, 1982, (Fourth printing) 1993.

——————. *The Footsteps of the Messiah.* Tustin, CA: Ariel Ministries, 2003.

Goldwater, Barry. *With No Apologies: the personal and political memoirs of United States Senator Barry M. Goldwater.* New York, New York: William Morrow, 1979.

Goodspeed, Edgar J. *The Apostolic Fathers.* New York, New York: Harper & Brothers, Publishers. 1950.

Green, Oliver B. *The Epistles of Paul the Apostle to the Thessalonians.* Greenville, South Carolina: The Gospel Hour, Inc., 1964, 1970 (Third printing).

Griffin, Des. *Fourth Reich of the Rich.* Colton, Oregon: Emissary Publications, 1976, 1981.

Hagee, John. *Beginning of the End.* Nashville, Tennessee: Thomas Nelson Inc., 1996.

Hunt, Dave. *How Close Are We?* Eugene, Oregon: Harvest House, 1993.

James, William T. *Storming Toward Armageddon.* Green Forest, Arkansas: New Leaf Press, 1992, second printing 1993.

Jeffrey, Grant, R. *Final Warning.* Eugene, Oregon: Harvest House, 1996.

——————. *Triumphant Return.* Roronto, Ontario: Frontier Research Publications, Inc. 2001.

Jones, Martyn-Lloyd, *Great Doctrines of the Bible.* Wheaton, Illinois: Quest Books, 1995.

Kah, Gary. *The New World Religion.* Noblesville, Indiana: Hope International Publishing, 1998.

Kirban, Salem. *Guide to Survival.* Huntingdon Valley, Pennsylvania: Salem Kirban, Inc. 1968, 1980 (Sixteenth printing).

Knox, John. *Historie of the Reformation of the Church of Scotland.* Glasgow, Scotland: Blackie, Fullarton, 1831.

LaHaye, Timothy. *The Beginning of the End.* Wheaton, Illinois: Tyndale House, 1972.

—————. *The Coming Peace in the Middle East*. Grand Rapids, Michigan: Zondervan Publishing House, 1984.

—————. *Tim LaHaye Prophecy Study Bible*. Chattanooga, Tennessee: AMG Publishers, 2000.

LaHaye, Timothy and Jenkins, Jerry. *Are We Living in the End Times?* Wheaton, Illinois: Tyndale House, 1999.

LaLonde, Peter. *One World Under Antichrist*, Eugene, Oregon: Harvest House Publishers, 1991.

Liddell and Scott. *Greek-English Lexicon*. Chicago, Illinois: Follett Publishing Company, 1927 (Twenty-sixth edition).

Lightfoot, J.B. *The Apostolic Fathers*. Grand Rapids, Michigan: Baker Book House, 1976 (Ninth printing).

Lindsell, Harold. *The Gathering Storm*. Wheaton, Illinois: Tyndale House, 1981.

Lindsey, Hal. *The 1980's: Countdown to Armageddon*. New York, New York: Bantam Books, 1980 (Bantam edition 1981).

—————. *The Late Great Planet Earth*. Grand Rapids, Michigan: Zondervan Publishing House. 1970, 1971 (Ninth printing).

—————. *Planet Earth 2000 A.D.* Palos Verdes, CA: Western Front Ltd., 1996.

—————. *Vanished Into Thin Air*. Beverly Hills, CA: Western Front Ltd., 1999.

Lockyer, Herbert. *All About the Second Coming*. Peabody, Massachusetts: Hendrickson Publishers, Inc. 1980, 2000 (Second Printing).

—————. *Rapture of the Saints*. Oklahoma City, Oklahoma: Southwest Radio Church, 1979.

Luther, Martin. *Commentary on Peter and Jude*. Grand Rapids, Michigan: Kregel Publications, 1990.

MacArthur, John. *The Second Coming*. Wheaton, Illinois: Crossway Books, 1999.

Martin, Malachi. *The Keys of this Blood*. New York, New York: Simon and Schuster, 1980.

McGee, J. Vernon. *I & II Thessalonians*. Pasadena, California: Thru the Bible Books, 1978.

Moore, Philip N. *The End of History the Messiah Conspiracy,* Atlanta, Georgia: The Conspiracy Inc., 1996.

Orwell, George. *1984*. New York, New York: The New American Library, 1963. Reprint of 1949 edition, Harcourt Brace Jovanovich.

Pentecost, Dwight. *Things to Come*. Findlay, Ohio: Dunham Publishing Company, 1958 (Third printing) 1959.

Perkins, Bill. *Steeling the Mind of America*. Green Forest, Arkansas: New Leaf Press, 1995.

Quigley, Carroll. *The Anglo-American Establishment: From Rhodes to Cliveden*. New York, New York: Books in Focus, 1981.

—————. *Tragedy and Hope: A History of the World in Our Time*. New York, New York: Macmillan, 1966.

Rassmussen, Roland. *The Post-Trib, Pre-Wrath Rapture*. Canoga Park, California: The Post-Trib Research Center, 1996.

Roberts, Alexander and Donaldson, James. *The Ante-Nicene Fathers*. Grand Rapids, Michigan: Eerdmans Publishing Company, 1956.

Rockefeller, David. *Memoirs*. New York, New York: Random House, 2002.

Scofield, Cyrus. *The First Scofield Study Bible*. Iowa Falls, Iowa: World Bible Publishers, Inc., 1986.

Smith, Chuck. *The Final Act*. Costa Mesa, California: Word for Today. 2007.

————. *Future Survival* Costa Mesa, California: Word for Today. 1978.

————. *Snatched Away!* Costa Mesa, California: Maranatha Evangelical Association of Calvary Chapel, 1976.

————. *The Soon to be Revealed Antichrist*. Costa Mesa, California: Maranatha Evangelical Association of Calvary Chapel, 1976.

————. *What the World is Coming to*. Costa Mesa, California: Word for Today. 1977.

Thayer, Joseph Henry. *Greek-English Lexicon*. Grand Rapids, Michigan: Zondervan, 1977 (Eighteenth printing).

Van Diest, John. *Ten Reasons Why Jesus is Coming Soon*. Sisters, Oregon: Multnomah Publishers, 1998.

Van Impe, Jack. *11:59...and Counting!* Royal Oak, Michigan: Jack Van Impe Ministries, 1983.

————. *Your Future*, Troy, Michigan: Jack Van Impe Ministries, 1989.

————. *Jack Van Impe Prophecy Bible*. Troy, Michigan: Jack Van Impe Ministries International, 1998.

Vine, W. E. *An Expository Dictionary of New Testament Words*. Chicago, Illinois: Moody Press, 1985, (Seventh printing).

Walvoord, John F. *Armageddon, Oil and the Middle East Crisis*. Grand Rapids, Zondervan Publishing House, 1974, (Sixteenth printing) 1980.

————. *The Church in Prophecy*. Grand Rapids, Zondervan Publishing House, 1964.

————. *The Rapture Question*. Grand Rapids, Michigan: Zondervan, 1973.

Webber, David and Hutchings, Noah. *Will Christ Come By 2001?* Oklahoma City, Oklahoma: Southwest Radio Church, 1978.

Webber, David, Hutchings, Noah and Gaverluk, Emil. *God's Timetable for the 1980's*, Oklahoma City, Oklahoma: Southwest Radio Church, 1978.

Wilson, Woodrow. *The New Freedom*. New York and Garden City, New York: Doubleday, Page and Company, 1914.

Wormser, Rene A. *Foundations*. Sevierville, Tennessee: Covenant House Books, 1993 (Third printing), Reprint of 1958 edition, Devin-Adair Company.

CPSIA information can be obtained
at www.ICGtesting.com
Printed in the USA
FSHW021235110920
73705FS